# McCALL'S SEWING FOR YOUR HOME

by the Editors of **McCall's Needlework & Crafts Publications**

SIMON AND SCHUSTER / THE McCALL PATTERN COMPANY • NEW YORK

Designed by Beri Greenwald
Manufactured in the United States of America
by Rand McNally & Company
1   2   3   4   5   6   7   8   9   10

Library of Congress Cataloging in Publication Data

Main entry under title:
McCall's Sewing for your home.
   1.  Sewing.  2.  House furnishings.  I.  McCall's
needlework & crafts.  II.  Title:  Sewing for your
home.
TT705.M15        1977        646.2′1        76-49510

ISBN 0-671-22372-0

# Contents

# 3
# WINDOW TREATMENTS

# 4
# CHILDREN'S ROOMS

# 5

# MORE GENERAL IDEAS

# McCALL'S
# SEWING
# FOR YOUR
# HOME

# Foreword

SEWING FOR YOUR HOME can be the most satisfying project you've ever undertaken. Simply by cutting and sewing fabric, you can transform a dull and unimaginative room, camouflage worn or faded furnishings, create a colorful new setting for yourself, your family and friends. What could be more inspiring than that? And what could give you a greater sense of accomplishment than making your home a welcome refuge of warmth and beauty from the many uncertainties of the outside world?

You can do it all—with a sewing machine and the marvelously flexible medium of fabric. That is why McCall's, the first name in sewing, now brings you this book devoted, almost exclusively, to sewing for your home. (A few additional techniques are included to make the things you sew even more effective; for instance, some of the "sewing" for special projects is done with a staple gun and staples—the fast, efficient way to cover many things with fabric, including walls.) This book shows you how to make everything you can sew for your home. Plus plenty of inspiring, full-color photographs that show you why you should!

# 1
# LIVING ROOMS

# Key Your Color Scheme to a Fabric

# Sew Custom Touches to Tie It All Together

If you can operate a sewing machine, you can pick and choose from a whole wide world of color schemes, each created by an artist. How and where? In fabric stores and departments, where a dazzling array of prints and patterns present infinite possibilities. Just pick a fabric you love and then plan your room around its professionally predesigned color scheme.

A dynamic color scheme was inspired by a sparkling print of stylized flowers. Walls and carpet are keyed to the vibrant orange background, while pillows, painting and plants pick up the touches of blue and green. The striking window treatment is simply alternating panels of print and sheer white curtain fabric tightly shirred on rods, both top and bottom. See drapery panel directions page 34.

If the fabric you fall in love with is a beauty you buy by the yard, you can use it any way and anywhere you please (provided its weight and weave are suitable for the purpose). If you find a piece of furniture already covered in the ideal fabric, simply purchase extra yardage when you buy the piece for your own custom-made additions. This multi-splendored color scheme was prompted by the sofa's upholstery; a tablecloth in the same vivid print makes a second splash of pattern. Directions for making round table covers begin on page 210.

# Start with Dramatic Draperies or Slipcovers

Simple, pinch-pleated draperies hung on wooden poles set a sunny, informal mood for a room keyed to their garden-flower colors. The intense orange that's an accent in the print is used prominently on the wicker furniture; the golds, greens and cooling white are repeated in the accessories. Directions for making draperies, page 124. Directions for making square bolster, page 223.

Infallible formula for a successful color scheme: pick a striking print to cover a large and important area, then key all your solid colors to it, right down to flowers and accessories. Fortunately, the windows and major pieces of furniture are among the most important elements in any room—fortunately because they're also the areas you can spotlight with attractive draperies and slipcovers.

What do you see first in this living room? The handsome sectional sofa—because it's slipcovered in a charming print. The vibrant colors that surround it and the verdant masses of greenery were all planned around it, insuring a smashing color scheme. Note how the pattern is placed on the sofa; see "How to Make Slipcovers," page 24.

# Black, White and Bright Can Be Contemporary or Traditional

Some of the best-looking prints to be found are invariably black and white. The best of mixers, too, they make other colors sparkle, add snap to any setting. In this traditional room, the black-and-white print used for wall covering, cornice and drapery, as well as slipcover, provides a dramatic counterpoint for the vivid rug and sparkling accessories.

See directions for covering walls with fabric on page 213; cornice directions on page 132; draperies, page 124; and making slipcovers on page 24.

If pattern-plus-pattern-plus-pattern is your kind of thing, begin
with black and white. The bold splashes of multi-color in the contemporary studio apartment above are framed by an equally bold
black-and-white print that panels two walls. The bed-platform doubles for sleeping and entertaining; directions for the floor cushions,
page 34, and the mattress cover, page 35.

# Black, White and Bright Can Be Boldly Dramatic

What's even more arresting than one bold black-and-white print? You guessed it—two! Black-and-white prints can be mixed very successfully; just keep the scale roughly the same (as here) or vary it widely (big black-and-white flowers, small black-and-white checks). Then add large expanses of white and staccato spots of strong color. Books and a barrage of bright cushions turn the trick here. All about covering cushions starts on page 220.

Begin with a black-and-white print and you can go *wild* with color—drench the rest of the room in a single blazing hue or keep everything sharp black and white except for a rainbow of small, brilliant accents. The living room goes the former route; everything but the zingy print (and a few frosty white touches) is red, red, RED. The round table covers that double the impact of the print are a cinch to make; see page 210. See directions for square bolster on page 223.

# Two Ways to Ignite White: Monotone or Multi-Color

Many color schemes *must* begin with white walls (when landlords rule the roost), but—happily—there's no better foil for many beautiful prints than pristine white. It makes an ideal backdrop for almost any color mix; just pick a pattern with some white in it and see how it sparkles against more white contrasted by a few bright accents keyed to other colors in the print. Here are two examples.

A whole garden of color blooms at the windows and on two of a well-tailored trio of slipcovers. The third picks up one potent hue from the print and makes a big splash of it. Flowers, a bowl of fruit and assorted bibelots take their cues from other colors in the print.

A boldly conceived pattern in strong blue and white is repeated over and over, and emphasized by still more blue-and-white pattern. A splash of solid blue and one splurge of multi-color make the monotone scheme explode. Directions for draperies, page 124; slipcovers, page 24.

# basic how-tos

## HOW TO MAKE SLIPCOVERS

You can give your living room a bright new personality simply by adding colorful new slipcovers. Don't be intimidated by the prospect of starting from scratch and producing trimly tailored covers for worn or faded furniture. No mystique is involved. Making well-fitted slipcovers takes time and patience, but the process is a logical and

A color-splashed print transforms a classic sofa, while a coordinated solid color slipcovers a typical chair. The directions for making slipcovers that follow are applied to this type of armchair, but the method of pin-fitting and cutting the fabric right on the furniture can be followed for any chair or sofa.

orderly series of steps anyone can follow. Those steps are outlined, complete with diagrams, on the next few pages.

## CHOOSING THE FABRIC

The very first step toward success in making slipcovers is choosing a suitable fabric. The key factor here is *firmness*. Be sure to choose a closely-woven fabric so the slipcover will hold its shape. Linen, sailcloth, velveteen, corduroy, chintz and many other fabrics made of cotton or synthetic fibers fill this requirement. The fabric should be wide enough to cover the widest section of a chair in one piece. (This is not possible, of course, in slipcovering a sofa.)

You'll find a solid color or a small all-over pattern easi-

est to work with because you won't have to worry about matching motifs at the seams. A large pattern must not only be matched, it must also be centered on each section of the slipcover, and its placement must be the same on opposite side sections. Stripes must be matched vertically at the seams, and plaids should be matched both vertically and horizontally.

Whatever fabric you choose, be sure the grainline is straight. You can check this before you buy by folding one end of the fabric back on itself diagonally and matching the selvages. If the end of the fabric has been torn, the torn end should be at right angles to the selvages. If the fabric has been cut across the end, you have to judge by following a single crosswise thread. Sometimes patterned fabrics are printed "off grain." If this is true of the fabric you have selected, forget it and make another choice. You can straighten a fabric which has been rolled or folded unevenly, and it is usually possible to straighten one which has been woven slightly off-grain, but there is nothing you can do about an off-grain print.

If it is necessary to straighten the fabric, place it on a flat surface and stretch it diagonally on the true bias from the corner opposite the higher end. Continue pulling until the crosswise threads are at right angles to the lengthwise ones.

### ESTIMATING THE YARDAGE REQUIRED

If the slipcover you plan to make is to replace a wornout one, you have a ready-made pattern which can also be used to estimate the new yardage required. Take the old slipcover apart and lay out the pieces in a space the same width as the fabric you intend to use. Be sure to place all pieces on the straight grain of the fabric.

If you have no such pattern, use the chart as an approximate guide. The yardages listed are average amounts for average-size furniture and average-size prints or patterns. If you have chosen a large pattern, allow at least one extra yard for matching it at all seams. If your fabric is 54" wide, reduce the amounts indicated for 48"-wide material by about 5%.

You can also estimate the yardage required to slipcover a chair by measuring the chair itself. Note the lengthwise measurement of each section and add 1" seam allowance on all sides; add 2" extra to seat, side and back sections (at the skirt line) and 5" tuck-in allowance across bottom of inside back, across bottom of inside arms, and across back of seat. Divide the total of these lengthwise measurements by 36 to estimate the number of yards required. If the slipcover is to have a "skirt," add the necessary yardage for that, depending upon its style.

### HOW TO BEGIN

If you are using an old slipcover as a pattern, simply use it as you would a paper pattern when making a garment. Pin each piece to the fabric, centering the major design motif (if other than an all-over) on each section.

If you are hesitant about working directly with the fabric, take a little extra time to make a muslin pattern. It will be good experience and will produce a permanent pattern that can be used again. In either case, the steps to be followed are the same.

### PIN-FITTING AND CUTTING

**Basic Procedure:** Whether you are making a slipcover or a muslin pattern, work on only one section at a time. Place the fabric on the particular section (in the order listed), and pin-fit and cut it before going on to the next section. Then assemble adjacent sections into units, and work on one unit at a time. (For instance, the inside back, side boxing above arms and outside back make up one unit.) Working in this way will eliminate any confusion about which pieces of fabric are to be seamed together.

Place the fabric right side up if there is any pattern to be matched. If you are working with muslin or a solid-color fabric, place it wrong side up on the chair to eliminate the step of unpinning and reversing the seams for stitching after the fitting is completed. Be sure the grainline is straight. The double-pointed arrows in the diagrams indicate the direction in which the lengthwise grain should go.

Pin-mark the center of each section of the chair at upper and lower edges. If you are using a fabric with a pattern, center the dominant motif on each section. If there is only one large motif repeated at intervals, center it horizontally on the section, but place it a little above center vertically. Pin the slipcover section in place, beginning at the center and pinning out to the seam lines, smoothing the fabric carefully so it lies flat and fits snugly at every point. Mark seam lines with pins as you fit. Trim away excess fabric, allowing 1" seam allowances except where deeper allowances are specified at skirt line and tuck-in points. As each section of the slipcover (or muslin) is cut, mark the center of top and bottom edges with a small notch.

## YARDAGE CHART FOR SLIPCOVERS

| Type | No. of Cushions | 48" Wide Plain | 48" Wide Patterned | 36" Wide Plain | 36" Wide Patterned | Cording |
|------|------|------|------|------|------|------|
| ARMCHAIR | 1 | 7½ | 8½ | 11½ | 12½ | 18 |
| WING CHAIR | 1. | 8 | 8½ | 12 | 13½ | 18 |
| BOUDOIR CHAIR | 1 | 5 | 6½ | 8 | 9 | 15 |
|  | 0 | 4½ | 5½ | 6½ | 7½ | 12 |
| OTTOMAN | 0 | 2 | 2½ | 3 | 3½ | 6 |
| SOFA (6-7') | 2-3 | 14 | 15½ | 21 | 23 | 36 |
|  | 1 | 13½ | 15 | 20½ | 22½ | 33 |
| LOVE SEAT | 2 | 10½ | 12 | 15 | 16½ | 24 |
|  | 1 | 10½ | 11 | 15 | 16½ | 23 |
| SOFA BED | 2 | 14½ | 16 | 20 | 21 | 40 |
| CUSHION | 1 | 1¼ | 1¾ | 2 | 2¼ | 5 |

**Inside Back:** Remove chair cushion, place fabric on inside back of chair in correct position and pin in place, beginning at center of section and working outward to seam lines. Make a 2″ fold at top edge and pin in place. Continue pinning fabric across top boxing and allow 1″ seam allowance beyond back edge of boxing; cut away excess fabric. Cut through center of 2″ fold. Allow 1″ seam allowance at side seams and around arms and cut away excess. Clip into seam allowances at corners of arms so fabric lies smoothly against inside back and pin along seam lines. Allow 5″ for tuck-in across bottom of section, between inside back and seat (Diagram 1).

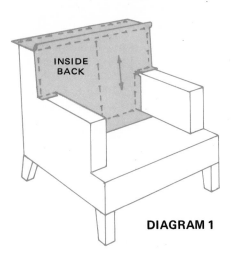

**DIAGRAM 1**

**Seat:** Place fabric on seat of chair and pin in place, smoothing and pinning from center out. Allow 5″ for tuck-in along back and inside arms. Allow 1″ seam allowance where front of arms meet seat and around front edge, clipping into seam allowance at corners (Diagram 2).

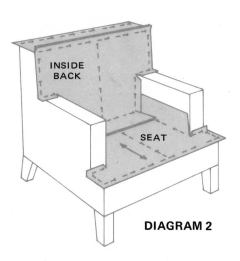

**DIAGRAM 2**

**Front Drop:** Place fabric across front in correct position (placement of pattern should correspond to that on inside back). Pin in place, beginning at center and continuing around corners. Allow 1″ seam allowance at sides and 2″ below skirt line along bottom edge (Diagram 3).

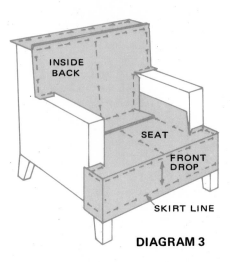

**DIAGRAM 3**

**Outside Back:** Place fabric on outside back in correct position and pin in place from center to side edges. Pin to top boxing across top edge. Allow a 1″ seam allowance along top and side edges and 2″ below skirt line along bottom edge; cut away excess fabric (Diagram 4).

**Side Boxing above Arms:** Place fabric in position and pin from center out. Pin to top boxing and to inside and outside back sections along seam lines. Allow 1″ seam allowances and cut away excess fabric (Diagram 4).

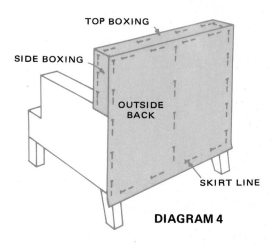

**DIAGRAM 4**

**Arm Sections:** Pin fabric to inside arms working from center out. Be sure the grainline is straight from top to bottom along front edge. Pin to inside back, allowing 1″ seam allowance where arms and back join. Allow a 5″

tuck-in along bottom edge; cut away excess fabric. Place fabric along top and down front of arms with grainline running from front to back. Pin in place, allowing 1″ seam allowance on all sides; cut away excess fabric (Diagram 5).

**Side Sections:** Pin fabric in place from center out, making sure grainline is straight along front edge. Pin to outside back, side boxing above arm, arm section and front drop on both sides. Leave 1″ seam allowance along these edges and 2″ below skirt line along bottom edge; cut away excess fabric (Diagram 5).

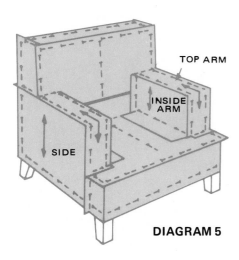

**DIAGRAM 5**

The slipcover is now pinned together except at tuck-ins. Now is the time to examine it carefully and make any adjustments required to make it fit smoothly. Check to make sure the grainline of fabric is straight on each section and pin out any unnecessary fullness.

## MARKING

While the pinned-together slipcover is still on the chair, mark both sides of each pinned seam with chalk or pencil on the wrong side of the fabric. If the slipcover has been pinned with the right side of the fabric out, spread the seams open to mark the wrong side (Diagram 6). On curved seams, make short cross lines 1″ apart to use as notch marks (Diagram 7).

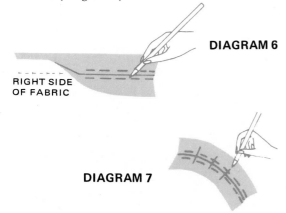

**DIAGRAM 6**

**RIGHT SIDE OF FABRIC**

**DIAGRAM 7**

## MAKING CORDED SEAMS

Corded seams are used to accent the lines of a chair or sofa, to give a tailored, professional-looking finish, and to strengthen the seam itself. Purchased cotton cable cord, available in various sizes, is covered with fabric to match or contrast the fabric of the slipcover. Cut bias strips of fabric, seam together and place cord on wrong side along center of strip. Fold fabric over cord, wrong sides together, and stitch along length close to cord, using a cording or zipper foot attachment. Trim seam allowances to ⅝″.

Before stitching seam to be corded, place cording on right side of one piece of fabric, raw edges of cording toward raw edge of fabric, and stitching line of cording on top of seam line of fabric. Using cording or zipper foot, stitch cording to fabric along stitching line of cording (Diagram 8).

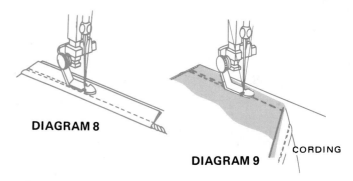

**DIAGRAM 8**

**DIAGRAM 9**    CORDING

Place the second piece of fabric over the corded piece, right sides together, and pin. With the corded piece uppermost, stitch just inside the first row of stitching. The first stitching line serves as a guide in stitching as close to the cording as possible; the double stitching line strengthens the seam and prevents the cording from slipping (Diagram 9). Grade the seams and press them away from the cording.

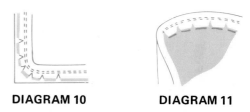

**DIAGRAM 10**      **DIAGRAM 11**

When placing cording around a corner, clip the seam allowance of cording so it lies flat (Diagram 10). When applying cording to a curve, clip seam allowances of both cording and fabric to prevent cupping (Diagram 11).

## PUTTING THE SLIPCOVER TOGETHER

Complete one unit of the slipcover at a time, stitching the plain seams first, then those with cording. Straighten pinned seams and correct markings, if necessary, before removing pins. Trim all seam allowances to ¾″ and press each seam open after stitching. As you complete each unit, try it on the chair to check seam placement and fit.

First, remove pins joining boxing sections to back and side sections. Remove back sections from chair. Stitch top boxing to top of each side boxing section with a plain seam (Diagram 12).

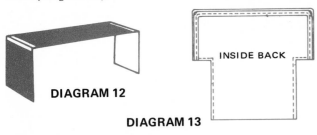

**DIAGRAM 12**

**DIAGRAM 13**

Stay-stitch around side and top edges of inside back section. Stitch cording around outside edge above cutouts for arms and across top (Diagram 13). With right sides together and raw edges even, pin corded edge of inside back to boxing strip. Stitch with corded section uppermost on machine.

Stay-stitch around side and top edges of outside back section, then apply cording to these three sides (Diagram 14). Pin outside back section to free edge of boxing strip, right sides together. Stitch up one side, across top, and down other side (Diagram 15). Place back unit on chair, check fitting and placement, and make any necessary adjustments.

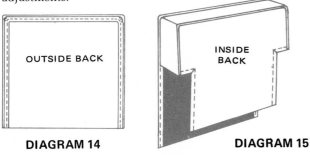

**DIAGRAM 14**          **DIAGRAM 15**

Remove arm sections from chair. Stay-stitch back edge of inside arm sections, and front and back edges of top arm sections. Stitch cording to top and front edges of side sections and to top and front edges of inside arm sections as far down front as tuck-in allowances. Join top arm sections to side and inside arm sections (Diagram 16). Try arm units on chair and adjust if necessary.

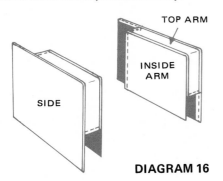

**DIAGRAM 16**

Join arm units to back unit, proceeding as follows on each side of slipcover: Pin side section to side boxing and top arm to inside back; stitch together. Pin inside arm to inside back on marked seam lines and stitch to beginning of tuck-in allowance. Pin side section to outside back section; stitch together on one side only; leave side where zipper will be inserted open (Diagram 17). When finishing the slipcover with a skirt, zipper is inserted after the skirt has been attached.

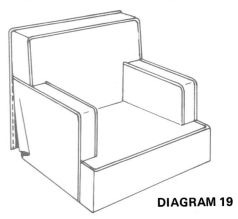

**DIAGRAM 17**

Stay-stitch front edge of seat section, going around corners to complete crossbar of "T" at each side. Stitch cording along front and side edges only. Stay-stitch side edges of front drop and stitch front drop to seat section (Diagram 18).

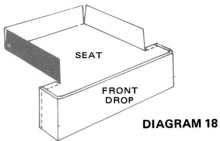

**DIAGRAM 18**

Join seat section to front panels of arm unit with plain seams. Join tuck-in allowance on each side of seat section to tuck-in allowance along bottom of inside arm, stitching to seam joining front panel of arm unit and seat section. Join tuck-in allowance along back of seat to tuck-in allowance along bottom of inside back (Diagram 19).

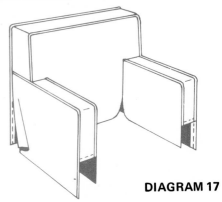

**DIAGRAM 19**

Now place the slipcover on the chair. If each section was carefully checked as it was finished, the slipcover should fit perfectly.

## FINISHING SLIPCOVER WITH A SKIRT

Most slipcovers are finished with a skirt, which may be gathered, pleated, or tailored with an inverted pleat at each corner. The last mentioned is the most popular style, but all are attached to the slipcover in the same manner.

The finished depth of the skirt should equal the distance from the skirt line of the slipcover to the floor. To this measurement, add 1″ for seam allowance and 1½″ for a hem. To determine the length of the strip required for a skirt, measure the distance around the chair at the skirt line. For a gathered skirt, allow one and one-half to two times this measurement. For a box-pleated skirt, triple the measurement. For a tailored skirt with corner pleats, add 70″, allowing an extra 16″ to make a full, inverted pleat at each corner, plus ¾″ seam allowances.

Cut the strips of fabric to make the skirt across the width of the fabric. If the skirt is to be pleated, space the pleats so that the seams joining the strips fall in the folds of the pleats.

For a tailored skirt with corner pleats, cut four strips of fabric the desired depth. Pin one strip to front of chair and mark fabric at corners (Diagram 20). Remove strip from chair and add 8¾″ at each marked corner. Trim away excess fabric; cut strips for sides and back of skirt in same manner.

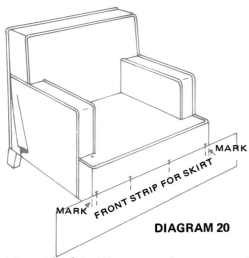

**DIAGRAM 20**

Join strips with plain ¾″ seams at three corners, leaving zipper corner open. Turn ¼″ at bottom edge of strip to wrong side, make another 1¼″ fold and hem, starting and stopping 2″ from zipper corner. (If fabric is very heavy, overcast raw edge and fold only once.)

Measure 8″ from both sides of each seam and mark fabric. To form pleats, fold fabric at marks and bring folds to meet at seams. Baste pleats in place and press.

Mark ¾″ seam allowances at edges left open for zipper. Measure 8″ in from seam allowances and mark. Fold fabric at marks and place folds along the seam lines. Baste in position and press.

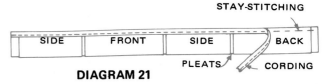

**DIAGRAM 21**

Stay-stitch ½″ from top edge through folded pleats. Stitch cording along top edge on right side of skirt (Diagram 21).

Pin skirt to slipcover along skirt line, right sides together, matching corners and centers on each side. Stitch together, beginning and ending at zipper opening (Diagram 22).

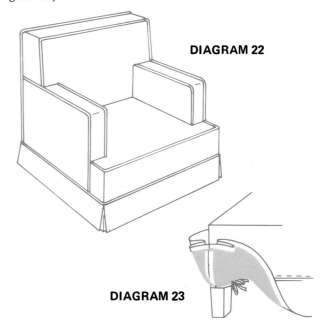

**DIAGRAM 22**

**DIAGRAM 23**

To hold cover firmly in place at lower edge, attach a piece of cotton twill tape to the inside seam at each corner and tie it around a leg of the chair (Diagram 23).

## INSERTING ZIPPER

A slipcover requires a special zipper with a wider tape and a heavier chain than those found in other zippers. Zippers of this type are available in 24″, 27″, 30″ and 36″ lengths. If the seam allowances along the opening for the zipper were not pressed flat earlier, do so now, and trim the corded seam allowance to ½″. Open the zipper and place it face down on the seam allowance of the corded seam, matching edge of zipper tape to edge of corded seam allowance, and with the top of the zipper 1½″ from the lower edge of the slipcover skirt. Using zipper foot, stitch along zipper close to teeth.

Close the zipper and turn the slipcover to the outside. Place folded edge of zipper opening over zipper teeth, against the corded seam; stitch across the end and down the side of the zipper. This gives the appearance of a lapped application. Finish hem at either side of zipper, enclosing ends of zipper tapes. You can now join the side section to the outside back section above the zipper.

## FINISHING SLIPCOVER WITHOUT A SKIRT

A slipcover which is not finished with a skirt can be given the look of upholstery by anchoring the bottom of the slipcover firmly under the chair. Tack one side of gripper snap tape to under edge of chair frame between legs (Diagram 24).

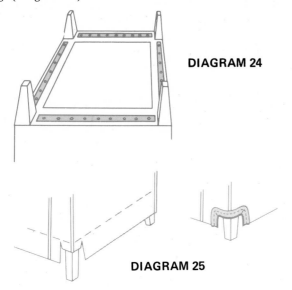

**DIAGRAM 24**

**DIAGRAM 25**

Pull the slipcover down firmly on all sides. Mark a line around the bottom edge of the chair on the fabric with chalk. At each chair leg, cut the fabric away ½" below chalk line. Stitch 1½" bias tape around cut-away corners on right side of cover (Diagram 25). Clip into seam allowances at corners and turn facing to wrong side.

Fold slipcover under along bottom edge of chair. Turn raw edges in so fold just covers gripper tape tucked to chair frame and pin. Remove slipcover and pin other half of gripper tape along folded edge; stitch securely in place.

## SLIPCOVERING THE CUSHION

With slipcover on chair and seat cushion in place, smooth fabric over top of cushion to determine the best placement of any pattern in relation to the pattern on inside back and arms of slipcover. When satisfied with placement, pin fabric in place at center of cushion and remove cushion. Pin fabric in place from center out to sides and mark seam lines along outer edges. Remove fabric, check measurements against cushion, and straighten seam lines if necessary. Add 1" seam allowance on all sides and cut two matching pieces. Pattern placement should be the same on top and bottom sections so cushion can be reversed.

Pin and stitch cording to the right side of each section along seam line, clipping seam allowance of cording to go around corners (Diagram 26). To join ends, cut covered cording ½" longer than required to make ends meet. Pull one end of cord out from covering and cut off ½". Turn edge of covering in ¼", slip over other end of cording and stitch closed.

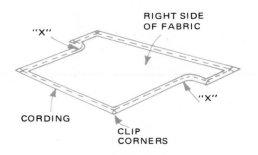

**DIAGRAM 26**

Cut a boxing strip 2" wider than depth of cushion and long enough to go around the T-shaped front of cushion from "X" mark on one side to "X" mark on the other side plus 2" (see Diagram 26). If using patterned fabric, center the pattern on front of boxing. Cut two strips 2" wider than one-half the depth of cushion and long enough to go around the back from "X" to "X", plus 2". Fold 1" under along one long side of each back strip. Place the two strips over zipper with folded edges meeting in center of zipper. Stitch along each side of zipper (Diagram 27).

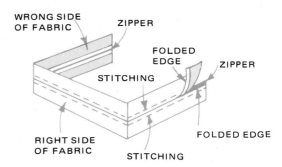

**DIAGRAM 27**

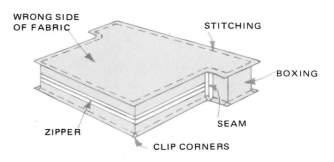

**DIAGRAM 28**

Stitch front and back boxing strips together to form a complete circle, taking 1" seams. Place boxing strip on top section of cover, right sides together and raw edges flush. Stitch along stitching line of cording (Diagram 28). Open zipper and join other edge of boxing strip to bottom section of cover in the same manner.

If your chair has a square or rectangular cushion, have zipper reach from the center of one side, around the back, to center of other side. Make boxing strips and join to top and bottom sections in the same manner.

## QUICK COLOR CHANGE: SEASONAL SLIPCOVERS

You don't have to redecorate your living room completely to give it an entirely new look. Simply changing the slip-covers can create a fresh new color scheme, transform the mood from serene to lively, or provide a change of pace to greet a new season. You can perform this decorating sleight-of-hand whenever your spirits—or your furnish-ings—need a lift. In fact, this face-lifting trick is so spirit-lifting as well, it's a good idea to have two sets of slipcov-ers—one for summer, one for winter. Here you see how much difference a change of slipcovers can make. Noth-ing was changed in this living room except the slipcover and the draperies. With the wealth of colors and patterns available, you can find two completely different fabrics that will complement the same walls and floorcovering. Don't overlook the piece goods departments where you buy dress fabrics. Just be sure the material you choose is sturdy and tightly woven, preferably of medium weight. See "How to Make Slipcovers" on page 24.

# HOW TO VARY A BASIC SLIPCOVER

The best-looking slipcovers are always trim and tailored, with crisp, straight cording and plain or pleated skirts. But there are many quick and easy ways to add a touch of individuality or make a slipcover suit the mood of a specific room. There are hundreds of handsome braids and fringes which, judiciously applied, will add a fashionable and expensive look to any slipcover you make. The covers that spruce up sofas shown are trimmed with braid in an almost identical manner, but one is crisply formal, the other colorfully casual. The fabrics and the types of braid make the difference.

Box-pleated skirts punctuated by covered buttons lend a very fashionable look to a boudoir chair and ottoman slipcovered in turquoise corduroy. To allow for good, deep box pleats, triple the measurement around the skirt line of any piece you're covering.

Bold black braid and four-inch-deep fringe border the skirt of a printed slipcover, adding a dramatic touch of contrast to suit the Spanish Provincial decor. Trimmed with less of a flourish, the same pattern would have a traditional flavor.

# directions for projects _____

## DRAPERY PANELS
### ON PAGE 15

MATERIALS NEEDED:
  Fabric; printed and solid-color sheer
  Two 7/16"-diameter casement rods for each panel
  Two 1½" projection brackets for each rod

Each panel should be at least twice as wide as the area of wall it is to cover. For example, to cover a 24"-wide section of wall using 36"-wide fabric (as shown in illustration on page 15), make both printed and solid-color panels in the following manner: Across full width of fabric, cut two pieces 6" longer than finished length of panels; cut printed pieces so pattern will match when pieces are seamed together. Cut one of the two pieces in half lengthwise; each half-width will be approximately 18" wide. With right sides together and fabric pattern matching, place raw edge of one half-width flush with selvage of full width; stitch together with a ½" seam and press allowances open. (If desired, stitch sheer pieces together with a French seam. Place wrong sides of fabric together and stitch ¼" from raw edges. Press flat, trim seam allowances to ⅛" and press seam open. Turn right sides of fabric together, fold on stitching line and press. Stitch on seam line.)

Make double 1" hem down each side. Turn 3" to wrong side along top edge and stitch across 1½" from fold to form top heading. Turn raw edge under ½" and stitch across close to fold to form 1" casing for rod. Make heading and casing at bottom in same manner (see diagram).

Insert rods in casings and place ends of rods in brackets.

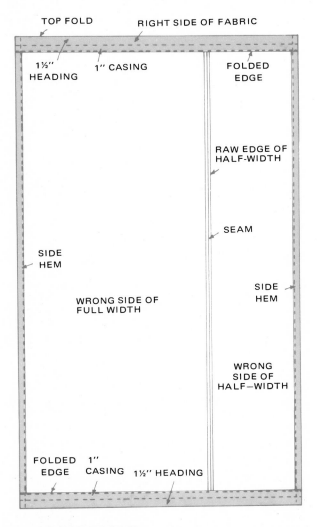

TOP FOLD    RIGHT SIDE OF FABRIC

1½" HEADING    1" CASING    FOLDED EDGE

RAW EDGE OF HALF-WIDTH

SEAM

SIDE HEM

SIDE HEM

WRONG SIDE OF FULL WIDTH

WRONG SIDE OF HALF—WIDTH

FOLDED EDGE    1" CASING    1½" HEADING

## COVERS FOR FLOOR CUSHIONS
### ON PAGES 18–19

MATERIALS NEEDED:
(for two cushions)
  3¼ yards 36"- or 44"-wide striped fabric
            OR
  1½ yards 54" plain or all-over print fabric
  5 yards pre-covered cording
  Two 22" x 22" x 4"-thick foam cushions

Cut four 27" squares of fabric for top and bottom sections of cushions. If fabric is striped, cut two pairs so stripes on top and bottom sections of each pair will match at center cording.

Mark edges of top and bottom sections for one cushion 2½" from each corner. To form corners, make a diagonal fold at each corner with right sides of fabric together and edges even, so 2½" marks meet. Stitch from marks to fold at each corner, forming a "box" 22" square and 2½" deep (Diagram 1).

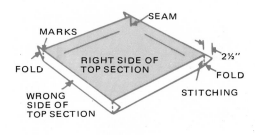

MARKS    SEAM

FOLD    RIGHT SIDE OF TOP SECTION    2½"    FOLD

WRONG SIDE OF TOP SECTION    STITCHING

**DIAGRAM 1**

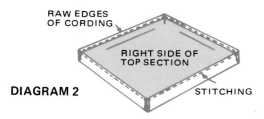

**DIAGRAM 2**

Trim corners ½" beyond stitching and press seam allowances open. Place cording around top section with stitching line of cording ½" in from edge and raw edges of fabric and cording together; stitch in place, following stitching line of cording (Diagram 2).

Place bottom section inside top section, right sides together, matching stripes if fabric is striped, and with seams meeting at corners. Stitch around three sides, following stitching line of cording; start and end stitching 3" from corners to leave a 28" long opening so cushion can be inserted (Diagram 3).

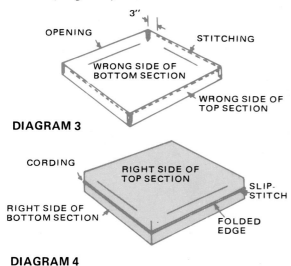

**DIAGRAM 3**

**DIAGRAM 4**

Turn right side out and insert pillow; fold unattached edge of bottom section to wrong side and slip-stitch opening closed along cording (Diagram 4).

## MATTRESS COVER
### ON PAGE 19

MATERIALS NEEDED:
(to cover 54"-wide mattress)
    10½ yards 44"-wide fabric
    7½ yards pre-covered cording

Across full width of fabric, cut piece 1½" longer than mattress. If fabric has a very decisive pattern (as in photograph on page 19), cut bottom edge ¾" below a full motif. Place this panel of fabric on remaining fabric, right sides

together, so pattern matches exactly along (or close to) selvages. Pin along exact centers of pattern motifs, where seam will be stitched, and baste in place. Turn right side out and check matching of pattern; adjust basting if necessary Stitch seam along basting line, trim allowances to ¾" and press open.

Place seamed fabric right side up on mattress with seam in center and full motif or motifs along bottom edge of mattress. Place cording around four sides, with stitching line of cording along top edge of mattress, clipping seam allowances of cording to go around corners. Stitch cording to top section, following stitching line of cording (Diagram 1). Trim away excess fabric along each side, ¾" beyond stitching.

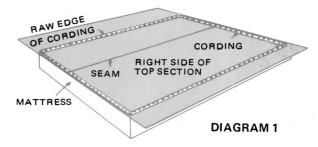

**DIAGRAM 1**

Make double side and end drops, placing pattern so it will match pattern on top section when seamed in place. Cut all drops twice depth of mattress plus 1½"; cut side drops 1½" longer than length of mattress and end drops 1½" longer than width of mattress. Fold drops in half lengthwise, right sides together; stitch across ends, ¾" from edges (Diagram 2).

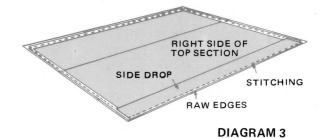

**DIAGRAM 2**

Turn drops right side out and press. Place side drop on top section with right sides together, raw edges even and pattern matching; stitch in place, following stitching line of cording (Diagram 3). Attach other side and end drops in the same manner.

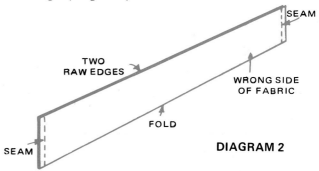

**DIAGRAM 3**

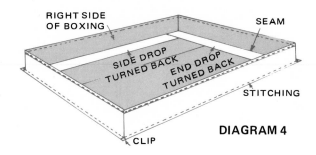

RIGHT SIDE
OF BOXING

SEAM

SIDE DROP
TURNED BACK

END DROP
TURNED BACK

STITCHING

CLIP

**DIAGRAM 4**

Using full width of remaining fabric, cut boxing strips 2″ deeper than height of mattress; seam strips together until boxing is long enough to go around entire mattress; seam ends together to form a complete circle. Turn ¼″ to wrong side along one long edge, then turn another 1″ to wrong side and stitch hem in place. Turn drops back onto right side of top section and place boxing around top section over drops, with right sides together and raw edges even. Clip seam allowance of boxing to go around corners and stitch in place along same line as before (Diagram 4).

Place cover on mattress, pull boxing down over sides and let drops fall over boxing (see photo).

# 2
# BEDROOMS

# Use Fabric
# to Bring
# Your Room to Life

If you had to confine your decorating efforts to only one medium, what would you choose? Paint? Great for walls and some pieces of furniture. Wallpaper or wallcovering? You can certainly do a lot with *that*, but its uses are still a little limited. Fabric? Ah, that's the answer! Colorful, flexible, adaptable fabric—patterned or plain, formal or informal, traditional or contemporary—can transform a whole room as nothing else can. Naturally, you think first of bedspreads when "doing" a bedroom. But don't stop there. Fresh, bright fabric makes everything it covers sparkle.

A pair of coordinated flower prints are used five different ways to transform a bedroom—inspiring its restful, feminine mood as well as its color scheme. The stripe used for the quilted coverlet and draperies also panels the walls (applied in a flash with spray adhesive); its all-over counterpart makes the dust ruffle and covers the seat of the Hepplewhite chair.

Directions for making bedspreads start on page 45. See directions for dust ruffle on page 53, and for draperies on page 124.

# Make a Bold Statement with One Strong Print

You can, of course, cover all four walls of a room with fabric—and the effect can be fabulous. But given the tremendous potential of a striking print, you can use a lot less fabric than that and still have eye-riveting impact. Here, two instances where simple panels of fabric—plain or pleated—serve as major design interest.

The drapery panels in this bedroom pretend they're covering big twin windows, but they're fool-the-eye fakes; the windows they conceal are small and mix-matched. The draperies lighten and brighten dark, paneled walls, while doubling the impact of the oversize sleeping well—and they do both admirably. The effectiveness of the whole idea is due largely to the fabric; a big, bold plaid lit up by blocks of sparkling white. (The same spectacular effect could be achieved with any emphatic pattern you fancy.) Another way fabric power adds to the picture: the barrage of bright toss pillows in coordinated solid colors. Directions for covering many types of pillows start on page 220.

An unadorned mattress and boxspring are given a dramatic "head-board" by simply running a panel of spread-matching fabric up the wall. The window shade and director's chair are done in the same dynamic pattern. And those two contemporary bedside tables are nothing but ordinary packing crates painted white! See directions for tailored bedspread with corner "pleats" on page 52; covering director's chair on page 56; how to apply fabric to walls starting on page 213; window shades starting on page 150; and square bolster on page 223.

# Go Wild with a Favorite Print . . . or Two

Daisy-printed fabric and coordinated checks collaborate on covering the walls of this lighthearted bed-sitting room, with the checks taking over when it comes to dressing up the wicker daybed. The big-eyed daisies also get another turn—blooming brightly on the circular tablecloth. It's a very happy marriage—one of many made in fabric heaven. (You can also choose and mate partners on your own.) Directions for making a fitted bedspread appear on page 52.

What else but fabric could cover a bedroom so completely with blooming color? Flower-strewn sheets were used to cover the walls and headboard and make the flirty dust ruffle and frilly pillow cases in this room, with coordinated wallpaper doing the same for the folding screen and bedside chest. Many fabrics with matching wallpaper are now available, but the screen could also be covered with fabric; the directions could be used for either. See page 58. Directions for the tiered dust ruffle start on page 57.

# basic how-tos

A graceful throw bedspread in a color-splashed print is the focal point of a predominantly white room. A cinch to sew, the throw is basically three straight panels; seams can be corded or accented with braid.

# BEGIN WITH A BASIC THROW BEDSPREAD

If you've never made a bedspread before, begin with a simple, easy-to-sew throw—two straight seams and a hem is all the making it takes! It's a good way to begin your color scheme, too; the versatile throw looks great in almost any print or pattern, practically any color or texture. (Choose a colorfast, firmly woven fabric with an easy-care finish.)

The first step in making any bedspread is to take accurate measurements—with the bed made up in the usual manner. For a throw, measure the top section from the foot of the bed to the edge of the pillow, allow for a generous tuck-in and add enough to go over the pillow. Add the distance from the top of the mattress to ½" above the floor for the drop at the foot of the bed, then add 1½" each for top and bottom hems. For a 75"-long bed, the total will be about 125".

Now measure the width of the mattress and add twice the distance from the top of the mattress to ½" above the floor. Add 3" for two 1½" side hems to determine the total width of the throw. Like all spreads, the throw is made in three lengthwise panels, with the center panel usually utilizing the full width of the fabric. (Exception: The center panel should not be wider than the mattress, so when using 48"- or 54"-wide fabric for a 39"-wide twin bed, cut the center panel 40" wide; cut it 1" wider than the mattress if the mattress is narrower than a standard twin size.) Allowing ½" for seam allowances, subtract the width of the center panel from the total width required; divide the remainder in half and cut two side panels to that width and to the same length as the center panel.

(When using 48"- or 54"-wide fabric for a twin-size throw, or 54" fabric for a full-size one, both side panels can be cut from one 125" length.)

You'll need 10½ yards of 35" to 45" fabric, or 7¼ yards of 54" fabric for either a twin or full-size throw. Seams can be corded or not, as you prefer; if you plan to use matching cording, you'll need 7½ yards of cord and an extra yard of fabric for cutting the bias strips you'll need to cover it.

Most fabrics used for a throw should be underlined to give them enough "body" to lie smoothly and resist wrinkling. Use lining fabric of the same width as the outer fabric, cut to exactly the same measurements. Underline each panel separately; stitch with wrong sides together and edges even.

If making corded seams, apply cording to the center panel before stitching it and the side panels together. Cut 2"-wide bias strips and cover cording (see page 209). Place the cording along both long edges of the center panel, raw edges of fabric and cording even. Stitch cording to panel along stitching line of cording. Now stitch the panels together, right sides facing, crowding the zipper foot against the cord and stitching slightly inside the first stitching line so the original stitching won't show on the right side.

Starting about 16" in from each corner along foot end and side edges, cut curved corners at foot end of throw (see diagram). Trace and cut curve on one side, fold throw in half and use first curved corner as pattern for second.

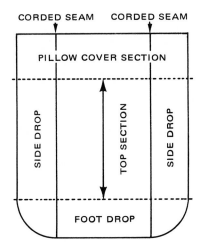

Now all that remains is to make a 1" finished hem on all four sides of the throw (or apply cording around three sides as seen opposite and hem the head end).

## THE BASIC THROW BEDSPREAD . . . MAKE IT MORE THAN BASIC

Having mastered the very simple mechanics of putting a basic throw together (see the preceding pages), you may want to do something a little different the next time around. Puffy "kimono" cording crisping the edge of the spread adds a bit of flair (as well as flare). Tufting is another custom touch that's literally as easy as tying a knot.

A pastel throw with kimono cording (above) brightens a young lady's bedroom. A panel of the same fabric makes the effective "headboard"; the mini-canopy is simply a ruffled strip of fabric tacked to the highest shelf of the storage wall.

A kimono-corded throw can have a casual country look or be considerably more formal, as you can see opposite. Either way, the wide, padded edging makes the spread hang beautifully. The one opposite is also tufted for a touch of contrast. You'll find directions for the window treatment on page 60; draped "headboard" on page 61; the bedspread on page 58.

## THE BASIC THROW BEDSPREAD . . . MAKE IT A WORK OF ART

No longer exactly basic, this bedspread gives you an idea of the many exciting ways you can embellish a basic throw. Yes, it's essentially the same simple, three-panel spread, made with two straight seams as described on page 45. But here it's splashed with big, brilliant flower-petals inspired by a Matisse painting. And although it has the much-prized look of painstaking hand-craftsmanship, the free-form petals and borders are appliqued by machine.

The center panel in this bedspread is only 36″ wide (after seaming) and the finished length 108″, so the appliqued pattern can be repeated evenly as indicated by the diagrams opposite. Notice that no two petals or mushroom shapes on the spread are exactly the same—which adds to its hand-crafted look. You can repeat the pattern given for each 36″ square or vary the shapes slightly as

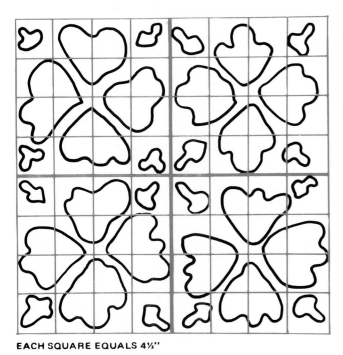

**EACH SQUARE EQUALS 4½"**

**DIAGRAM 1**

Diagram 2 grid (small initials at corners = mushroom shapes; large initials in center of each square = petals):

| D | P | P | D | D | A | A | D |
|---|---|---|---|---|---|---|---|
| **D** | | **L** | | **P** | | **R** | |
| P | N | P | D | D | D | A | P |
| P | D | D | D | A | D | A | P |
| **D** | | **L** | | **P** | | **R** | |
| P | N | P | D | D | D | A | P |
| P | D | D | P | N | D | A | P |
| **Y** | | **A** | | **Y** | | **N** | |
| D | A | A | N | N | D | D | D |
| P | D | D | D | N | N | D | D |
| **D** | | **F** | | **P** | | **R** | |
| D | P | P | N | N | A | A | N |
| N | D | P | D | N | N | D | N |
| **Y** | | **R** | | **Y** | | **P** | |
| N | D | D | A | D | D | D | A |
| D | P | A | P | D | D | P | D |
| **A** | | **N** | | **L** | | **F** | |
| D | D | D | D | D | D | D | D |

SIDE PANEL     CENTER PANEL     SIDE PANEL

**DIAGRAM 2**

you cut them out or applique them. In addition to giving the end result a highly artistic effect, varying the shapes as you go along means you don't have to be too careful when cutting or stitching. The directions and diagrams are for a full-size spread; you can easily adapt them to a twin-size (or narrower) spread by cutting narrower side panels and using single rows of petals; keep the center panel the same.

For a full-size spread you'll need 9¾ yards of 44"-wide white fabric; 3½ yards of dark green; one yard each of pink, red, yellow and light green; ¾ yard each of aqua, French blue and navy blue. We used a heavy cotton faille that required no underlining; if using lightweight fabric, underline panels separately after appliqueing.

Cut three pieces of white fabric 3¼ yards long. Cut one of them 38" wide for the center panel; cut two remaining pieces 35" wide for side panels. Cut six strips of dark green fabric 3" wide by 3¼ yards long for the border appliques.

On 38"-wide center panel, mark off 1" seam allowance along each long edge; mark off 4½" across top and bottom edges for hem allowances. Fold panel in half lengthwise and press fold. Divide length between hem allowances into six 18" sections by folding and pressing or with basting stitches.

Cut a piece of heavy paper 36" square. Draw lines 4½" apart horizontally and vertically as shown in Diagram 1; then draw outlines of petals and mushroom shapes as indicated by diagram. Cut out these shapes to use as patterns for appliques. Cut each applique 1" larger than pattern all around; stitch appliques to panel as indicated by Diagram 1 and trim away the extra 1" allowance as close

to stitching line as possible after stitching has been completed.

Diagram 2 indicates colors used in each 18" square of spread. Four petals in center of each square are identified by large initials; small mushroom shapes in corners are identified by small initials. N = navy; L = light green; R = red; Y = yellow; D = dark green; A = aqua; P = pink; F = French blue.

Starting at lower edge of center panel, cut four petals each of navy, light green, red and yellow, cutting each 1" larger than pattern. Pin each in place and satin-stitch to panel with matching thread, 1" in from edge. Cut away 1" allowance along stitching. Add mushroom shapes in colors indicated, appliqueing as before. Continue to applique petals and mushrooms in all twelve squares of center panel.

On each 35"-wide side panel mark 1" seam allowance along long edge to be joined to center panel. Then mark off one row of six 18" squares and applique with petals and mushroom shapes in colors indicated in Diagram 2. Place center panel on bed, centering it on width, and pin one side panel to it, overlapping seam allowances, to determine width of side panels. Mark hemline ½" above floor and hem both side panels. Baste three 3"-wide dark green strips to each side panel, spacing them evenly between appliques and hemline. Measure ½" in from both edges of each strip and draw irregular, slightly wavy lines parallel with straight edges (see photograph). Satin-stitch along wavy lines and trim excess fabric along stitching. Stitch side panels to center panel with 1" seams; turn ½" to wrong side along top and bottom edges, then make 4" finished top and bottom hems.

# MAKE A HANDSOME
# TAILORED BEDSPREAD

You may prefer the trimly fitted effect of a tailored bedspread—and although it has an expensive "custommade" look, it's not much harder to make than the more casual throw. A tailored spread with separate end and side drops that part company at the corners is the one to choose for a four-poster bed; it fits smoothly around the bottom posts without bunching or wrinkling. The photograph shows how perfectly a well-tailored spread fits—as well as how effective a room done in one pretty fabric can be.

Starting with accurate measurements is of utmost importance when making a tailored spread; the cording should fall precisely along the edge of the mattress when sheets and blankets are in place. To make a tailored spread for a standard 54" x 75" double bed, you'll need 8 yards of 55"-wide fabric, 7 yards of the same width fabric for lining, 7 yards of lightweight flannel for interfacing if

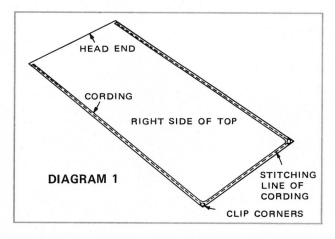

**DIAGRAM 1**

HEAD END
CORDING
RIGHT SIDE OF TOP
STITCHING LINE OF CORDING
CLIP CORNERS

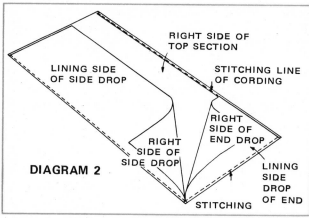

**DIAGRAM 2**

RIGHT SIDE OF TOP SECTION
LINING SIDE OF SIDE DROP
STITCHING LINE OF CORDING
RIGHT SIDE OF SIDE DROP
RIGHT SIDE OF END DROP
LINING SIDE DROP OF END
STITCHING

you want to interface spread, and 7½ yards of cord if you plan to make corded seams (see page 209 for directions for covering cording). (If you don't use corded seams, you must be careful to match any pattern along seam lines.) With sheets, blankets and pillows in place, measure width of bed; measure length from foot of bed to 8" under pillows, then back out and over top of pillows down to mattress in back. Cut top section 1" wider and 1" longer than these measurements. Cut lining and interfacing to same size. (If it is necessary to seam lining and interfacing to obtain width, cut and join pieces so seams do not fall on top of each other; press seams open.) Cut 2"-wide bias strips of fabric and cover cording; trim covering ½" beyond stitching.

Place top section, right side up, over interfacing and pin together. Place cording around three edges on right side of top section, with raw edges of cording, fabric and interfacing flush; clip seam allowance of cording to go around corners. Stitch cording to fabric and interfacing, following stitching line of cording (Diagram 1). Leave head end open.

Place top section on bed and measure from stitching line of cording to floor. Cut two side drops 1" wider than this measurement and to same length as top section. Cut one end drop to same depth as side drops and to same width as top section. Cut lining and interfacing to match each drop. Place drop right side up on interfacing; place lining, wrong side up, over drop. Stitch the three layers together around three sides, ½" from raw edges. (Do not stitch across upper edges.) Turn drop right side out and press so seam is exactly along edge of fold. Baste raw edges together across top.

Place one side drop along side edge of top section, right sides together and raw edges of drop and top section flush. Stitch drop to top section, following stitching line of cording. Stitch end drop to top in same manner (Diagram 2). Stitch remaining side drop to top section in same manner.

Turn side and end drops up over top section and smooth flat. Place lining for top section over drops, wrong side up, with raw edges flush; baste together around three sides, following stitching line of cording. (Do not baste across head end.) Turn right side out and check to be sure spread lies smoothly. Turn wrong side out and stitch lining in place. Turn right side out and press. Turn raw edges of fabric, interfacing and lining to inside across head end of spread and blind-stitch opening closed.

A tailored spread for a bed with a headboard but no footboard (and no posts) is made the same way, but with the addition of two lined pieces going around the bottom corners beneath the drops to give the effect of pleated corners without the bulk. Directions for this version are on page 52.

## MAKE A TAILORED SPREAD WITH CORNER "PLEATS"

Directions for making a tailored spread to be used on a four-poster bed appear on page 50. This variation is for a bed without posts or footboard, as seen on page 85. It also has an attached pillow-cover section so pillows can be placed on top of the spread and the pillow cover placed over the pillows from back to front and tucked under at the front. This makes the side drops hang to the same length all the way to the head of the bed, instead of the drops on the pillow section being shorter than the other drops. (If you prefer using a bolster with this type of spread, as shown on page 41, omit the pillow-cover section.)

A full-size spread takes 8 yards of 55"-wide fabric, 7 yards of the same width for lining, and 7½ yards of cord. Cut top section 1" wider and 1" longer than mattress with sheets and blankets in place. Cut lining same size. Cut 2"-wide bias strips of fabric (see Cutting Layout) and cover cording (see page 00); trim ½" beyond stitching. Pin cording around side and foot edges on right side of top section, raw edges of fabric and cording even. Clip seam allowance of cording to go around corners. Stitch in place, following stitching line of cording.

**CUTTING LAYOUT**

Place top section on bed and measure from stitching line of cording to floor. Cut two side drops 1" wider than this measurement and same length as top section. Cut one end drop to same depth as side drops and to same width as top section. Cut lining to match each drop. Place lining for each drop on right side of fabric and stitch around three sides, taking ½" seams. (Do not stitch across upper edges.) Turn right side out, baste raw edges together across top and press. Place side and end drops on top section of spread, right sides together, and stitch in place, following stitching line of cording.

Turn side and end drops over top section. Place lining for top right side down over drops, all raw edges even, and baste around three sides, following stitching line of cording. Turn right side out and check to be sure spread

lies smoothly. Turn back to wrong side and stitch lining in place around three sides; trim any excess ½" beyond stitching. (If omitting pillow cover, stitch across head end, leaving room to turn; turn, then slip stitch opening closed.)

Cut fabric for two corner "pleats" 17" wide and to same depth as drops. (Although they will look like pleats, these pieces will actually be underlays, to avoid the bulkiness of pleats at the corners.) Cut lining pieces to same size, place on right sides of fabric pieces, and stitch around side and lower edges. Turn right side out and press. Clip seam allowances at center of top edge. Place pleat sections wrong side up over lining sides of drops, with center clip of pleat section at each corner and bottom edges even. Stitch in place along same stitching line as before. See Diagram 1.

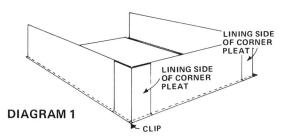

**DIAGRAM 1**

To make pillow-cover section, place spread on bed and put pillows in place on top of it. Measure over pillows from back to front and allow for tuck-in; measure over top of pillows from side to side, from bottom of one side drop to the other. Cut fabric and lining 2" wider and 2" longer than these measurements. Place lining on fabric, right sides together, and stitch around all four sides, leaving opening the width of the bed centered on one long side

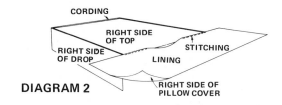

**DIAGRAM 2**

and taking 1" seams. Turn right side out and press. Turn raw edges of fabric and lining to inside across opening and press. Insert end of spread into opening, with lining side of pillow cover section on top. See Diagram 2. Stitch fabric and lining to the spread across the opening.

# MAKE A GATHERED DUST RUFFLE

The top section (or underlay) of a dust ruffle fits over the boxspring and under the mattress, and is usually made of muslin. Cut muslin 1″ wider and 1″ longer than boxspring, seaming at center if muslin is not wide enough. Cut muslin for two end sections 1″ longer than width of spring and 1″ wider than depth of spring. Cut muslin for two side sections 1″ longer than length of spring and same width as end sections. Make a ½″ hem along three edges of each side and end section, leaving one long side of each unhemmed. Stitch a 10″ strip of ½″-wide twill tape to each finished corner and a 20″ strip, folded in half, to the center of each side section if the bed has center legs. Place one end section across head of top section, right sides together and raw edges even, with top section extending ½″ at each side. Stitch end section to top section, taking a ½″ seam. (See Diagram 1.)

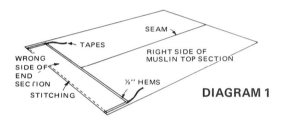

**DIAGRAM 1**

To determine depth of ruffle, measure from top of spring to floor. Cut pieces 4″ deeper than this measurement across width of fabric so pattern will match when pieces are seamed together. Seam pieces together, matching pattern, to form one strip 2½ times the length of three sides of spring plus 4″. (This assumes head of bed will be placed against wall; if bed will be placed in corner, you may wish to make strip 2½ times the length of only *two* sides of spring.) Make a 2″ hem on each short end of strip; turn bottom edge under ½″ and then make a 3″ finished bottom hem.

Using buttonhole twist in the bobbin, make two rows of machine gathering along top (unhemmed) edge of ruffle, placing them ¼″ and ½″ in from edge. Make a mark every 12″ along three sides of muslin top section and every 30″ along top edge of ruffle. With wrong side of ruffle toward you, start at right end and pull up bobbin threads of gathering until marks on ruffle correspond to those on one long side of top section. Place ruffle on top section with wrong side up and raw edges even; place muslin side section on top of ruffle with wrong side up and raw edges even. Stitch along side ½″ from edges through all thicknesses. (See Diagram 2.)

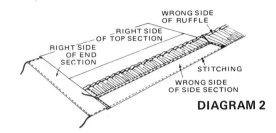

**DIAGRAM 2**

Gather ruffle and continue around other two sides in same manner, joining muslin end section across foot of top section and other side section along remaining side edge. Turn ruffle and muslin sections down and smooth seam allowances to underside of top section. Edge stitch through top section and seam allowances around all four sides. (See Diagram 3.) Place dust ruffle on spring and tie tapes around legs of bed.

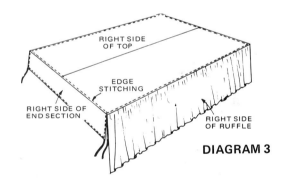

**DIAGRAM 3**

NOTE: For a four-poster bed, make ruffle in three sections, each 2½ times length required plus 3½″ hem allowances at bottom corners. Turn short ends under ½″, then make 3″ finished hems and seam to top section with corresponding muslin sections as above, stitching through all thicknesses.

## SHOW-OFF SHEETS AND PILLOWCASES

If you're tired of wildly printed sheets or just prefer to sleep on pristine white, add borders of expensive-looking Venice lace to the hems of sheets and pillowcases.

The pretty pink pair were embroidered by machine, using a decorative ball stitch and a delicately scalloped design. Step-by-step directions follow.

You've decided on the perfect bedspread, draperies and all the other touches that will earn you decorating plaudits from family, friends and visitors? Great—but don't stop your decorating there. How about the bedroom only you (or the lucky occupants) will see? When that beautiful spread you plan to make is turned down, will the view still be delightful? Pretty sheets and pillowcases have a very special elegance—like lovely underthings. And it doesn't take much effort to add a distinctive personal touch to purchased bedclothes.

For the elegant lace-trimmed set, far left, a one-inch band of lace was stitched across the sheet and another around the pillowcase, one inch from the edges. Then two rows of satin stitching were machine-embroidered along both edges of the lace, ¾″ from the lace and ¼″ apart.

To embroider a sheet and pillowcase as shown in the second picture opposite, you'll need a small amount of organdy and size 50 thread in the desired color. A ball stitch set for ³⁄₁₆″ at the widest point was used for the embroidery in the photograph, but almost any decorative stitch or a plain satin stitch could be used with an equally attractive result.

We suggest working on the pillowcase first because the procedure is a little simpler. The first step is to remove the stitching from the hem. Then trace the design below and transfer it to the pillowcase. Use dressmaker's tracing paper and place the scalloped design midway between the fold and the original stitching line (on the outside, not the inside) of the hem. Cut a 2½″-wide strip of organdy and baste it to the wrong side of the pillowcase, in back of the scalloped design. Using a ball or other embroidery stitch, and stitching through the single layer of pillowcase and organdy backing only, stitch along the marked lines of the design, following the upper row of smaller loops first, and then the lower row of larger loops and deeper scallops. Remove the basting stitches and turn

the hem back in place, enclosing the organdy backing. Then straight-stitch along the original stitching line to re-hem.

To embroider the hem of a sheet, it is necessary to cut off the hem (and replace it later) so the entire sheet does not have to be turned while doing the embroidery. Remove the top hem by cutting through the sheet ¼″ below the stitching line of the hem. Then remove the stitching from the hem. Transfer the traced design to the outer side of the hem as before, centering it between the cut edge and the fold. Cut a 2½″-wide strip of organdy and baste it to the hem, in back of the scalloped design. Using the same decorative stitch as before, stitch along the marked lines, stitching through the single layer of hem and backing only. Remove the basting stitches. Turn under the cut edge of the hem so the new folded edge is even with the original folded edge and press. Sandwich the raw edge of the sheet between the two folded edges of the hem and stitch through all layers, as close to the folded edges as possible (see diagram).

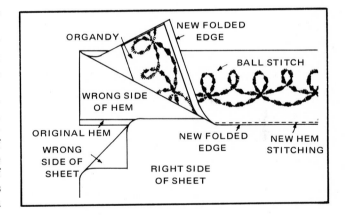

# directions for projects

## DIRECTOR'S CHAIR
### ON PAGES 41, 93, 182

NOTE: Directions given are for covering existing fabric seat and back (so lightweight or loosely-woven fabric can be used). If you do not wish to use existing seat and back, new ones should be made of corduroy, canvas or equally strong fabric, using old seat and back as patterns.

To cover seat, before removing original fabric seat, draw a line from front to back along each side edge indicating width of wooden frame. Remove seat from frame and measure width across seat between marked lines; measure depth from front to back edges (Diagram 1).

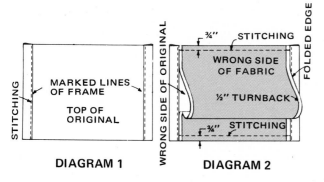

**DIAGRAM 1**  **DIAGRAM 2**

Cut new fabric 1″ wider than distance between marked lines and 3″ deeper than distance from front to back, with fabric design in desired position if fabric is patterned.

Duplicate marked lines indicating width of frame on underside of original seat. Fold ½″ to wrong side along each side edge of new fabric and place right side against underside of original seat, with folded edges along marked lines and raw edges even with front and back edges of original seat. Stitch across front and back edges, ¾″ from each edge (Diagram 2).

Turn seat right side out and stitch across each side as close to folded edge as possible, making sure folded edges exactly meet marked lines on original seat (Diagram 3).

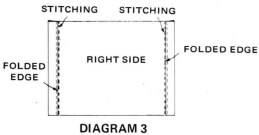

**DIAGRAM 3**

To cover back, remove original back from frame. Cut new fabric to cover wrong side of back as deep as original

back and as wide as distance between stitched edges of casings. Stitch in place to original back ½″ in from top and bottom edges (Diagram 4).

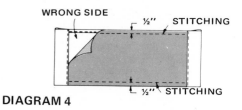

**DIAGRAM 4**

Place original back on fabric for new back so design on right side (if any) is in desired position. Cut fabric 1½″ beyond top and bottom edges, and wide enough to go around each side edge and overlap covering on wrong side of back. Place this piece, right side down, with raw edge along top of wrong side of original back and stitch ¾″ from edge, starting and ending stitching at vertical stitching on original back. Clip through raw edge at each end of stitching 1½″ down from top edge (Diagram 5). Stitch across bottom edge and clip in same manner.

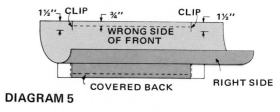

**DIAGRAM 5**

Turn back right side out. Diagram 6 shows view from back at this point with back covered, a ¾″-wide edging of new fabric across top and bottom edges and extending ¾″ past top and bottom edges at each end. Turn that ¾″ to wrong side along top and bottom edges of one end and wrap around to back so fold goes along top and bottom edges of original cover. Trim so raw edge of new fabric overlaps back covering ½″ and zigzag stitch over raw edge from top to bottom (Diagram 7). Finish other end in same manner.

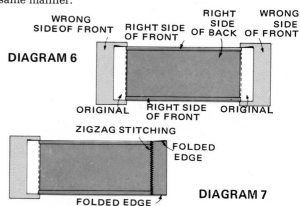

**DIAGRAM 6**

**DIAGRAM 7**

# TIERED DUST RUFFLE
## ON PAGE 43

MATERIALS NEEDED:
(for 54″-wide bed)

    Two queen-size printed sheets (or 10 yards 54″-wide fabric)

    Buttonhole twist or nylon thread

    Four yards ½″-wide twill tape

Remove stitching from top hem of each sheet and press to remove fold. From one she t, cut strips 105″ long as follows: five 10¼″ wide for ruffle A; five 5¾″ wide for ruffle B; two 4¾″ wide for ruffle C. From other sheet, cut three 4¾″-wide strips for ruffle C and use remainder for top and sides of cover.

To make ruffle A, join five strips into one long strip by making French seams in following manner: Place two strips with wrong sides together and stitch across 10¼″ ends ⅛″ from edge; turn right sides together with seam along folded edge; press and stitch ¼″ from fold, enclosing raw edges. Press to one side (Diagram 1).

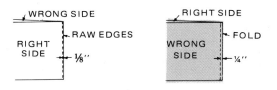

**DIAGRAM 1**

Hem bottom edge of ruffle by turning ¼″ to wrong side along one long edge, then turning another ¼″ and stitching. Hem each short edge in same manner. At top edge, turn ¾″ to wrong side, and make a row of gathering stitches ½″ from folded edge, using buttonhole twist or nylon thread in bobbin. Finished width of ruffle A is 9″ (Diagram 2).

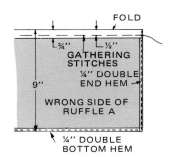

**DIAGRAM 2**

Make ruffles B and C in same manner so finished width of B is 4½″ and finished width of C is 3½″

Place sheet for top and sides on bed spring, wrong side up, so sheet hangs at least 1″ below bottom of spring on all four sides. (If using 54″-wide fabric, seam two 74″ lengths of fabric together for top section.) Pin down each

corner and mark position of bottom edge of spring. (If spring is attached to a headboard, pin fabric down as far as possible and leave remainder open.) Cut away excess fabric 1″ below marked line on all four sides and ½″ beyond pinned corners (Diagram 3).

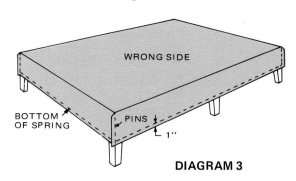

**DIAGRAM 3**

Remove cover and stitch along pinned corners. Make a double ½″ hem along four sides so bottom edge of cover is even with bottom of spring and stitch in place. (If corners at head of bed are to be left partly open, stitch hems along both edges below corner seams.) Cut six 24″ lengths of twill tape; fold each in half, and stitch through fold to bottom edge of cover, placing one at each corner leg and one at each center leg of spring. (If corners are left open at head, cut two of the tapes in half and stitch a 12″-long piece to each side of opening.) Replace cover on spring, right side up, and mark three lines along both sides and foot; mark bottom line A 9″ up from floor; mark line B 1″ above line A; mark line C 2½″ above line B. Top of spring in photo is 15½″ from floor; if your spring is a different height, adjust placement of lines B and C.

Measuring along top edge of ruffle A, place a pin 192″ from each end. (This amount of ruffle is to go along each side of cover, with remainder across foot end.) Starting at one end, pull up gathering stitches until ruffle between end and first pin fits along side of cover. Pull stitches until ruffle between pins fits foot end of cover. Pull stitches from other end until remainder of ruffle fits other side of cover. Pin ruffle A on cover with gathering row along line A; remove cover from spring and stitch ruffle in place, following gathering line (Diagram 4).

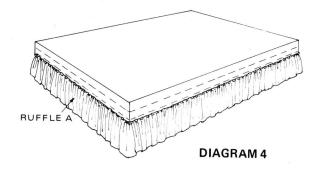

**DIAGRAM 4**

Gather and attach ruffle B, then ruffle C, in same manner. Place cover on spring and tie tapes around each leg to hold it in place.

## WALLPAPER-COVERED SCREEN
## ON PAGE 43

MATERIALS NEEDED:
    One screen, 84″ high with three 17″-wide
    panels
    Nine yards 21″-wide pre-pasted wallpaper
    Six 120″ lengths ¼″ x ½″ half-round rope molding
    1″ wire brads
    Twenty-two yards ¾″-wide cloth tape

Using full width of wallpaper, cut three 96″-long strips. Remove hinges from screen to separate panels. Following manufacturer's directions, apply one strip of wallpaper to front of one panel so equal amounts project beyond each side of panel and 6″ projects beyond top and bottom edges. Wrap wallpaper around side edges of panel and stick to back. Cut away top corners as shown in Diagram 1, leaving 2″ side flaps. Clip to front corners.

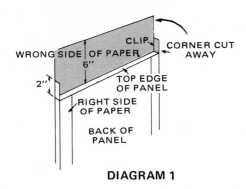

**DIAGRAM 1**

Fold 2″ flaps down onto top edge at each side and stick in place (Diagram 2).

Pull 6″ over top edge and stick to back of panel (Diagram 3). Cut, clip and cover bottom corners in same manner. Cover other two panels in same manner.

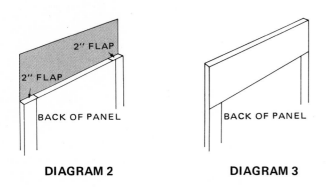

**DIAGRAM 2**        **DIAGRAM 3**

Place strips of cloth tape (#1 and #2) down each side edge, with edges of tape ⅛″ in from edges of panel. Place strips (#3 and #4) across top and bottom edges in same manner. Place two strips (#5 and #6) across panel so there is 25½″ clearance between #3 and #5 and between #4 and #6. Place two strips (#7 and #8) across panel so

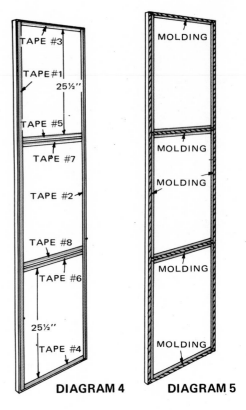

**DIAGRAM 4**        **DIAGRAM 5**

there is ¼″ between #5 and #7 and between #6 and #8 (Diagram 4).

From each 120″ length of molding, cut one 84″ piece and one 17″ piece. Cut a 45° angle at each end of each piece so that angles of two 84″ pieces and two 17″ pieces will meet at corners when placed around outside edges of each panel. Paint molding and nail in place. From remaining pieces of molding, cut pieces to fit across each panel between tapes #5 and #7 and between tapes #6 and #8. Paint and nail in place so equal amount of tape shows on each side of molding (Diagram 5).

Replace hinges to connect three panels.

## BEDSPREAD WITH "KIMONO"
## CORDING
## ON PAGE 47

MATERIALS NEEDED:
(for 96″ x 115″ bedspread to fit double bed 54″ x 75″ with 21″ drop)
    8¾ yards 48″-wide fabric
    6½ yards 48″-wide lining
    Polyester fiberfill
    4-ply yarn for tufting
    Tapestry needle

NOTE: The finished length of this spread is only 115″ because the pillows are flat and don't require much tuck-in; be sure to measure your own bed with everything in place and adjust the length accordingly.

Using full width of fabric, cut two pieces 113½" long. Cut one of these pieces in half lengthwise to form two 24" x 113½" side panels. Place a 24"-wide panel at each side of full-width piece, right sides together, selvages even and pattern of fabric matching; stitch together with ½" seams along selvages. Press seams open. Trim 1" along each side to form piece 92" wide x 113½" long. Cut 113½" lengths of fiberfill and join together to form 1 piece 92" wide, butting edges of fiberfill together and catch-stitching to form flat joining. Cut two 113½" lengths of lining and join with one seam at center; press seam open and trim lining to 92" width. Pin fabric, fiberfill and lining together with all edges even, and cut curved corners at foot end (Diagram 1). Unpin.

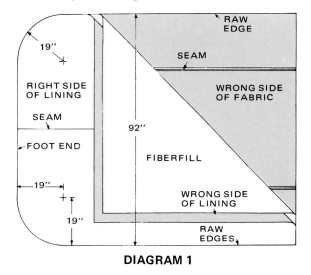

**DIAGRAM 1**

From remaining fabric, cut four lengthwise strips, each 6" wide, for kimono cording, cutting them so fabric pattern will match when strips are joined across 6" edges. Stitch strips together with ½" seams. Cut 6"-wide strips of fiberfill and join together as before until they are same length as fabric strip. Place fiberfill on wrong side of fabric strip, then fold in half lengthwise so right side of fabric is on the outside and raw edges are even; stitch along entire length ½" from raw edges, stopping stitching 1" from end. At this end, turn ½" of fabric to inside of cording and slip-stitch end closed (Diagram 2).

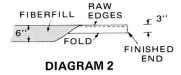

**DIAGRAM 2**

Trim fiberfill as close to seam line as possible. Place kimono cording around side edges and foot of spread on right side of *fabric only,* with raw edges even and finished end of cording ½" from head of bedspread on one side. Baste cording around three sides, easing in fullness at curved corners so cording will lie flat when turned; cut

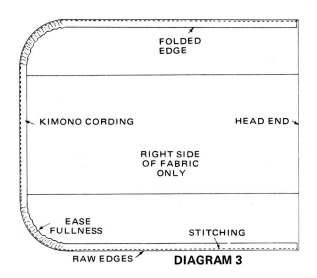

**DIAGRAM 3**

cording and turn in raw edges of fabric so finished end of cording is ½" from head end of spread on other side. Stitch around three sides ½" from raw edges, following stitching line of cording (Diagram 3).

With cording turned back against right side of fabric, place lining on fabric with right sides together and all raw edges even, covering cording. Place fiberfill over lining with all edges even; baste the three layers together. Stitch around three sides, following stitching line of cording. Stitch across head end, ½" from edge, leaving a 48" opening at center. Turn right side out through opening; slip-stitch opening closed. Press.

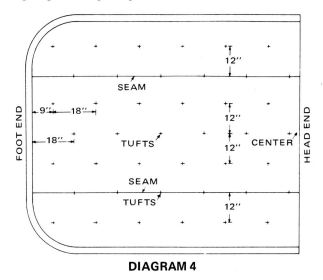

**DIAGRAM 4**

Smooth bedspread out flat and mark positions of tufts in following manner: Along center line and each seam, mark every 18" from foot to head. Along lines 12" each side of center and 12" beyond seams, mark 9" from foot, then every 18" (Diagram 4). Make tuft at each mark in following manner: Using three strands of yarn and tapestry needle, insert needle through all thicknesses from right side of fabric to wrong side and back up to right side. Tie yarn securely and trim ends ¾" from knot.

# WINDOW TREATMENT
## ON PAGE 47

MATERIALS NEEDED:
(for room with 96″ ceiling)

    Two "2 x 4" clear pine x 96″ for A and B

    Eight 2½″ angle irons with sixteen 1″ and four
       1¾″ flat head wood screws and four toggle bolts

    Two 1⅜″-diameter closet poles, width of window
       plus 36″

    Two pairs closet pole brackets, 1 open and 1
       closed bracket in each pair

    Six yards 48″-wide fabric for draperies

    Basecoat and paint

Attach four angle irons to inside face of A with two screws through each, so back of each angle iron is flush with back edge of A. Place one flush with top of A, one flush with bottom, and two equally spaced along length (see Diagram 3). Attach one open pole bracket to inside face of A so opening is facing up and top of pole will be

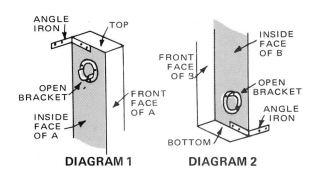

**DIAGRAM 1**   **DIAGRAM 2**

1″ from top of A when pole is in place (Diagram 1). Attach closed bracket to bottom of A in same relative position. Attach angle irons to inside face of B in same manner. Attach closed pole bracket to top inside face of B in same position as open bracket at top of A. Attach open bracket to bottom inside face of B so opening is facing front face of B with just enough of the lip of bracket on top to hold pole firmly in place when in position (Diagram 2).

Apply basecoat and paint to A and B, angle irons and brackets, following manufacturer's directions. Attach A to wall with one 1¾″ screw through top and bottom angle irons and one bolt through each of the other two angle irons, placing inside face of A 18″ to right of window. Attach B 18″ from left side of window in same manner (Diagram 3).

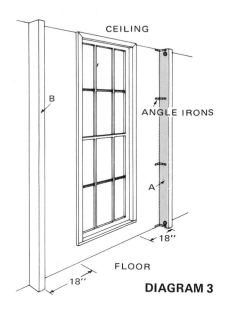

**DIAGRAM 3**

Across entire width of fabric cut two 105″ lengths for side draperies. Along each side edge, turn ½″ to wrong side, then turn 2″ to wrong side and stitch to form side hems. Along each top edge, turn 4″ to wrong side and stitch 1″ down from fold to form 1″ heading; turn ½″ under along raw edge and stitch across along fold to form 2½″ casing for pole.

Paint poles, let dry and insert one through top casings of draperies. Place one end of pole into closed bracket at top end of B, then slip other end of pole into open bracket at top end of A. Place other pole in position in bottom brackets in same manner. Pull draperies taut and wrap unfinished bottom edges around bottom pole to determine placement of 2½″ bottom casings (without headings). Mark and pin in place. Remove draperies from poles, turn ½″ to wrong side and stitch casings.

# DRAPED "HEADBOARD"
## ON PAGE 47

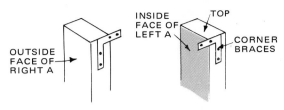

**DIAGRAM 1**

MATERIALS NEEDED:
(for room with 96″ ceiling)

Two "2 x 4"s, each 96″, for A

Four 3″ corner braces with eight 1″ and four 1¾″
flat-head wood screws

Two spring-tension curtain rods to fit between A
and B

8¾ yards 48″-wide fabric

Basecoat and paint

Attach corner braces to A with 1″ screws so two A form a pair; place braces flush with top and bottom ends of each A with braces centered on A and projecting past inside faces (Diagram 1).

Apply basecoat and paint to each A, including projecting braces. Place left A against wall and attach with 1¾″ screws through corner braces into wall; attach right A in same manner, having space between them equal to width of bed plus 4″ (braces will be covered by drapery later). Across entire width of fabric cut three 103″ lengths and seam together with ½″ seams to form one wide piece. Along each side edge, turn ½″ to wrong side, then turn 2″ to wrong side and stitch to form side hems. Along top edge, turn 3″ to wrong side and stitch 1″ down from fold to form 1″ heading; turn ½″ under along raw edge and stitch along fold to form 1½″ casing for rod. Complete drapery in same manner as for drapery in window treatment (page 60). Place rods through casings and place in position between two A.

# How to Capture the Charm of a Canopied Four-Poster in Today's Tiny Rooms

You're a child of today and manage to cope with living in a hectic, worried world, but your natural propensity is for a calm, well-ordered environment in which you can live graciously. Well, at least in your own home, you can. You can create a setting of quiet comfort inspired by the best of the past, when good design flourished and fine workmanship was a matter of pride. You can put the same thought and care into creating necessities (and comforts) for your home as did your forebears, and the result will be even more outstanding today. Happily, the wide choice of fabrics now available and the miraculous sewing machines that no longer amaze us make sewing for one's home more enjoyable than ever.

Your bedroom may be smaller than the master bedroom in an affluent 18th-Century home, but your bed can still have the luxurious look—and yes, even the stately effect—of a canopied four-poster without overwhelming the rest of the room. This bed treatment, with its scalloped valance and coverlet, its softly pleated drapery and back panel, is an inspired adaptation of a traditional favorite. It has an almost regal air, but there's still something lighthearted about the big, wavy scallops and the fanciful print of stylized flowers. You can find many prints of this type that have an authentic 18th Century flavor; any one would be just as effective used the same way. You'll find directions for making the valance, drapery and coverlet beginning on page 72, and directions for the gathered dust ruffle on page 53.

# How to Have the Traditional Look of an 18th-Century Bedroom

If you love the gracious charm of the period when fine furniture-making reached its peak and decorative design of all kinds flourished as never before or since, you'll thrive on the 18th-Century look. And if your bedroom is a reasonably generous size, you can indulge yourself all the way and have a private retreat as entrancing as the one glimpsed here. If you don't already own a traditional four-poster bed with a gracefully arched canopy, you really should have one—and dress it in a charming Chinoiserie print instead of the usual dainty but innocuous sheer white. And don't settle for a smooth-topped canopy; a luxuriously-gathered one is far more effective. Reproducing the bed treatment seen here may seem like an ambitious undertaking, but actually it's amazingly simple. The ruffled canopy is made entirely of straight pieces of fabric—and so, for that matter, are the coverlet and dust ruffle. So all the sewing is straight, easy seams. And you'll find step-by-step directions for making the ruffled canopy starting on page 74. The coverlet is simply a short version of the tailored spread described (with complete directions) on page 50. Making the gathered dust ruffle is also a snap; directions for that are on page 53.

# How to Have the Traditional Look of a French Provincial Bedroom

If you have a strong feeling for tradition, but an informal country look suits your life style, consider the many charms of French Provincial. "Country French," as it's sometimes called, combines the best of two worlds. The provincial pieces created by local craftsmen for the rustic chateaux and manor houses of 18th-Century France copied the elegant court furniture of the period, but the country cabinetmakers concentrated on the wood they worked with, omitting the gilding and other elaborate detailing of the Parisian models while retaining their grace and timeless quality. The result was furniture of simple country charm, sturdy enough for family use and tasteful enough for a country estate. That same feeling of simplified elegance is reflected in the bedroom here, and may be just the look you'd like to live with. The mini-canopy suggests a curtained poster bed without the formality or the all-enclosed feeling. The whole room has an airy, open look, and the latticed floral print used for the valances, drapery and bedspread adds a fresh, country-garden air. You'll have no trouble finding a similar print in a color scheme that pleases you, plus a coordinated solid. Directions for making the mini-canopy and the bed drapery are on page 74; see page 132 for valances, page 124 for draperies, and page 210 for round table covers.

# Dramatic Canopies Provide an Easy Touch of Tradition

Would you have believed it possible to make such commanding canopies by draping fabric over poles? The one at the left marries a touch of tradition to a clean-swept modern look. One wooden pole with brackets was attached to the wall behind the bed, another with finials to the ceiling. Cut to the width of the bed plus side hems, the fabric panel was doubled at one end to make the overhang.

Above, a neo-classic bedroom designed by an individualist who tempered a touch of tradition with sophisticated taste. The canopy was inspired by a Napoleonic campaign bed (the original was made of mosquito netting) and hung on drapery rods wound with striped ribbon. These, the satin-striped fabric and the round bolster all have a decidedly French Empire look. Directions for bed canopy are on page 76. Directions for drapery pole are on page 77. See how to make a round bolster on page 223.

# A Mini-Canopy in an Exotic Mood Marries Tradition to Today

If you're torn between a traditional look and the contemporary concept of uncluttered line and a minimum of ornamentation, have the best of both. There's nothing more dramatic than one magnificently decorative piece in a coolly contemporary setting. This updated version of a canopied bed, with its soaring panel of richly patterned fabric topped by a miniature canopy that repeats the scalloped motif of the bedspread, is doubly effective because everything else in the room is so understated. The exotic print sparkles as though paved with jewels against snowy white walls, a fluffy white carpet and simple white-painted furniture. The only other splashes of color are supplied by nature: ferns in rustic wicker baskets, garden flowers in plain white containers. The beauty of this decorating strategy is that it doesn't depend on a particular fabric; any vividly colored print would sparkle just as vibrantly against a sea of white. The pointed scallops that edge the canopy and the bedspread were inspired by this specific print, but could easily be adapted to follow the design-line of another pattern. (On a medallion-printed fabric, for instance, make rounded scallops.) Just alter the outline shown in the directions for Mini-Canopy that begin on page 77. Directions for making the bedspread and bolster cover are given on pages 78–79. Here again, they're for the twin bed photographed, but adjusting the dimensions to suit other sizes is a very simple matter. To make the dust ruffle, see page 53.

# directions for projects

## BED DRAPERY AND BEDSPREAD
### ON PAGE 62

MATERIALS NEEDED:
Three pine "1 x 3"s, each·width of bed plus 20" for A, B, and C
Nine toggle bolts
Snap tape
½"-diameter cording
Four ½" brass rings
Finishing nails
Two curtain rods
Pin-on hooks
Fabric
Flannel interfacing
Lining fabric (sateen, muslin or polished cotton)

**Pleated Panel Behind Bed:** Nail A to B with finishing nails as shown in Diagram 1. Tack snap tape around three edges of A and across B, having snaps as close to ends as possible and placing tape on B as close to corner as you can (Diagram 2). Attach A and B to wall and ceiling with three toggle bolts through each piece. Attach lower strip C to wall with toggle bolts in the same manner, so it is located 3" below the top edge of mattress (Diagram 3).

Cut fabric lengths to height required (top of A to bottom of C) plus 2" and seam pieces together to make one piece three times length of B plus 2". Press seams open. Make 1" hem down each side. Make 2" deep pleats across top and bottom edges, keeping seams on the inside of

pleats. Stitch snap tape across top and bottom edges on right side so snaps match those on tape attached to B and C, having inside edge of tape 1" in from edge of fabric (Diagram 4).

Tack snap tape along bottom edge of C, then snap tapes on the pleated panel to tapes tacked to B and C (Diagram 5).

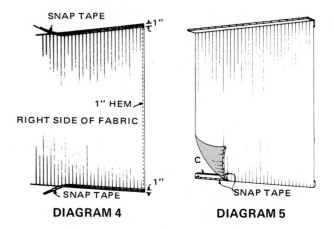

**DIAGRAM 4**          **DIAGRAM 5**

**Coverlet:** Measure top of bed from head to foot and from side to side with sheets, blankets and dust ruffle in place. Cut fabric, flannel interfacing and lining fabric to fit top of bed plus ⅝" seam allowance on all four sides, seaming if necessary. If necessary to seam outer fabric, make top in three sections, with wide center panel (usually full width of fabric) flanked by two side panels of equal width. Cut panels so pattern will match exactly when seamed together. If necessary to seam interfacing and/or lining, make sure seams will not fall on those of the outer fabric.

Cutting across the width of the fabric, cut strips of outer fabric one-half the depth of dust ruffle and seam together until long enough to go around three sides of the bed. Cut and seam interfacing and lining fabric to the same size. Press all seams open.

Draw scalloped design on outer fabric so a scallop goes around each corner at the foot and one is in the center. Continue scallop design along both sides.

Cut bias strips and cover cording (see directions for covering cording on page 209). Place cording along scalloped edge and stitch, clipping seam allowance of cording as needed to go around curves. Trim fabric ⅝" outside of stitching line (Diagram 6).

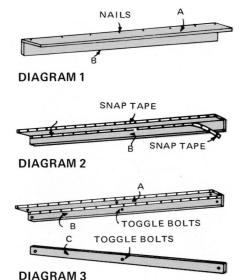

**DIAGRAM 1**

**DIAGRAM 2**

**DIAGRAM 3**

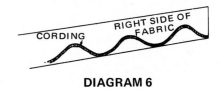

**DIAGRAM 6**

Place lining fabric wrong side down on interfacing; then place outer fabric right side down on lining. Be sure to stagger seams so they do not fall on top of each other, then baste all three pieces together. Stitch 5/8″ seam down each side, then stitch along scalloped edge following stitched line where cording was applied. Trim away extra lining fabric and interfacing (Diagram 7). Clip inner curved edges and turn right side out, then press.

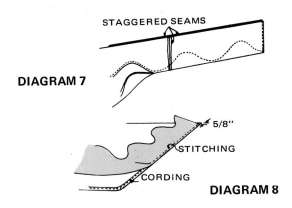

**DIAGRAM 7**

**DIAGRAM 8**

Baste interfacing to wrong side of top piece. Stitch cording to three edges, taking a 5/8″ seam and clipping seam allowance of cording to go around corners. Stitch scalloped drop to top along same stitching line (Diagram 8), keeping ends of drop 5/8″ in from head end of top piece.

Fold scalloped drop back over top, then baste lining fabric (right side down) along three edges of top, enclosing drop. Turn right side out to make certain top lies smooth and flat. When sure that lining is properly basted to top, turn wrong side out and stitch around three sides on same stitching line as before. Turn right side out and press. Turn under edges across head of bed and blind-stitch (Diagram 9).

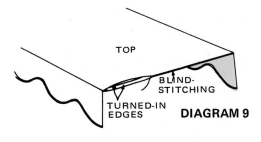

**DIAGRAM 9**

**Drapery Panels: (Make two)** Cut fabric to desired width (usually 2½ times finished width) plus 4″ for side hems and 1¼″ seam allowance, and to desired length plus 3″ for hem and 5/8″ seam allowance. Cut lining 3″ shorter than outer fabric and 8″ narrower. Turn up 3″ hem in outer fabric and a 1″ hem in lining. Matching side and top edges, right sides together, seam from top to bottom of lining hem (Diagram 10). Press seams open and fold so seams are same distance from side folds on both sides. Stitch 5/8″ seam across top (Diagram 11). Turn right side out and press. Make pleats across top edge.

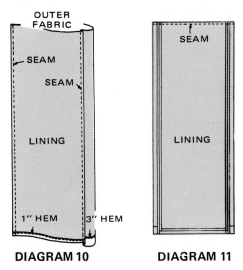

**DIAGRAM 10**     **DIAGRAM 11**

To make tie-backs, cut two pieces of outer fabric and two pieces of lining as shown in Diagram 12. Trim cording allowance to ½″ and stitch across top and bottom edges on right side of outer fabric, raw edges of fabric and cording flush. Place lining on each piece of outer fabric, right sides together, and stitch along same stitching lines. Turn tie-backs right side out. Turn in raw edges across ends and blind-stitch closed. Sew brass ring to each end (Diagram 13).

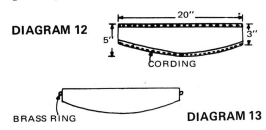

**DIAGRAM 12**

**DIAGRAM 13**

Attach curtain rod to each end of B and hang draperies. Screw cup hook to wall at each side of bed and hook rings of tie-back over them.

**Valance:** Cut strips of fabric, interfacing and lining to same depth as scalloped drop for spread and long enough to go around three sides of A plus seam allowances. Space scallops so lowest points are at equal thirds of width. Assemble in same manner as for scalloped drop of spread.

Sew snap tape across top edge of valance on right side so snaps match those on tape attached to A. Turn taped edge under and snap valance in place on A (Diagram 14).

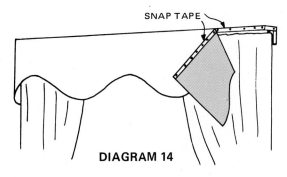

**DIAGRAM 14**

## RUFFLED BED CANOPY
### ON PAGE 65

MATERIALS NEEDED:
  55″-wide fabric
  55″-wide lining fabric
  Snap tape
  Upholsterers' tacks

Unscrew finials from tops of posts and remove tester frame. Measure length of tester frame along top edge of one curved side. Using full width of fabric, cut a piece 1¾ times this length. Cut piece of lining fabric to same size. Cut two strips of snap tape 1″ longer than length of frame and two 3″-wide strips of lining fabric the same length as tape.

Turn ½″ to wrong side along both ends of fabric and lining and press. Place fabric on lining, wrong sides together, with both folded ends and selvages along both sides flush. Stitch across each end ¼″ from folded edges. Stitch two rows of machine gathering stitches along each side, placing them ¼″ and ⅝″ from edges. Make a mark every 12″ along each strip of snap tape and every 21″ along each side edge of canopy on lining side. Gather fabric and lining so marks on lining match marks on tape. Fold ½″ under at each end of tape and place tape on lining, flush with edge of lining and leaving ½″ of lining without tape at each end. Stitch *only* along inside edge of tape (Diagram 1).

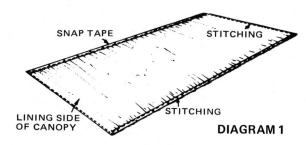

SNAP TAPE    STITCHING

LINING SIDE OF CANOPY    STITCHING

**DIAGRAM 1**

Fold the two 3″-wide lining strips in half lengthwise; turn ½″ under at each end and press. Insert raw edges of lining strip between tape and lining, then stitch along outside edge of tape through all thicknesses. Place canopy on top of frame and mark position of finial hole at each corner. Make a buttonhole in each corner at these positions (Diagram 2).

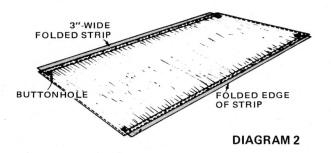

3″-WIDE FOLDED STRIP

BUTTONHOLE    FOLDED EDGE OF STRIP

**DIAGRAM 2**

Measure around entire outside edge of canopy and multiply by two for length of ruffle. Cut 9¾″-wide strips of fabric so pattern will match when seamed together across short ends. Seam strips together until length of piece equals above measurement. Cut and seam lining pieces together to same size. Place lining on fabric with right sides together and all edges even. Stitch along one long side ½″ in from edge, and along the other long side ¼″ in from edge. Turn right side out and press so a seam is along each edge. Turn under raw edges on one end and slip-stitch over raw edges of other end to form a circular piece. Run two rows of machine gathering stitches along edge with ¼″ seam, placing them ¼″ and ⅜″ from edge (Diagram 3).

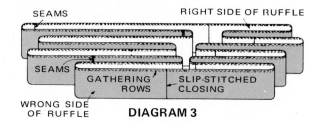

SEAMS    RIGHT SIDE OF RUFFLE

SEAMS

GATHERING ROWS    SLIP-STITCHED CLOSING

WRONG SIDE OF RUFFLE    **DIAGRAM 3**

Mark every 12″ along edges of canopy and every 24″ along gathering line of ruffle. Place ruffle right side down on right side of canopy with gathering line ½″ in from edge of canopy along ends and along folded strip of lining, close to edge of snap tape. Pull up gathers so marks match and pin in place; then stitch ruffle to canopy along pinned line. (Stitching ruffle to folded strip of lining fabric, instead of directly to top section, eliminates excessive bulkiness and makes ruffle fall gracefully.) Using upholsterers' tacks, attach other side of snap tape to tester frame, along top of curved edges. Place canopy on frame and replace finials on tops of posts.

## MINI-CANOPY AND BED DRAPERY
### ON PAGE 66

MATERIALS NEEDED:
(for double-bed size)
  ½″ x 4′ x 6′ sheet of plywood for A, B and C
  "1 x 2" pine:
    one 60″ for D
    two 11″ for E
  1⅓ yards 50″-wide fabric for canopy plus 10¾ yards for drapery
  Flannel for padding
  1½″ flat-head wood screws
  1½″ finishing nails
  2″ common nails
  Seven 3″ toggle bolts
  White glue
  Staple gun and staples

Basecoat and paint
Molding to match existing molding
Lath stripping or decorative braid
Two wooden dowels, 1⅜″ diameter, 15″ long
Two sets of inside casing sockets to fit poles (dowels)
Eighteen wooden pole rings, 1¾″ diameter
¼ yard 36″-wide interfacing for tiebacks
Four brass rings and two cup hooks

**Mini-canopy:** From ½″ plywood, cut one 14½″ x 61″ piece for A, one 15″ x 61″ piece for C, and two 14½″ x 14½″ pieces for B.

Drill pilot holes in A. Using 1½″ flat-head wood screws, glue and screw A to outer ends of B with all outer edges flush, as shown in Diagram 1. Drill pilot holes in C and glue and screw C to top edges of A and B with all outer edges flush. Following manufacturer's directions, apply basecoat and paint to inside surfaces of A, B and C.

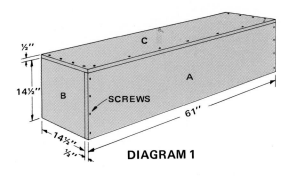

**DIAGRAM 1**

Cut one piece of fabric 19″ deep x full 50″ width to cover front of canopy. Cut two 19″-deep x 22″-wide pieces from remaining fabric to cover sides of canopy, being careful to cut these pieces so that pattern will match across all three pieces after they are seamed together with ½″ seams. Matching pattern, stitch one 19″ x 22″ piece to

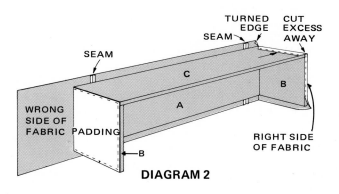

**DIAGRAM 2**

each side of 50″-wide piece. Cover front faces of A and B with flannel padding; staple in place. Center fabric on front of A, bring to back edges of B and staple in place (Diagram 2). (Strip of fabric 92″ long allows exactly ½″ of fabric to staple to ½″-wide back edge of each B.)

At top edge of fabric, clip fabric diagonally to front corners of C and turn clipped edges under; cut away fabric at back corners of C. Bring fabric to top of C and staple in place (Diagram 2). Clip and wrap fabric around lower edges of A and B in same manner, and staple to inside faces of A and B. (19″-wide piece of fabric, centered on 15″-wide face of canopy, allows 2″ extra at top and bottom.) Cover raw edge of fabric and staples on inside surfaces of A and B with decorative braid or lath stripping.

If walls of room are finished with soffit molding as shown in room photographed on page 66, remove a 61″ length of it along wall where canopy is to be placed. Center D lengthwise within this measurement, ½″ down from top edges of remaining molding. Mark positions for five evenly-spaced toggle bolts on D and on wall. Using marks as guide, drill pilot holes for 3″ toggle bolts in D and in wall. Bolt D to wall. Place one E at each end of D, at right angles to D and with outer edges flush (Diagram 3). Mark positions for two toggle bolts on each E and on wall. Using marks as guide, drill pilot holes for 3″ toggle bolts in each E and in wall. Bolt E to wall.

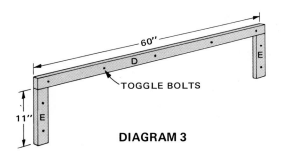

**DIAGRAM 3**

Place fabric-covered canopy over D and E with inside face of C resting on top edge of D and inside faces of B against outside edges of E. Using 2″ common nails, nail through C into top edge of D. Using as few 1½″ finishing nails as practical, nail through B into edges of E; pull fabric carefully back over nailheads. Cut matching soffit molding to lengths required and nail along top edges of A and B with finishing nails. (Length of finishing nails will be determined by thickness of molding.) If walls are finished with ceiling molding only, same effect can be achieved by placing top of canopy against ceiling and applying matching molding along top edges of A and B.

**Bed Drapery:** NOTE: If using a fabric with a one-way pattern such as that shown on page 66, all lengths must be stitched together with the pattern going in the same direction (in this case, with all flowers growing upward). To match the pattern perfectly when making seams, align pattern along edges of both pieces with right sides together and place pins horizontally into the seam. Do not remove pins until seam has been completed.

Cut four 92″-long panels of fabric across full width, matching placement of pattern on all panels. With right sides together, match two panels carefully and stitch 1″ seams along both long edges, forming a tube. Press seams open. Make a 1″ hem along edge of tube which will be bottom of drapery. Still working on the wrong side, bring seamlines to center of tube and stitch across top ½" from raw edges (Diagram 4).

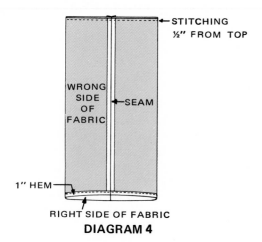

DIAGRAM 4

Turn drapery right side out and press seam along top edge, but do not press folds along sides of drapery. Sew nine rings to top of drapery, placing one at each end and others 6" apart. Seam remaining two 92" panels of fabric together and finish in same manner.

Completed draperies are approximately 90" long. Inside the mini-canopy, screw two casing sockets to wall and two to inner face of A, approximately 1" from inner face of each B and 90½" from floor. Insert dowels through wooden rings; hang draperies in place by inserting dowels in casing sockets.

# BED CANOPY
## ON PAGE 69

MATERIALS NEEDED:
(for 39"-wide bed)
    Three 1⅜" diameter wooden poles, each 39" long
    Three screw-on wooden finials
    Three 6" wooden discs
    Three lengths of gold chain: 18½", 24½" and 42½"
    Gold paint
    Three 1½" flat-head wood screws
    Six molly bolts or toggle screws
    Two lengths of 54"-wide sheer fabric, as required, to go from floor behind headboard, over 3 poles to floor at foot
    Solid color fabric
    Striped fabric or 1"-wide striped ribbon
    Tacks
    Staple gun and staples
    1"-wire brads

NOTE: Ceiling in room shown is 8 feet high; tops of poles are 12", 18" and 36" down from ceiling. Their positions, lengths of chains and length of sheer canopy will vary depending upon the height of your ceiling.

**Poles:** Measure circumference of pole; cut a strip of solid color fabric 1" wider than circumference of pole and 1" longer than length of pole. Turn ½" to wrong side along one long edge and, with fabric extending ½" beyond each end of pole, wrap fabric around pole, covering raw edge with folded edge. Staple in place close to folded edge. Fold excess ½" of fabric at each end flat against end of pole, pleating it to make it lie flat; staple in place.

For wrapping pole, use 1"-wide striped ribbon or cut a 2"-wide strip of striped fabric 64" long. If using ribbon, turn ½" to wrong side across each short edge; if using fabric, turn ½" to wrong side along all edges. Press folds flat. Starting at one end of fabric-covered pole, place one end of ribbon or strip of fabric on folded edge of fabric around pole and tack in place; wrap around pole in spiral fashion, keeping spirals evenly spaced and pulled smoothly in place. Tack to other end at folded edge of fabric (Diagram 1).

DIAGRAM 1

Paint finial with gold paint. Drill pilot hole in one end of pole and screw finial in place. Drill pilot holes in other end of fabric-wrapped pole and in center of wooden disc for 1½" screws; drill another hole in the disc ½" from outer edge for molly bolt or toggle screw. Paint disc with gold paint. Screw disc to pole with 1½" screw through pilot hole in center of disc. Attach disc to wall with molly bolt or toggle screw through remaining pilot hole so top of pole is desired distance from ceiling and staples face toward ceiling. Nail other side of disc to wall with 1" wire brads. Make a 6½" loop in one end of chain and catch finial end of pole in this loop; attach other end of chain to ceiling with molly bolt or toggle screw to hold pole in level position. Paint head of bolt or screw and touch up disc, if necessary.

**Canopy:** Make a ½" hem across each 54" end of each length of fabric. Drape lengths over poles side by side as shown in photo and adjust folds on each pole so selvage edges are hidden.

## DRAPERY POLE
### ON PAGE 69

MATERIALS NEEDED:
- One 1⅜″-diameter wooden pole in required length
- Two screw-on wooden finials
- Two wooden brackets
- Wooden drapery rings with 1¾″ inside diameter
- Two 3⅛″ diameter decorative brass holdbacks with 3⅜″ posts
- Gold paint
- Tacks
- Solid-color fabric
- Striped fabric or 1″-wide striped ribbon
- Staple gun and staples

Cover pole in same manner as for preceding Bed Canopy. Paint finials, brackets and rings with gold paint. Attach finial to one end of pole, put drapery rings on pole and attach finial to other end of pole. Attach brackets to wall at each side of opening, put pole in place and hang draperies from wooden rings. Hold conventional pinch-pleated draperies back with decorative brass holdbacks as shown in illustration on page 69.

## MINI-CANOPY AND WALL PANEL
### ON PAGE 71

MATERIALS NEEDED:
(for 47″-wide unit)
- Two pine "1 x 2"s, each 84″, for A, B, C
- Two ⁷⁄₁₆″ x 1¾″ x 84″ lattice strips for D
- Four ⅝″-wide x 84″-long pieces of rope molding for E
- Two ¼″ x ½″ x 84″ lattice strips for F
- Two 3″ angle irons with four 1″ and two 1¾″ screws
- 2″ finishing nails
- ¾″ brads
- Six yards 52″-wide fabric
- ½ yard scrap of 48″-wide fabric for dust cover on top of canopy
- Three yards precovered cording
- Staple gun and staples
- Wood glue
- Basecoat and paint: white and desired color

Across full width of fabric, cut four 10″ strips for scalloped valance so pattern matches across all four and will be in desired position when ½″ seam is taken along scalloped or pointed lower edge. Seam two widths together along 10″ ends, matching pattern. Trim to 82″ length, centering scallops so placement is the same at both ends. Place cording along lower edge on right side of seamed piece with stitching line of cording following fabric pat-

tern or desired scallop design; clip seam allowance of cording to go around points or scallops. Stitch, following stitching line of cording (Diagram 1). Trim fabric flush with cording allowance.

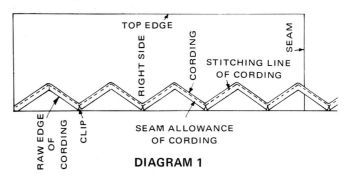

**DIAGRAM 1**

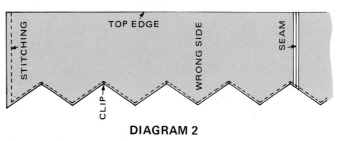

**DIAGRAM 2**

Seam remaining two pieces together and trim as before. Place second seamed piece over first, with right sides together, covering cording. Stitch ½″ from ends and along pointed lower edge, following same stitching line as before. Trim seam allowance ¼″ beyond stitching and clip at inside points (Diagram 2).

Turn valance right-side out and press so cording is along lower edge. Stitch across valance ¾″ below top edge; set aside.

Starting at a point 85″ above floor line, mark two vertical lines 46″ apart to designate sides of fabric for wall panel (finished width of panel will be 47″). Across full width of fabric, cut an 85½″ length; trim to 46″ width so pattern is centered. With top edge 85″ from floor and side edges along marked lines, staple fabric to wall along top and side edges; turn ½″ under along lower edge and staple in place. Determine positions of wall studs along top edge of fabric.

From *each* "1 x 2," cut one A, 17″; one B, 45½″; one C, 15½″. Nail A to ends of B so ends of A are flush with outside faces of B. Hold frame at top edge of fabric on wall with ends of frame extending ½″ beyond fabric on both sides; mark positions of studs on one B. Place two C inside frame so they are centered on the two stud positions nearest A; nail through B into ends of C (Diagram 3).

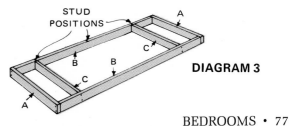

**DIAGRAM 3**

Across full width of fabric, cut a 22″ length; cover underside of frame by wrapping fabric around it and stapling to top edges of A and B. Using 1″ screws, attach two angle irons to top edges of B and C so outside faces of angle irons are flush with back face of B (Diagram 4).

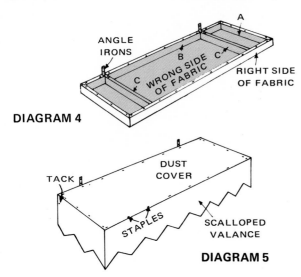

**DIAGRAM 4**

**DIAGRAM 5**

Place scalloped canopy valance around front and sides of frame so stitching line ¾″ below top edge of valance is along top edge of frame; staple valance to top edges of A and B. Using ¾″ brads, tack valance to frame at lower back corner of each A. Staple ½ yard scrap of fabric to top edges of A and B to form dust cover (Diagram 5).

Using 1¾″ screws through angle irons into studs, attach canopy to wall so fabric-covered underside is 84″ from floor and sides of canopy extend ½″ beyond fabric panel on both sides.

Following manufacturer's directions, apply basecoat to D, E and F. Paint D and E white; paint F desired color (maroon in photograph). Glue two E to face of D, one along each side; glue F between E. Position D/E/F along each side of fabric panel, covering edges of fabric and aligning outside edges of D/E/F with sides of canopy; nail to wall with 2″ finishing nails placed between E and F, placing nails at each end and about 24″ apart (see photograph on page 71). Touch up with paint.

# BEDSPREAD AND BOLSTER COVER
## ON PAGE 71

MATERIALS NEEDED:
(for 39″ x 75″ bed and 4″ x 18″ x 39″ bolster)
    11½ yards 52″-wide fabric
    6½ yards 44″-wide lining (sateen, polished cotton or muslin)
    Nineteen yards pre-covered cording
    One 40″ or two 20″ zippers for bolster cover
    One 4″ x 18″ x 39″ foam bolster pillow
    Nylon thread

**Bedspread:** Cut pieces for lining as shown in Diagram 1: A and B, each 6½″ x 234″; C, 10″ x 234″; two D, each 21″ x 78″. From fabric, cut following pieces so fabric pattern is centered and will match when seamed: top E, 41″ x 78″; five scalloped borders F, each 10″ x full width; two bolster tops G, each 20″ x 41″; three bolster boxings H, each 5½″ x full width; eight ruffles J, each 24″ x full width.

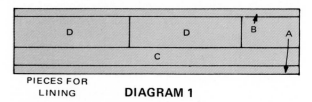

**PIECES FOR LINING**    **DIAGRAM 1**

Join five F together along 10″ edges so fabric pattern will match; press seams open. Using F and lining C, make scalloped border with finished length of 223″ in same manner as for scalloped valance of mini-canopy, Diagrams 1 and 2, page 77; omit stitching across ends and ¾″ below top edge.

Seam eight J together along 24″ edges, matching fabric pattern. Using nylon thread in bobbin, run two gathering rows ⅜″ and ¾″ from top edge. Pull up nylon gathering threads and pin wrong side of J along raw edge of lining A, adjusting gathers evenly. Place raw edge of lining B flush with edges of A and J; stitch ½″ from edge through A, J and B (Diagram 2).

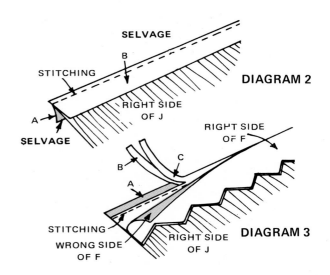

Turn A and B up so selvages are flush above edge of J; baste together along selvages. Mark positions of corners of bed on A/B. Place A and B flush with lining C on scalloped border, forming two 3½″-deep inverted pleats at each corner (see photo). Leaving F free, stitch across 1¼″ from edge through A, B and C *only*; stitch from head end down one long side to fold of corner pleat, then stitch other side in same manner. Stitch across foot end from fold of pleat at one corner to fold of pleat at other corner. Trim away B and C ½″ beyond stitching (Diagram 3).

Smooth F so scalloped border lies flat; baste A and F

together across top edge. This procedure eliminates bulky seams around top edge of bedspread.

Taking a ½" seam, join two lining D together along 78" length; press seam open. Place top E and lining D with right sides together and all edges flush; baste around all four sides. Place cording around three edges on right side of E (do not place it across head end); place stitching line of cording ½" in from edges of E and clip seam allowance of cording to go around corners. Stitch together, following stitching line of cording (Diagram 4).

Place joined ruffle and scalloped drop around three sides of E, right sides together, covering cording and keeping all edges flush. Stitch A and F to E, following stitching line of cording (Diagram 5).

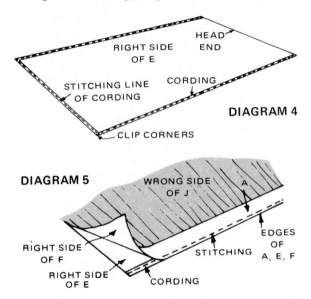

Place spread on bed and mark lower edge of ruffle J; hem. Hem across edge of one ruffle, top E and other ruffle at head end.

**Bolster:** Cut one G in half lengthwise to form two 10" widths; fold ½" to wrong side along one long edge of each. Place folded edges along center of zipper so they meet, and stitch along each side of zipper. Trim other G to same size.

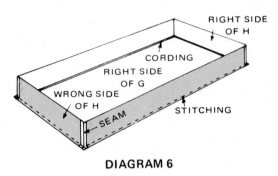

Place cording around all four edges of each G in same manner as for cording on Bedspread; stitch in place. Trim two H to 40" and cut remaining one into two 19" pieces. Alternating 19" and 40" lengths and taking ½" seams, stitch four H together across short ends to form complete circle. With right sides together, raw edges even and a seam at each corner, place H around G. Stitch together, following stitching line as before (Diagram 6).

With zipper open a short distance, stitch unattached edge of H to other G in same manner. Open zipper all the way, turn cover right side out and insert bolster.

# Four-Poster Pizzaz Without Any Posters

You love the drama of a decorative four-poster but don't see any prospect of owning one? Fake it! The fabulously effective "four-posters" seen here haven't a post between them. It's all done with fabric and molding attached to an easy-to-construct frame which, in turn, is attached to the ceiling. To make it even easier, printed bedsheets were used in lieu of by-the-yard fabric for the beauty at the left—which means a lot less seaming. (The directions for the Fake Four-Poster that start on page 94 tell you exactly how many, and how to use them.) A coordinated sheet wraps up the mattress for an ultra-trim look and makes a bedspread superfluous. If you'd rather use a bedspread, see the version below; a double-bordered 55"-wide print was used for the tailored bedspread (see page 50).

# Contemporary Four-Posters You Can Construct and Cover

Yes, you can. You can have a four-poster bed that's as contemporary as tomorrow by simply constructing a "3 x 3" frame and covering it in any fabric you please. You can have a boldly avant-garde look like the one above to star in a room that's all silvery shimmer and shine, or you can build the same basic frame and cover it with almost-traditional flowers for the softer look at the left. Directions for the four-poster frame above, complete with headboard, start on page 95. Because the square-cut posts stand free of the bed, the coverlet opposite is a short-cut version of a tailored spread with pleated corners (see page 52); the one above is made the same way without the pillow section, and the ruffle-less "dust ruffle" is a duplicate of the coverlet.

# Make a Fabric-Covered Headboard to Make the Most of Your Bed

Has it ever occurred to you that you can start with only a mattress and boxspring and end up with a complete, custom-made bed? The difference is only a headboard and a bedspread to match—both of which you can turn out yourself without too much effort. These two simple additions can transform the bare bones of a bed into a stunning focal point a professional decorator would be proud to produce. The decorative assets are obvious. You don't have to settle for a heavy-looking headboard, or have a completely matched "set" of furniture. What you *can* have is a bed completely covered in any color and pattern that pleases you and works with the rest of the room.

See what we mean by a stunning focal point? Instead of a stereotyped piece of furniture that's merely functional, the bed opposite is a major asset to the decorative plan of the room—as well as to its color scheme. The lively blend of blues and greens laced generously with white, and the mixture of geometric and floral patterns, gives the room a fresh, contemporary look in spite of the rather heavy, conventional furniture. (A dark wood headboard against the white-laquered Kashmiri screen would have killed the whole effect.) And the curved headboard isn't hard to make and cover, as you'll see when you turn to the directions on page 98. Directions for the tailored bedspread with corner pleats are on page 52.

# Fabric-Covered Headboards Transform Studio Couches into Decorative Daybeds

Close your eyes a moment and picture an undressed studio couch in its ticking-striped birthday suit. Would you believe these decorative daybeds both started out in life that way? An unadorned studio couch is a functional piece of furniture that looks the part, and adding a store-bought slipcover in one of the unimaginative tweeds or plaids most ready-mades come in doesn't help its utilitarian appearance one bit. But give it a good-looking headboard and footboard, dress it up in a dashing print or pattern, add a pair of trimly covered bolsters, and that plain-Jane studio couch becomes a handsome daybed.

Below left, the reincarnation of a dull studio couch. This one was brought to life by the addition of two tailored headboards and *two* zippy fabrics. Start-and-stop stripes cover the headboards; a coordinated version covers the rest of the bed and the squared-off bolsters. If you like the lean look of these headboards, you're in luck; they're even easier to make than the padded ones below. Two 37″ x 39″ panels of ¾″ plywood were simply glued and screwed together with flat-head wood screws to make each one. In this case, the edges of the headboards weren't padded, and contrasting fabric was used for the boxing, to match the cording on the daybed cover and bolsters. Otherwise, the daybed cover was made the same way as the flowered one; see page 101. Directions for covering the square, foam rubber bolsters are on page 223.

Posy-striped fabric and two padded headboards transformed a characterless studio couch into this charming daybed below. The same whimsical print was used to cover the walls and make the draperies, visually expanding the limited space of a tiny bed-sleeping room. (White-painted furniture and shutters also help in visually opening up the area.) The headboards that give the bed a sofa's status by day were made by wrapping muslin and then the decorative fabric around simple frames constructed of "1 x 3" pine. Directions for headboard and footboard are on page 99, and are followed by directions for making the daybed cover. See directions for round bolsters on page 223.

# Ingenious Use of Fabric Makes Inventive Headboards

Whoever said a "headboard" has to be literally a board? Fabric is certainly more decorative than almost any wood, and far easier to manipulate into something dramatic or unusual. And instead of being an extraneous element, a headboard made of or covered with fabric can be completely incorporated into your decorating scheme. Say, for instance, you're dotty about dots, and would like a bedroom done completely in polka dots of different sizes for a fresh approach to the pattern-on-pattern idea. The headboard above would be a real smash, and is easier to make than you'd think. You simply cut diamond shapes out of fiber board, pad them and cover them with fabric printed with large, medium and small-size dots in a preplanned pattern, and then nail them to a plywood base. The padding gives the headboard a sort of quilted, cushiony look. Turn to diamond headboard on page 103 to see how easy it is to do. Polka dots are a very basic pattern, and several fabric houses have color-coordinated dots in as many as four or five different sizes season after season and year after year, so you should have no trouble finding a coordinated trio. These happen to be in white on navy blue, but white on fire-engine red or stinging green would also be spectacular. And if you like the patchwork look, you might even try using three different-size dots on three different brilliant colors.

If you want something soft and feminine, try this one on for size. There's certainly nothing board-like about the gathered folds of flower-splashed fabric (although there *is* an unseen panel of plywood bracing the painted wooden poles). You can make this imaginative softie from a single full-size sheet; the padded table cover takes a queen-size one (see directions on page 103). Directions for fabric "headboard" are on page 102.

# Make It More Than a Bedroom

How many hours a night do you sleep? Enough to warrant devoting a whole room (or rooms) to nothing but? We'll wager not. In today's usually-cramped living quarters, it's downright wasteful to squander even a hundred square feet of living space (to say nothing of your decorating dollars) on a room you use only when your eyes are closed. Every room should be a "living" room, especially if your family spans varied ages and interests. Everyone needs a private spot where he (or she) can get away from the rest of the clan occasionally—and not just at bedtime. Providing such a retreat doesn't require any more space—just a little more planning. Here is one of the ways you can turn any sleeping-room, however small, into more than a bedroom. Also see some bright ideas for a teenager's home-within-a-home on pages 92–93.

Designed for a couple (with an exuberant brood of teenagers) who like to read, write letters and watch TV where they can relax in quiet comfort, the room at the right doubles for a non-existent library—and is done in a strong, non-bedroomy color. What's more, it has a clever hidden asset: the round table cover is cut so a front panel flips up to reveal an otherwise-out-of-sight TV screen. Made with four decoratively-corded slits, the back panel of the tablecloth can also be lifted so there's no danger of the set overheating. The fabric-covered panel that conceals the recessed radiator was cut two inches shorter than the opening and then cut away at the bottom (like a chest on short legs) to allow for proper circulation. Four magnetic cabinet catches, applied to edges of the panel and to side walls of the recess, hold it in place. Note that the bedside table is big enough to hold all the necessities for writing or telephoning in comfort. You'll find step-by-step directions for making the TV table cover on page 104. To make the fitted coverlet with pleated corners, just follow the directions for a tailored spread on page 52, cutting the side and end drops as short as you want them.

# Young Version of the Twenty-Four-Hour Bedroom

Is it a bedroom? Well, yes—but only for six or eight hours out of every twenty-four. The rest of the time it's a study, playroom, living room and, most important of all, a prestigious spot for a teen-ager to entertain her friends. The status accrues because the decor is so obviously "with it"—and because it doesn't *look* like a bedroom. Except for a little judiciously-used paint, it's all done with fabric— a lively combine of printed and plain corduroy in swinging colors. (The fabric could just as well be any sturdy, washable material.) Even the whimsical wall hanging is made of fabric—and made on a sewing machine at that. Directions for the snoozing-flower hanging are on page 105; the mattress covers on page 106; the directions for re-covering a director's chair on page 56 were used for this one, too. Directions for pillow covers start on page 220.

# directions for projects

## FAKE FOUR-POSTER
### ON PAGE 80

MATERIALS NEEDED:
(for bed 54" x 76")

    Printed sheets:
        Three twin-size for draperies and
        canopy
        One twin and one full-size to cover
        walls
    Solid-color sheets:
        Two twin-size for lining of draperies
    "1 x 2" pine (cut to exactly 1⅜" wide):
        Two 58¼" for A and E
        One 79½" for B
        One 81" for F
    "1 x 3" pine:
        One 53¾" for J
        Two 59" for G
        Two 75¾" for H
        Lengths required for C and D
        (see Diagrams 2 and 3)
    1⅛" x 2¼" solid crown molding:
        One 60"
        One 84"
    Eighteen ⅝" x 1½" corrugated fasteners
    1¾" flat-head wood screws as required for
        attaching C and D
    Twenty 1½" flat-head wood screws
    1" finishing nails
    2¼" common nails
    72" eyelet rodding
    One ½" button, to be covered, if desired for
        rosette
    Four ⅜" brass rings
    Two brass cup hooks
    Drapery hooks
    Staple gun and staples
    Basecoat and paint
    White glue (optional)

NOTE: Project is designed for a bed placed in the corner of the room. Canopy is 5" wider and 5" longer than bed to allow draperies to hang straight and free of bed. When attaching A, B, C and D, stagger nails or screws along length to avoid splitting the wood. Eyelet rodding is made of flexible aluminum and is used for oddly-shaped and/or stationary drapery installations. If 100% cotton sheets are used, wash to eliminate shrinkage.

Measuring from corner, remove 59" of molding along ceiling line at head end of bed and 81" along side of bed. Using common nails spaced about 9" apart, attach A to head wall at ceiling line; attach B to side wall in same manner (Diagram 1).

Determine positions of ceiling joists above bed area and mark each one.

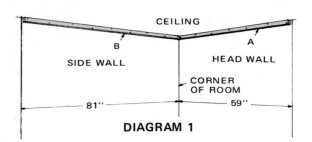

**DIAGRAM 1**

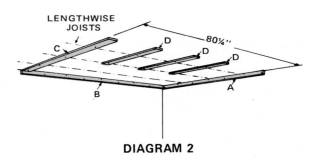

**DIAGRAM 2**

If joists run lengthwise, cut one C, 57½" long, and three D so each D is long enough to cross two joists when measuring from end of A (Diagram 2).

If joists run crosswise, cut one C, 79½" long, and two D so each D is long enough to cross two joists when measuring from end of B (Diagram 3).

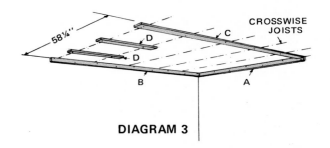

**DIAGRAM 3**

Drill pilot holes for 1¾" screws in C and D, placing them so screws will go into joists. Attach C and D to joists, spacing D about 18" apart where there are lengthwise joists (see Diagram 2) and about 17" apart where there are crosswise joists (see Diagram 3).

Using common nails, attach E either to long edge of C or to ends of B, D and C; attach F either to ends of C, D and A or to long edge of C (Diagram 4).

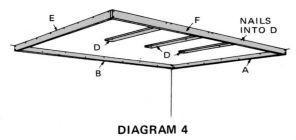

**DIAGRAM 4**

Using three fasteners at each joining, make frame from "1 x 3" pine (G, H and J) so that it has the same outside dimensions as the underside of the canopy (Diagram 5). Drill pilot holes for 1½" screws, placing them ⅜" in from outside edges of frame; on G, place holes 1" from each end and 19" apart; on H, place holes 4" from ends of frame and about 18" apart.

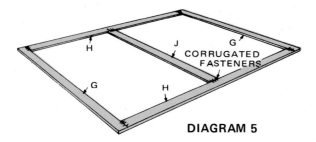

**DIAGRAM 5**

Place a printed, twin-size sheet on frame; wrap it around onto side edges, trim and staple in place. Make a small slit through sheet at position of each pilot hole. Attach an 18" strip of eyelet rodding at two opposite corners of frame and a 36" strip around third corner, following manufacturer's directions and placing strips close to edge (Diagram 6).

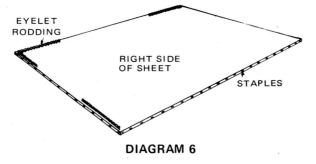

**DIAGRAM 6**

Cover walls in following manner: Remove stitching from top hem on a twin-size sheet and press flat; place sheet against head wall so cut edge is along bottom edge of A and selvage is flush with right side of canopy. Staple along top and down side; trim so left side of sheet extends 2" around corner onto side wall and bottom edge extends 2" below top of bed. Staple left side and bottom edge in place. Hammer staples flat. Attach a full-size sheet to side wall in same manner, placing selvage flush with end of canopy and folding edge under at corner. Pull down tightly to hold fold snugly in place; you may wish to further secure fold with small dots of white glue (Diagram 7). Hammer staples flat.

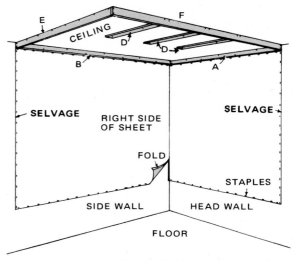

**DIAGRAM 7**

Start screws through holes in frame and attach frame to A, B, E and F; screw tightly enough so screw heads go through slits in fabric and do not show. Cut molding to fit against existing molding on walls and miter front corner. Paint molding and attach to E and F, using a nailset and 1" nails (see photo on page 80).

Cut one printed and one solid-color twin-size sheet in half lengthwise to make draperies next to wall. Use entire width of remaining printed and solid-color sheets to make corner drapery. Make tiebacks from scraps of printed sheets left over from those used to cover walls. Attach a cup hook to each wall at selvage of fabric on wall so draperies will be held back at desired height.

## FOUR-POSTER FRAME
### ON PAGE 83

MATERIALS NEEDED:
"3 x 3" pine:
Four, room height, for A and B
Two, width of bed, for C
Two, length of bed, for D
Two clear pine "1 x 3"s, each 108", for E and F
Two 36" lengths of ¾" dowel
Twenty-two 1¼" flat-head wood screws
Eight 2" angle irons with twelve 1" and twelve 1¾" flat-head wood screws
1¾" finishing nails
¾" wire brads
1½ yards of muslin
56"-wide fabric, length of A plus length of D plus 32"
Staple gun and staples or upholsterers' tacks
Wood glue

NOTE: Be sure to purchase "3 x 3"s which are finished on all four sides (S4S) and be sure they are straight and

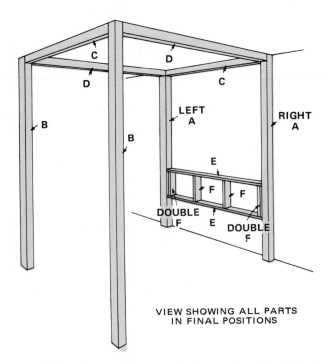

VIEW SHOWING ALL PARTS
IN FINAL POSITIONS

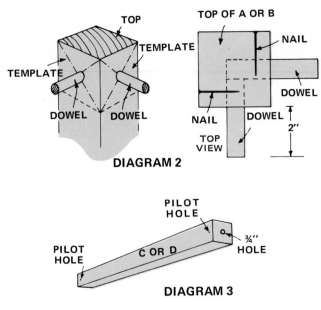

DIAGRAM 2

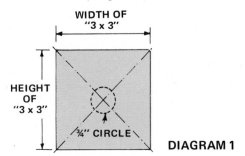

DIAGRAM 3

true. Allow them to dry at room temperature for at least two weeks before starting construction.

Make a template to fit end of "3 x 3" and mark a ¾" circle in ex*act* center (Diagram 1).

**WIDTH OF "3 x 3"**

**HEIGHT OF "3 x 3"**

¾" CIRCLE

**DIAGRAM 1**

Place template on one face of A, flush with top, and mark center of ¾" hole. Bore a ¾" hole 2" deep in position marked. Repeat on one *adjoining face* of A, placing template flush with edges of A on three sides. Bore two holes in same manner at top of other A and each B. Cut twelve 4" lengths of dowel. Apply glue and insert a dowel into each hole in A and B, pushing the first dowel in the full 2", and the second dowel up against the first one. Trim dowels so all project 2" from faces of A and B. Bore pilot holes into two remaining faces of each A and B for finishing nails, placing them 1" in from side edges so nails will go through dowels; drive nails in place (Diagram 2).

Using 1" screws, attach two angle irons to each B, placing them flush with bottom and at center of each face with the dowels.

Using template, mark center of ¾" hole on both *ends* of each C and D. Bore ¾" holes 2" deep in positions marked. On each C and D, bore two pilot holes for finishing nails 1" in from each end, placing both on the same face (Diagram 3).

Place one C between two A and check to be sure top edges line up when dowels go into ends of C. *Do not attach.* Mark this C for head end. Place second C between two B, checking to make sure top edges are even, and mark for foot end. Place one D between each A and B and mark for right and left sides.

From each "1 x 3," cut one E 54" long and three F 16½" long. Glue and screw two F together so all edges are flush. Bore two ¾" holes through both F, placing them 4" from each end. Repeat to form a second double F (Diagram 4).

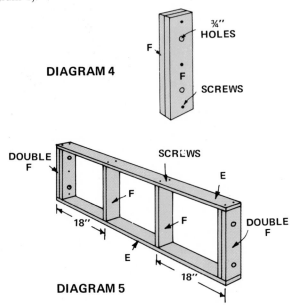

DIAGRAM 4

DIAGRAM 5

Assemble frame for headboard as shown in Diagram 5, using two screws through E into F at each joint.

Measure from floor to top of bed for dimension "X". Draw a line across left A at "X" to determine position of bottom of headboard. Place headboard against A with bottom of E on line and mark positions of two holes in F on A. Bore ¾" holes 2" deep at these positions; apply glue and insert 4" length of dowel in each hole. Repeat on second A, placing holes on inside face of each A as shown in Diagram 6.

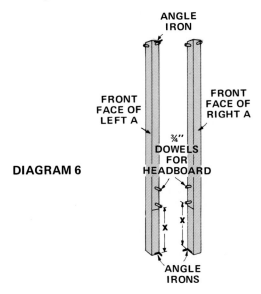

**DIAGRAM 6**

With 1" screws, attach two angle irons to left A on same face with ¾" holes, placing one flush with top end and back face, the other flush with bottom end and back face. Attach one angle iron to right A in the same manner, at bottom end only.

Cut a full width of fabric 2" longer than A; then cut lengthwise into four 14" wide strips. Cover two A as follows: Staple or tack fabric along length of face which will be against wall, with edge of fabric ½" from one corner. Cutting holes to accommodate dowels, wrap fabric around A; fold second edge under and overlap first edge along corner of A where you started. Nail in place with wire brads and staple to top and bottom, mitering corners. Cover two B in the same manner, starting at corner between dowels, and finishing by driving brads at an angle through fabric; then work fabric threads back together to cover heads. Staple to top and bottom as on A (Diagram 7).

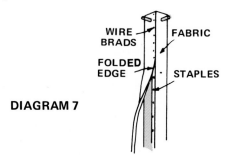

**DIAGRAM 7**

Cut a full width of fabric 2" longer than D, then cut lengthwise into four 14" wide strips. Cover two C and two D in the same manner as A and B, cutting away excess at ends.

Mark lines on wall to locate positions of A, using plumb bob to be sure they are vertical. Hold left A in position against wall and attach angle irons to wall with 1¾" screws. Attach an angle iron to right end of C for head end, keeping it flush with back face of C. Apply glue and place hole in other end of C over dowel on left A and push in place. Attach angle iron on C to wall with 1¾" screws (Diagram 8).

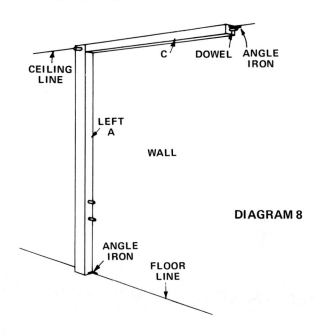

**DIAGRAM 8**

Cover front face of headboard with muslin, taking it over top and bottom edges and stapling to back of E. Trim away excess along each end, flush with outside edge of F. Cover with decorative fabric in the same manner, allowing fabric to go over ends onto F and mitering corners. Place headboard in position with dowels of left A through holes in double F and left end of C. Apply glue to dowels on right A and place in position with dowels of A going into holes in headboard. Nail through pilot holes in C so nails go through dowels; then work fabric threads together. Attach angle irons at bottom of A to wall with 1¾" screws (Diagram 9).

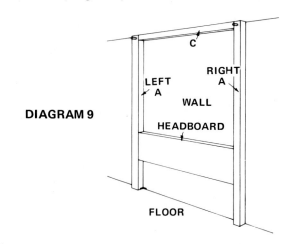

**DIAGRAM 9**

Apply glue to remaining dowels on left A and left B; place D against A, then B against D with dowels going into holes in D; nail through pilot holes in D. Attach angle irons on B to floor with 1¾" screws (Diagram 10).

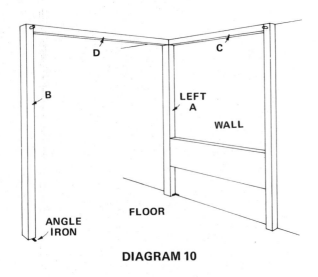

**DIAGRAM 10**

Assemble the other B, C, D in same manner to complete frame.

# CURVED HEADBOARD
## ON PAGE 85

MATERIALS NEEDED:
(for double bed)

Two pieces of plywood, each ⅜" x 37" x 54"

"1 x 4" pine:
   One 168"
   One 54"

Three carriage bolts with washers, and lock
   washers (see instructions)

Four yards cording, to be covered

¼"-thick padding

Two yards 44"-wide muslin

Four yards upholsterers' tape or ½" cardboard
   strips

Two yards 44"-wide cambric or glazed chintz (to
   cover back—optional)

Two yards 55" decorative fabric

Upholsterers' tacks or staple gun and staples

Wood glue

Thirty-eight 1" flat-head wood screws

On one piece of plywood, mark off 1" squares and draw outline of top edge of headboard, following half-pattern given in Diagram 1. Cut plywood, then trace outline on second piece of plywood and cut.

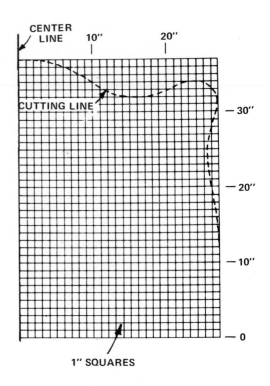

**DIAGRAM 1**

Cut thirteen 12" lengths of "1 x 4" for spacer blocks. Apply glue to 54" length of "1 x 4" and place along lower edge of one piece of plywood, keeping edges flush. Glue the spacer blocks in place as close to curved top and side edges as possible (Diagram 2).

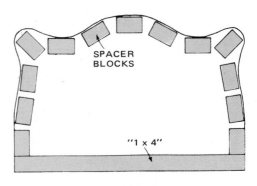

**DIAGRAM 2**

After glue has dried, screw through plywood into each spacer block with one screw, and into "1 x 4" along bottom with six screws spaced about 9" apart. Apply glue to spacer blocks and place second side of headboard in position so all edges are flush. Screw through second side of headboard in same manner as through first side.

Cover front face of headboard with padding and then with muslin. Tack muslin to back of headboard, clipping edges to go around curves and overlapping edges where necessary to keep muslin smooth and taut (Diagram 3).

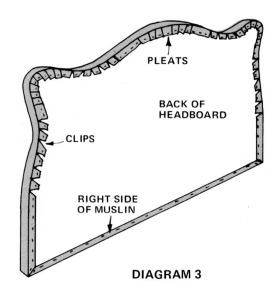

PLEATS

BACK OF
HEADBOARD

CLIPS

RIGHT SIDE
OF MUSLIN

**DIAGRAM 3**

# HEADBOARD AND FOOTBOARD
## ON PAGES 86–87

MATERIALS NEEDED:
"1 x 3" pine:
    Four, width of bed, for A and B
    Four, height desired for headboard less 1½",
      for C
    Two, width of bed less 1½", for D
    Two for E (see directions)
Eight 3" angle irons with sixteen 1" and eight
    1½" flat-head wood screws
Eight 2½" molly bolts
Thirty-two 1½" No. 10 flat-head wood screws
Pre-shrunk medium-weight muslin
½" cording
Upholsterers' tape or cardboard strips
½"-thick polyester fiberfill
Tacks or staple gun and staples
Curved needle and heavy nylon thread
Decorative fabric

Determine width of headboard by measuring across bed with sheets and blankets in place.

Attach A and B to C with two screws at each corner. Attach D to inside of frame at height 3" below top of mattress, using two screws through each C into D. Cut E to fit between B and D and attach with two screws through D and B into E (Diagram 1).

NOTE: Drill pilot holes for screws, apply glue to both faces of wood and dip screws in glue before driving. Countersink all screw heads flush with outer faces of frame.

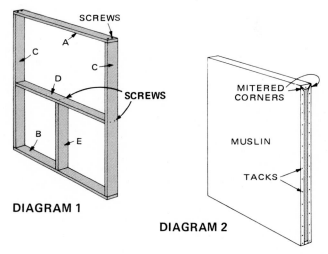

SCREWS

A

C

C

D

SCREWS

B

E

**DIAGRAM 1**

MITERED
CORNERS

MUSLIN

TACKS

**DIAGRAM 2**

Cover front face of headboard with decorative fabric, keeping line of fabric design parallel with bottom edge, or centering design on front, and tacking to side edges. Cut 2"-wide bias strips of fabric and cover cording (see page 209). Place cording around headboard with stitching line of cording along front edge (Diagram 4A). Cut 4"-wide strips of fabric, following design line carefully, and

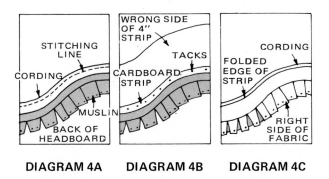

STITCHING
LINE

CORDING

MUSLIN

BACK OF
HEADBOARD

**DIAGRAM 4A**

WRONG SIDE
OF 4"
STRIP

TACKS

CARDBOARD
STRIP

**DIAGRAM 4B**

CORDING

FOLDED
EDGE OF
STRIP

RIGHT
SIDE OF
FABRIC

**DIAGRAM 4C**

seam together until long enough to go around edge of headboard. Place right side down over cording with raw edges of fabric and cording flush. Place upholsterers' tape or cardboard strips over fabric with edge of tape or strip tight against cording; tack in place (4B). Turn fabric back over tape and pull onto back of headboard; tack in place so top edge remains smooth (4C).

Bore three holes for bolts along back of headboard, placing them 2" above lower edge with one 2" from each end and one at center. Hold headboard in place against box spring and mark locations of the three holes on box spring. Bore holes in box spring and attach headboard with bolts going through headboard into spring. Secure with a lock washer on each bolt. Cover back of headboard with cambric or chintz, if desired, by turning in edges and tacking all around.

Cut muslin to width of frame plus 4" and long enough to wrap around from underside of B, up outside face of frame, over A, down other side to underside of B, plus 4". (Seam if necessary and press seam open.) Tack or staple excess muslin in place along front and back edges of C, mitering corners at top edges of C (Diagram 2).

Cut fabric 4″ wider and 4″ longer than frame; cover outside face by tacking or stapling excess to outer surfaces of A, B and C, mitering corners as for muslin.

Cut 2″-wide bias strips of fabric and cover cording (see page 209); trim seam allowances to ½″. Tack cording temporarily in place around three sides of frame, placing stitching line of cording along front edges of C and A, with seam allowances of cording against outer surfaces of C and A. Cut 4″-wide strips of fabric to double the length of C plus A plus 4″ and seam together. Place strip right side down over cording, with raw edges of fabric and cording flush. Place upholsterers' tape over fabric along stitching line of cording and tack or staple in place (Diagram 3).

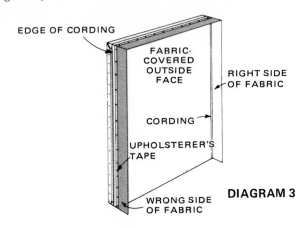

DIAGRAM 3

Cut strips of padding 2½″ wide and place along A and both C, covering raw edges of fabric and cording. Turn fabric back over padding and tack to inside edges of A and C, then tack cording along the same edges. Attach angle irons to edges of B, C, D and E with 1″ screws (Diagram 4).

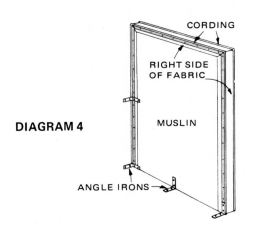

DIAGRAM 4

Cut fabric 4″ wider and 4″ longer than frame to cover inside face of frame. Place fabric over A, right side down, with raw edge flush with seam allowances of cording. Place upholsterers' tape over raw edge of fabric, tight against cording, and tack in place (Diagram 5).

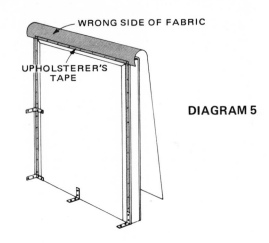

DIAGRAM 5

Turn raw edges of fabric under down both sides and blind-stitch along stitching line of cording; tack to underside of B (Diagram 6).

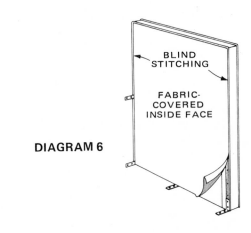

DIAGRAM 6

Make second frame and upholster in the same manner, reversing outside and inside faces to form a pair.

Place bed in desired position with a headboard at each end; mark locations of holes in angle irons on floor and wall. Screw angle irons to floor with 1½″ screws and attach to wall with one molly bolt through each angle iron. Be sure to allow enough clearance to move bed in and out when making or changing the bed.

# DAYBED COVERS
## ON PAGES 86–87

MATERIALS NEEDED:
(for daybed 75″ long, up to 39″ wide)
      6½ yards 44″-wide fabric
      6½ yards cording, to be covered
      6½ yards 44″-wide lining fabric
      2¼ yards flannel for interfacing
      ½″ elastic

Cut fabric for top section of cover 1½″ wider and 1½″ longer than the bed. (Be sure to have sheets and blankets in place when measuring.) Cut flannel and lining fabric to same size. From ¾ yard of fabric, cut 2½″-wide bias strips and cover cording; trim seam allowances to ½″. Place flannel on wrong side of outer fabric, smooth flat and pin together around all sides. Place cording on right side of fabric with raw edges of fabric, flannel and cording even, clipping seam allowances of cording to go around corners; stitch together along stitching line of cording (Diagram 1).

**DIAGRAM 1**

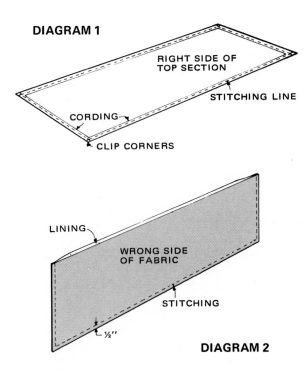

Cut fabric for front drop 5″ longer than bed and 5″ wider than distance from top of bed to floor. (If using patterned fabric, cut drop so pattern will match pattern of top section when drop and top are seamed together.) Be sure drop will have 2½″ overhang at each end. Cut lining fabric same size. Place lining on fabric with right sides together and stitch ½″ from edge across two short sides and one long one (Diagram 2). Turn right side out and press.

Measure depth of mattress. Cut strips for boxing twice as deep as this measurement plus 4½″ and long enough to equal the length of one long side and two short ones minus 2″ when seamed together. Fold strip in half lengthwise, right side out, and stitch ¾″ from folded edge to form casing. Cut elastic 18″ shorter than length of strip. Run elastic through casing and stitch at each end (Diagram 3).

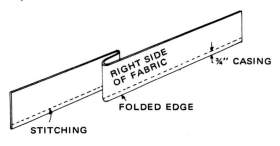

**DIAGRAM 3**

Place front drop on top section, right sides together, with raw edges flush. Check to make sure that pattern will match when top and drop are seamed together. Drop will extend 2″ around each front corner.

Place boxing strip around three other sides in same manner, turning under ½″ on each end so it overlaps front drop by only ½″ on each side. Stitch front drop and boxing to top section, following stitching line of cording (Diagram 4).

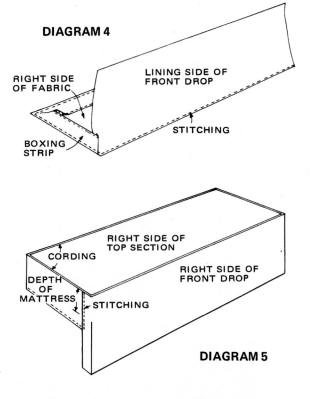

On right side, stitch front drop and boxing together at each side (Diagram 5).

Turn front drop and boxing up over right side of top section. Place lining on top with all edges flush and baste three sides in place, leaving one short side open. Turn right side out to be sure fabric, interfacing and lining lie flat and smooth. Turn wrong side out, make any necessary adjustments, and stitch together along stitching line of cording. Turn right side out. Turn in edges along unstitched end and slip-stitch opening closed (Diagram 6).

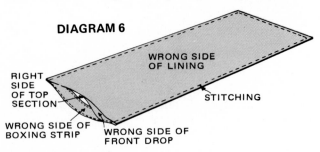

**DIAGRAM 6**

WRONG SIDE OF LINING

RIGHT SIDE OF TOP SECTION

STITCHING

WRONG SIDE OF BOXING STRIP

WRONG SIDE OF FRONT DROP

Place cover on bed, mark hem ½" from floor and hem lower edge.

# FABRIC "HEADBOARD"
## ON PAGE 89

MATERIALS NEEDED:
(for 39"-wide bed)

One full-size flat sheet (or 2½ yards 45"-wide fabric)

One piece of plywood, ¾" x 18" x 42", for A

Two 2¾"-diameter wooden poles, each 72" long, for B

Two screw-on wooden finials

Four 1½" angle irons with sixteen ¾" flat-head wood screws

Two 1¾" angle irons with two toggle bolts and two ¾" flat-head wood screws

Two ⅜"-diameter solid brass rods, each 43½" long

Basecoat and paint

Attach two 1½" angle irons to top edge of A, placing them so outside edges of angle irons are flush with side edges of A. Attach other two 1½" angle irons to bottom edge in same manner (Diagram 1).

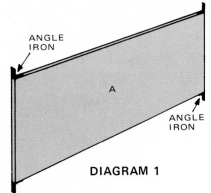

ANGLE IRON

A

ANGLE IRON

**DIAGRAM 1**

Attach angle irons on A to both wooden poles B so bottom edge of A is 22" from bottom ends of B, making sure A is straight along center of each B. Bore two ½"-diameter holes in each B to receive brass rods; bore each 1½" deep, placing one directly below lower angle iron on each B and one 12" down from top end of each B on a straight line with A (Diagram 2).

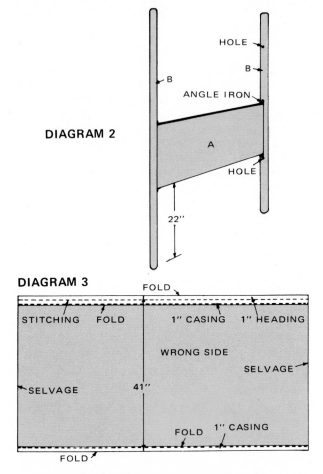

HOLE

B

B

ANGLE IRON

**DIAGRAM 2**

A

HOLE

22"

**DIAGRAM 3**

FOLD

STITCHING  FOLD

1" CASING  1" HEADING

WRONG SIDE

SELVAGE

SELVAGE  41"

FOLD  1" CASING

FOLD

Across full width of sheet, cut one piece 45" long. Turn ½" to wrong side across bottom edge, then turn another 1" to wrong side and stitch close to fold to form 1" casing. Turn 2½" to wrong side across top edge and stitch 1" down from fold to form 1" heading. Turn raw edge under ½" and stitch close to fold to form 1" casing. Finished length of panel is 41" (Diagram 3).

Drill a pilot hole in top end of each B and screw finials in place. Apply basecoat and paint, following manufacturer's directions. Place headboard against wall in desired position. Placing them 3" below bottom edge of A, attach two 1¾" angle irons to wall with toggle bolts so outside edges are flush against inside of B. Attach angle irons to B with ¾" screws.

Place rod through 1" top casing of panel; insert one end of rod all the way into upper hole in one B. Push other end of rod ¾" into corresponding hole in opposite B. Place rod through bottom casing of panel and insert rod into lower holes in same manner.

## PADDED TABLE COVER
### ON PAGE 89

MATERIALS NEEDED:
(for table 30″ in diameter, 27″ high)

    One queen-size flat sheet (or 4½ yards 45″-wide fabric)

    Five yards 4-cord shirring tape

    Staple gun and staples

    Padding to fit table top

Across full width of sheet, cut two pieces, each 30½″ long (or 3½″ longer than height of table) for ruffle. Stitch the two pieces together with a ½″ seam along one 30½″ edge of each to form one flat piece 30½″ x 179″. Press seam open. Turn ½″ to wrong side along each remaining 30½″ edge and stitch in place. Turn ½″ to wrong side along bottom edge, then turn up a 3″ hem and stitch. Turn ½″ to wrong side along top edge and press. Cut shirring tape in half lengthwise, and place one strip along top edge of fabric so top edge of tape is 1/16″ from folded edge. Knot drawstrings at ends, and stitch across tape on both sides of both drawstrings, being careful not to stitch through them; there will be four rows of stitching in all (Diagram 1).

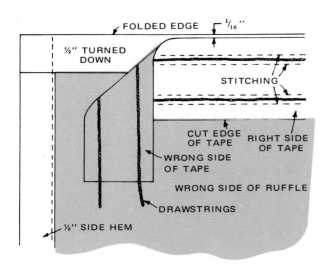

**DIAGRAM 1**

From remaining fabric, cut a 35″ square; cut padding to fit top of table and staple in place. Place fabric on table top; smooth fabric over edge and staple to underside.

Place ruffle against edge of table with top edges flush, and tack ruffle to edge of top at center seam. Pull up drawstrings on tape from both sides until ruffle fits snugly around table; knot ends of drawstrings to hold gathers in place. If you want to be able to stretch fabric out flat for laundering, pin excess cord out of sight; otherwise, cut it off. Tack ruffle to top in a few places around edge to hold in place.

## "DIAMOND" HEADBOARD
### ON PAGE 88

MATERIALS NEEDED:
(for headboard for 39″-wide bed)

    One piece of plywood, ¾″ x 24″ x 48″, for C

    One piece of fiber board, ½″ x 24″ x 48″

    One clear pine "1 x 2", 133″ long, for D, E

    44″-wide fabric:

        One yard small dot

        ½ yard medium dot

        ½ yard large dot

    One yard ½″-thick padding

    1″ wire brads

    2″ finishing nails

    Two large flat-head nails

    Two saw-tooth picture hangers with nails

    Staple gun and staples

    White glue

    Basecoat and paint

    Cardboard

To make quarter diamond pattern, make triangle 5⅝″ tall, 4⅛″ wide at base, with 7″ hypotenuse (Diagram 1).

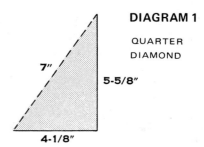

**DIAGRAM 1**

QUARTER DIAMOND

7″  5-5/8″

4-1/8″

Using quarter-diamond pattern, make cardboard patterns for full-diamond, half-diamond A, half-diamond B and quarter diamond (Diagram 2).

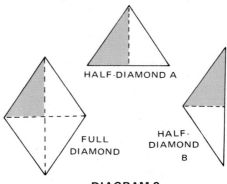

HALF-DIAMOND A

FULL DIAMOND

HALF-DIAMOND B

**DIAGRAM 2**

Using cardboard patterns and following layout in Diagram 3, mark lines on fiber board and cut out fourteen full diamonds, eight half-diamonds A, two half-diamonds B and four quarter diamonds. Cut padding to cover each piece. Place padding on front of each diamond or partial diamond, and secure with dots of glue. Cut fabric 2″ larger than each diamond or partial diamond, and wrap fabric around it, keeping rows of dots straight across front and clipping away excess fabric at points so there is only one layer of fabric in back. Staple fabric to back of fiber board. Cover ten full diamonds with small dots, two with medium dots and two with large dots. Cover four half-diamonds A with medium dots and four with large dots. Cover one half-diamond B with medium dots, and one with large dots. Cover two quarter diamonds with medium dots and two with large dots. Place covered pieces on plywood C in positions shown in Diagram 3.

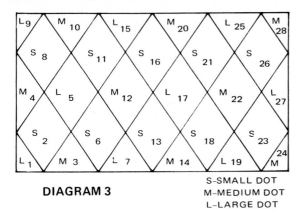

**DIAGRAM 3**

S—SMALL DOT
M—MEDIUM DOT
L—LARGE DOT

Remove diamonds and partial diamonds one at a time, outlining position of each on plywood. Trim away excess plywood. Using two 1″ wire brads through three (where possible) or two edges of each diamond or partial diamond, nail them obliquely in place on plywood; begin with #1 as shown in Diagram 3 and proceed in order to #28 (#27 will be nailed in place along one edge only).

From "1 x 2," cut D and E to fit around plywood so E will cover ends of D. Sand lightly; apply basecoat and paint following manufacturer's directions. Nail D to top and bottom edges of plywood so back edge of D and back face of plywood are even. Along each side, nail E to plywood and ends of D (Diagram 4).

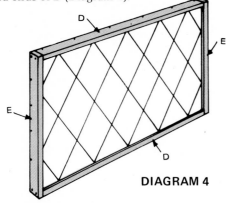

**DIAGRAM 4**

Nail two saw-tooth picture hangers to back edge of upper D, placing them 4″ from each corner. Hammer nails into wall at desired positions and hang headboard in place.

# TV TABLE COVER
## ON PAGE 91

MATERIALS NEEDED:
(for table 30″ high, 30″ in diameter):
    5¾ yards of 48″ or wider fabric
    5¼ yards of 48″ or wider lining fabric
    Eleven yards of cording, to be covered

Cut one 48″ x 93″ piece of fabric. With right sides together and raw edges even at one end, seam this piece to remaining fabric, stitching ½″ from selvage edges. Keeping right sides together, fold 93″ piece in half so three raw edges are together 46½″ from fold, and remaining piece extends 21″. Make sure all selvage edges are exactly even (Diagram 1).

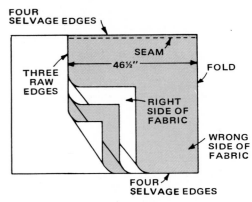

**DIAGRAM 1**

Make a string compass by tying a knot at one end of string, then tying a second knot 45″ from first one. Pin first knot of string at intersection of seam line and fold. Mark a circle at second knot for cut line, pinning through all four thicknesses (Diagram 2).

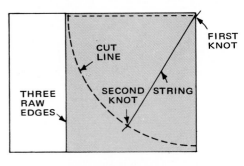

**DIAGRAM 2**

Cut along line through all four thicknesses to make circular cover.

Seam lining fabric and cut to same size circle in same manner.

With cover still folded in quarters, mark a line from intersection of seam line and fold to a point at exact center of curved lower edge. Mark Point A on this line 29″

from lower edge. Cut through all four thicknesses to make a slit from lower edge to Point A (Diagram 3).

From single thickness of remaining fabric, cut 1½" wide bias strips as shown in Diagram 4. Sew strips together as shown in Diagram 5 to make strip 384" long.

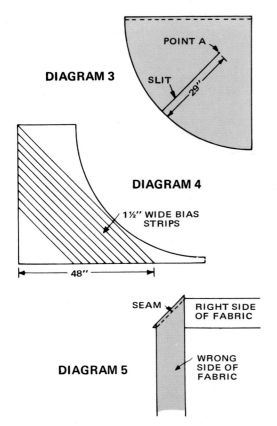

**DIAGRAM 3**

POINT A

SLIT

29"

**DIAGRAM 4**

1½" WIDE BIAS STRIPS

48"

**DIAGRAM 5**

SEAM

RIGHT SIDE OF FABRIC

WRONG SIDE OF FABRIC

Trim ¼" beyond stitching and press seams open. Cover cord by placing it along center of wrong side of strip, folding fabric over cord, wrong sides together, and stitching along length close to cord, using a cording foot attachment. Trim seam allowance of cording ½" beyond stitching line.

Pin cording along edge on right side of cover, raw edges together, clipping to go around corners at bottom of slits and at Points A, and with stitching line of cording ¼" above Points A at tops of slits (Diagram 6).

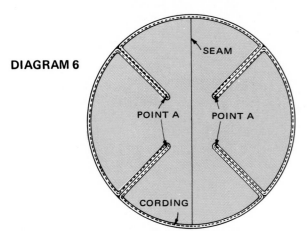

**DIAGRAM 6**

SEAM

POINT A

POINT A

CORDING

Stitch cording to cover, following stitching line of cording.

Place lining on cover with right sides together so lining covers cording. Pin in place so two pieces are smooth. Stitch lining in place, following stitching line on wrong side of cover. Leave an opening in one section large enough to turn cover right side out. Turn cover right side out, then close opening by turning raw edges under and slip-stitching in place.

## FABRIC WALL HANGING
### ON PAGE 92

MATERIALS NEEDED:
(for 28" x 36" wall hanging)
    ⅛ yard green fabric for stem, leaves and grass
    ¼ yard fuchsia fabric for face
    ¾ yard purple fabric for petals, mountain and hill
    One yard orange fabric for background
    ⅔ yard 44"-wide or wider turquoise fabric for cloud and borders
    One yard 44"-wide or wider black fabric for backing
    Polyester fiberfill
    Polyester batting
    One lath strip, ¼" x ⅞" x 28"

NOTE: Each fabric used for wall hanging should be a firm cotton or cotton blend; very lightweight fabrics might have a tendency to pucker.

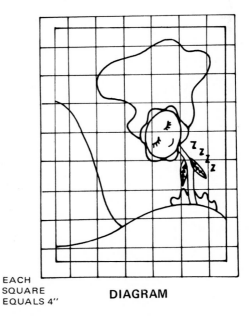

EACH SQUARE EQUALS 4"

**DIAGRAM**

Press all fabrics. Enlarge graph as indicated and draw pattern for each section of hanging as follows: Trace outlines for stem, two leaves and grass section on green fabric, extending top and bottom of stem, base of each leaf and bottom of grass section by ½″ for overlapping of appliqued sections. Trace outlines for mountain and hill on purple fabric, extending left side and bottom of mountain and both sides and bottom of hill by ½″. Trace outline of face on fuchsia fabric, same size as indicated on graph; trace connected outline of petals on purple fabric (forming a circular section with scalloped edges); next, trace outline of complete cloud on turquoise fabric (connecting two points at bottom edge of cloud which are interrupted by outline of face and petals). Cut out all sections.

Draw eyes and mouth on flower face with pencil; using purple thread, embroider eyes and mouth with a tight machine zigzag stitch. Center flower face on scalloped purple circle; using fuchsia thread, applique face to purple petals with zigzag stitch. Cut 1″ slit at back of scalloped purple circle and stuff evenly with fiberfill; overcast slit closed.

Following placement shown in graph and overlapping adjoining edges by ½″ as allowed for when cutting out sections, applique sections in the following order, using a zigzag stitch and matching thread. Stitch turquoise cloud, green stem, leaves and grass, and purple mountain to orange background. Stitch stuffed flower face with purple petals to turquoise cloud, orange background and green stem. Stitch purple mountain to orange background. Stitch purple hill to purple mountain, orange background and grass.

Cut two 3″ slits in background fabric, at back of mountain and hill, and stuff evenly with fiberfill; close slits with overcasting stitch.

Draw four ''Z''s on background as shown in graph and zigzag stitch over each.

With right sides together and taking ½″ seams, stitch border strips to background, mountain and hill. Press seam allowances flat. Cut batting same size as background with borders; place hanging, right side up, on batting, with all edges even. Stitch hanging to batting. With right sides together, stitch backing to hanging along three sides. Turn right side out; press and stitch remaining side by hand.

## MATTRESS COVERS
### ON PAGES 92–93

MATERIALS NEEDED:
(to cover two 38″ x 75″ x 6″-thick mattresses)
    10¼ yards 44″-wide corduroy or 11¾ yards other
       44″ fabric
    10¼ yards 1½″-wide washable trim
    Twenty-six yards cording, to be covered
    Thirteen yards ½″-wide heavy elastic

Following Cutting Layout for corduroy, cut two 39½″ x 76½″ A to cover tops of mattresses, four 7½″ x 49½″ C and four 7½″ x 49½″ E to cover ends of mattresses, four 7½″ x 79½″ B and four 7½″ x 79½″ D to cover sides of mattresses, and three 2″-wide strips, two full length of yardage listed and one 216″ long, to cover cording. Cut with long edges of all pieces parallel to selvages.

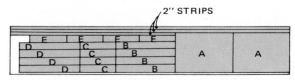

**CUTTING LAYOUT FOR CORDUROY**

Fold 2″ strips in half lengthwise, wrong sides together, to cover cording; stitch close to cord. For fabric other than corduroy, use bias strips for covering; see page 209.

To make one mattress cover, place one A on mattress right side up; place cording completely around A, clipping seam allowance at corners, so that stitching line of cording is along edge of mattress with seam allowance of cording toward raw edges of A. Stitch in place, following stitching line of cording.

Cut four lengths of trim, two 64″ long and two 27″ long. Place trim in position on right side of A, 6½″ in from edge on all four sides; baste in place, mitering corners, and machine-stitch close to edges along both sides of trim (Diagram 1).

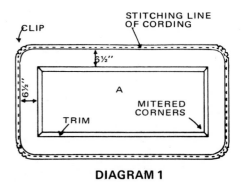

**DIAGRAM 1**

With right sides together and raw edges even, place one B along each side of A and one C along each end; pin in place. Holding ends of B and C together at each corner,

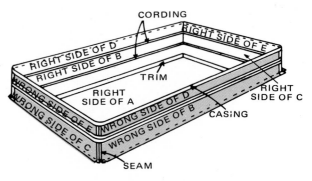

**DIAGRAM 2**

mark placement of seam so boxing fits smoothly along cording. Stitch seams at corners; stitch B and C to A, following stitching line of cording. Place another length of cording along raw edges of B and C with stitching line of cording ¾" from raw edge of fabric; stitch in place. With right sides together, pin and stitch one D to each B and one E to each C, following stitching line of cording and seaming together at corners as before. Turn 1" to wrong side along bottom edge of D and E for a casing, leaving a 2" opening in which to insert elastic. Insert elastic in casing; turn cover to right side and place on mattress; pull elastic tight enough to hold cover in place and still allow cover to be removed. Stitch ends of elastic together (Diagram 2). Make second cover in same manner.

# 3
# WINDOW TREATMENTS

# Make Every Window Part of Your Decorating Plan

The walls, floor and ceiling make up the "shell" of a room—the basic spatial entity that must be considered first when making a decorating plan. But one or more walls are almost always broken up (or taken up) by windows, and since most walls are solidly colored or covered with a repetitive pattern, the eye is always attracted to these interrupting spaces. So the windows automatically become an important focal point. It follows, therefore, that what you do with your windows may be the make-or-break factor in your decorating plan. Fortunately, there are many interesting, creative ways to treat any window, many fabulous-looking fabrics and coverings and paint colors to play with. One of the best possible ways to begin a decorating scheme is to *start* with the windows. At very least, make them an integral part of your plan.

One easy (and dramatic) way to tie a window treatment in with the rest of the room is to repeat a striking fabric used elsewhere in some interesting way. In this vibrant living room, the sunny, flower-splashed fabric used for upholstery also covers the wall-wide lambrequin and makes the Roman shades. Played against boldly contrasting colors, the result is spectacular. Directions for making lambrequins begin on page 218; for Roman shades, see page 153.

# Coordinate Your Window Treatment with Your Decorating Plan

This dining room was planned around a can't-fail color scheme: bold black-and-white print against a blaze of solid color. In this case, high-key lemon yellow is the sizzling solid—and only by covering walls, floor *and* windows in the same stinging hue could the result be this dramatic. Directions for making the corner cornice, page 136.

Reverse the formula and cover one wall, including the windows, in a blaze of *pattern*, and the result will be every bit as dynamic. Especially if you cool the blaze with lots of frosty white and shiny black (repeating the white background and black accents of the print), and tie the whole thing together with chair cushions covered in the same exuberant pattern. In the dining room below, the fabric splashed with super-size poppies covers the wall between the windows and the corner extensions that were built to form an architectural bay. But the idea would work just as well with a perfectly flat wall—and with any equally eye-catching fabric. Directions for making the pinch-pleated draperies that are such an important element in both decorating plans begin on page 124.

# Coordinated Draperies — An Important Part of Your Decorating Plan

A stylized Paisley print is used for these straight-hanging draw draperies and also to cover the traditional wing chair, as well as the cushion on the cane-back side chair. Repetition of the decorative fabric creates a unified and inviting grouping around the desk. (Notice how the curving scrolls of the pattern repeat the carved S-curves of the desk—another subtle but unifying factor.)

Of all the many ways to make your window treatment part of your decorating plan, graceful pinch-pleated draperies are probably the most popular. Their fluid, even folds are a softening influence on the architectural severity of modern rooms, and they can unify diverse elements with eye-filling splashes of pattern or color. In addition to their obviously decorative assets, they're extremely practical from a functional point of view. With sheer glass curtains underneath (or even without), they let in any desired amount of light by day, and can be closed completely at night to make any room a warm, cozy, enclave. Here you see the same type of pleated draperies used two different ways. Directions for draperies start on page 124.

The same type of pinch-pleated draperies have a totally different effect when held back by tie-backs. This contemporary pattern is also used for draperies and cushions, as well as the slipcover on the comfortable easy chair. The print's attractive medley of lime, turquoise and green inspired the whole color scheme.

# Contrast-Lined Draperies Tie a Color-Scheme Together

Contrast-lined draperies may add just the slightly "different" look you'd like a room to have, and since fabric colors and patterns are virtually unlimited, you can make them the perfect finishing touch for any color scheme.

Covering all four walls (see directions for covering walls on page 213) and furniture in one attractive pattern—and not necessarily a small one—creates a restful, intimate ambiance that's perfect for a bedroom and, surprisingly, may make a small room look larger. But some relieving touch of contrast is essential, and coordinated, solid-color draperies lined in matching pattern are just what's needed. If the pattern is a monotone, as here, add a sharp jab or two of accent color. Directions for making draperies start on page 124.

Here, sill-length draperies match the walls (always good tie-it-to-gether strategy), but the flash of vivid pattern provided by linings and tie-backs that match the flamboyantly-printed sofa is a gay and unexpected touch.

# Cafe Curtains Can Be Used Many Ways

Don't dismiss cafes as kitchen-only curtains. They're a very versatile means of having both privacy and daylight in many different rooms. They can be made several ways and combined with window shades as well as long draperies. See directions for laminating shades starting on page 150.

Here, strap-topped cafe curtains on gleaming brass rods team up with matching shades for an interesting arrangement in a Provincial dining area. Part of a big kitchen here, it could also be the dining room of a country house.

Here, a double tier of scallop-topped cafe curtains take care of the privacy-plus-light problem for a bay window that's too close to the street for comfort. The independent tiers offer the maximum adjustability and control. You can make your own pattern for this type of scallop-topped curtains or use scalloped pleater tape (the easy way) if you'd like your cafes scalloped *and* pleated. Directions for making draperies and curtains begin on page 124.

# Ruffled Curtains
# Come Out of the Kitchen

Even if your taste runs mainly to contemporary, you may like the "homey" touch of quaintly ruffled curtains softening utilitarian counters and cabinets in the kitchen, or adding a froth of filmy white to bedroom windows. But have you ever considered how dramatic they could be sweeping across a wide expanse of living room or sunroom wall? With the country look so fashionable right now, and relaxed at-home living the rule, they might be just the thing to give a room that needs re-doing a fresh new outlook. And in spite of their rather special look, they're not much harder to make than straight-hanging curtains or draperies, because even the ruffles are all straight strips of fabric.

Above, see ruffled curtains in their traditional role—adding a frilly, lighthearted touch to the functional plainness of a kitchen, where the windows are usually rather small. But now take a look at the garden-like living room at the left, and see how the whole room bursts into flower with ruffled curtains dramatizing one window wall. The two adjoining walls are also covered with the same full-blown pattern of rosy-red peonies and carnations to give the room a faintly Victorian flavor. (You can find lots of prints in the same nostalgic mood, and the lacy wicker furniture couldn't be more *au courant*.)

The directions for making ruffled tieback curtains start on page 137. See page 213 for directions for covering walls with fabric.

# Window Dressing with a Difference

Dress a window with plants instead of draperies! In this dining room, inconspicuous steel standards and brackets were installed on both sides of the window recess and glass shelves placed at irregular intervals. A variety of potted plants flourish in the sunlight, surrounded by fern-sprayed walls and crisp white shutters.

Fed up with frilly kitchen curtains? Cover wooden blinds with the same gaily printed paper that covers the walls. It takes a little patience, but practically no tools. Single-edge razor blades and a rubber-based glue are all you need; see page 138.

Mini-awnings are more fun for a family playroom or a sunroom than a serious (and conventional) window treatment. In this sun-filled family room, zigzag-striped cotton corduroy makes a trio of tiny, scalloped awnings edged with contrasting braid. They're surprisingly easy to make, and almost as easy to install. You'll find complete directions on page 138.

# basic how-tos

## HOW TO MAKE DRAPERIES AND CURTAINS

Draperies and curtains are the basic components of most window treatments—and therefore a vital factor in decorating. In most rooms, they can do more than any other single element to create a mood, define a style, or emphasize a color scheme. They can be formal or informal, simple or elaborate, vivid or subdued, patterned or plain. They can let light in or keep it out, draw attention to a lovely view or disguise an unattractive one. They can even camouflage a poorly-sized window or change the apparent proportions of a room.

What kind of fabric should you choose to perform these decorating miracles? First of all, one you love and will enjoy living with for more than a season. Be practical about it, too: choose a fabric that's colorfast and treated to repel soot and stains. Fabrics with body are best for full-length draperies; lighter weights and sheers are fine for short curtains. Remember that dress fabrics and even sheets come in stunning patterns and are comparatively inexpensive. (And the wide widths sheets come in mean less seaming.)

Actually, you get a lot for your effort when you make curtains or draperies. Seams and hems are all straight sewing, and even lined draperies can be stitched together quickly. If you've invested in a good drapery fabric, spend the extra time and money it takes to make linings. They'll protect the draperies from fading and add extra body, making the draperies more likely to hang in deep, even folds. In fact, well-made draperies or curtains are well worth your very best efforts. Just follow the directions given here; even a sewing novice should have no trouble making well-tailored draperies or curtains to be proud of.

### START WITH CORRECT MEASUREMENTS

Be sure to measure each window for which you are making draperies or curtains individually. Windows in the same room may not be identical in size even though they appear to be. For that matter, many floors are not level across the entire width or length of floor-length draperies. Always have the proper fixtures and rods in place before measuring and measure from the top of the fixture down. Draperies, curtains and linings must be cut on the true lengthwise and crosswise grains of the fabric to hang correctly.

For *finished length*, measure from the top of the rod to the sill, the apron or the floor, depending upon how long finished length is to be. (These three lengths are the only correct ones.) For *finished width*, measure the length of the rod including the "returns," or the distance the rod

extends out from the wall on both sides; to this measurement, add 6″ for center overlap (3″ on each panel).

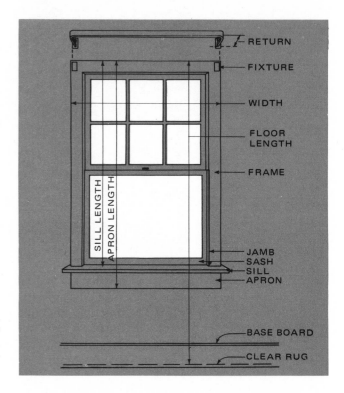

### ADD THE NECESSARY ALLOWANCES

To determine the amount of yardage you'll need, first decide how full you want the draperies or curtains to be. The general rule is to allow two to 2½ times the width of the area to be covered if the fabric is of heavy or medium weight; allow three times the width if the fabric is sheer.

Where headings are used, add 1″ to the finished length (unless a ruffled effect such as seen on pages 148–49 is desired). Then add the following allowances for top and bottom hems:

TOP HEMS:
　　Pleated Heading on lined draperies or curtains ...... 4″
　　Pleated Heading on unlined draperies, curtains ... 4½″
　　Pleated Heading made with pleater tape ........... ½″
　　Shirred Heading made with 4-cord shirring tape .... 3″
　　Shirred Heading with a casing ..................... 3″
　　Plain Hem for clip-on rings (no heading) ...... 1¼″–4″

| BOTTOM HEMS: | Single Hem | Double Hem |
|---|---|---|
| Floor-length Draperies, Curtains ...5″ | | .............9″ |
| Glass Curtains ....................3¼″ | | ...........6″ |
| Cafe Curtains ...................2¼″–3¼″ | | .....4″–6″ |
| Ruffled Curtains ................¼″ | | |

(Subtract width of ruffle from finished length, then add ¼″ for hem)

To finished *width* of each panel, add 1½″ on each side for single hems, 2″ on each side for double hems. In addition, add ½″ seam allowances if more than one width of fabric is required for each panel.

## DETERMINE THE NUMBER OF PANELS

To determine the number of panels needed for each window, divide the *total* width of drapery by the width of fabric being used. Buy lining fabric of the same width as the drapery fabric, and count on the same number of panels as for draperies.

## ALLOW EXTRA FABRIC FOR MATCHING

If patterned fabric is used, extra yardage will be needed for matching the pattern on all panels (unless the pattern is a small, all-over design). The amount depends upon the size of the "repeat," which is usually noted on drapery fabric. A notation that the fabric has a 21″ repeat means that the design is repeated every 21″. If the repeat is not indicated, measure the distance from one point on the design to exactly the same point on the next design directly above or below it. Divide the total length of the drapery by the length of the repeat. For example, if the total length is 105″ and the repeat is 21″, exactly five repeats would be needed for each panel, and there would be no waste involved in matching this particular pattern. However, if the repeat were 20″ and the total length 105″, 5¼ repeats would be needed for each panel. To match *this* pattern, it would be necessary to buy six repeats for each panel, or 120″, because each panel must begin and end at the same points in the design.

In addition to matching a patterned fabric, the design should be placed so that the effect will be pleasing. On long draperies, an unbroken repeat should be at the finished top of the drapery. A broken repeat will be less noticeable at the floor. But on short draperies, the opposite is true. A broken repeat at the bottom is more noticeable because it's more nearly at eye level. After determining how much extra yardage is required for matching the pattern on all windows in a room, add one more extra repeat to allow for the best placement.

## CUT AND MARK FABRIC ACCURATELY

Accuracy is extremely important when cutting draperies. Pull a crosswise thread to straighten the end of the fabric. If the end is not square, pull fabric on the true bias in the direction opposite the higher corner. Continue stretching until the crosswise threads are at right angles to the lengthwise threads. Trim off all selvages and press fabric to remove wrinkles.

Place the fabric on a large flat surface, right side up, and study the pattern to decide in which direction the design should go. All panels must be cut in the same direction.

Use a yardstick or steel tape measure and chalk pencil to measure and mark the fabric. Mark the finished top edge, keeping in mind the best placement of the design if

the fabric is patterned. Measure upward from this line to mark the top hem allowance. Measuring down from this line, add the heading allowance to the finished length of drapery and mark a line indicating the finished bottom edge of drapery. Measuring down from *this* line, add the bottom hem allowance. You have now marked off the total length required for the first panel. Use this length as a pattern for all remaining lengths. To mark each succeeding one, place the cut length right side down on the fabric, matching the design carefully at all points if the fabric is patterned.

## SEAMING LENGTHS OF FABRIC TOGETHER

In most cases, each drapery panel requires more than one width of fabric, so the lengths have to be joined by seams. Excessive finishing on these long seams may cause puckering, so make them the simplest way possible.

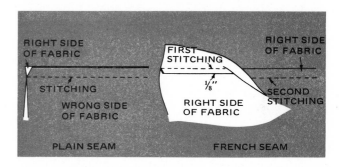

Plain seams can be used on most fabrics. Pin right sides of the two lengths together, carefully matching any pattern, and stitch ½″ from edges. Press allowances open.

French seams should be used on sheer fabrics or ones that ravel. Place wrong sides of the two lengths together and stitch ¼″ from edges. Press as stitched and trim seam allowances to ⅛″, then·press allowances open. Turn right sides of fabric together, press so seam is along exact edge, and stitch ¼″ from first seam, enclosing raw edges.

From here on, the construction of lined and unlined draperies and curtains differs.

## UNLINED DRAPERIES AND CURTAINS

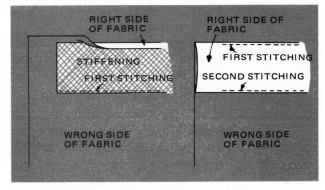

The upper edge is finished with a stiffening such as crinoline or buckram, or with pleater tape. Four-inch-wide buckram is standard, but if draperies are extra-long, you may want to use 5″ width. (If so, add the extra 1″ to the total length.) Place stiffening on wrong side of fabric ½″ from upper edge, starting and stopping 1½″ from the side edges of panel. Stitch along lower edge of stiffening.

Turn top edge of panel over stiffening and press. Turn stiffening to wrong side to form top hem. Stitch along what is now lower edge of stiffening through all thicknesses.

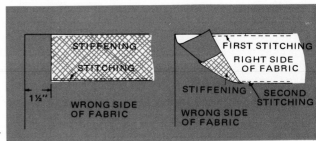

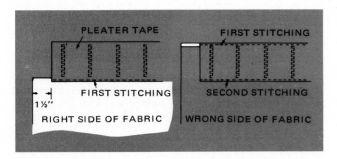

To finish upper edge of panel with pleater tape, place tape along top of panel, both right sides up, with tape overlapping top edge of fabric by ½″. Measure the return on the rod and position pockets in tape so that the first pleat on side edge of panel will come at the corner of the rod. Top-stitch tape in place. Turn pleater tape to wrong side of panel and stitch along what is now lower edge of tape through all thicknesses.

Finish side edges of panel next. Turn under ½″ down each side and press. Turn another 1″ to wrong side, mitering upper corners, and pin in place. Slip-stitch hems by hand (preferably) or machine-stitch to within 6″ of finished length.

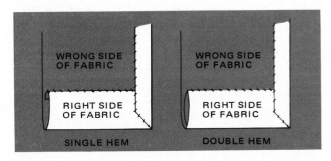

Finish lower edge with a single or double hem according to allowance planned earlier. For a single hem, turn ½″ to wrong side, then turn up a 4½″ hem.

For a double hem, turn 4½″ to wrong side, then turn up another 4½″. Pin and baste hem in place. Let the finished drapery hang for several days. If the fabric stretches, adjust length; if not, slip-stitch hem in place as basted. Turn unfinished side hems over the bottom hem, mitering corners, and finish stitching side hems in place.

## LINED DRAPERIES AND CURTAINS

The upper edge can be finished with stiffening as for unlined drapery, but the placement changes. Place stiffen-ing on wrong side of fabric with upper edges even and ends 1½″ from side edges of panel. Stitch along lower edge of stiffening. Turn stiffening to wrong side to form top hem and stitch along what is now lower edge of stiffening through all thicknesses.

To finish the upper edge with pleater tape, apply the tape in exactly the same manner as for unlined drapery. With right sides of both tape and fabric up, place tape so it overlaps top edge of fabric by ½″ and top-stitch in place. Turn pleater tape to wrong side and stitch along what is now lower edge of tape through all thicknesses.

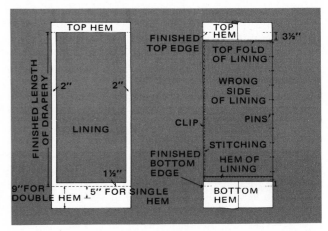

Straighten end of lining fabric in same manner as for drapery fabric. Cut lengths of lining 1½″ shorter than finished length of drapery. Stitch lengths of lining together with plain seams. Lining should be 4″ narrower than drapery panel, so cut 2″ off each side of lining panel so that seams of both fall in same place.

Turn ½″ of lining to wrong side along both upper and lower edges and press. Turn up a 2″ hem along lower edge of lining and stitch in place. Place lining over drapery panel, right sides together. Place folded top edge of lining 3½″ down from finished top edge of drapery panel.

Pin side edges of lining and drapery panel together, with right sides still facing. Since lining is narrower than drapery panel, the panel will not lie flat. Stitch side edges together with ½″ seams. Clip seam allowances every 3″ to 4″ to prevent puckering and press open.

Turn panel to right side and center lining over drapery

fabric. Pin seams to drapery fabric and press; if panel is made of more than one width of fabric, pin seams of lining and fabric together and press. There will be a 1″ hem of drapery fabric showing along either side of the lining.

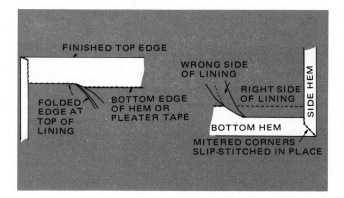

Pin the top edge of the lining over the lower edge of the hem or pleater tape and slip-stitch lining in place. Turn side hems to inside above the lining, mitering top corners, and slip-stitch side hems to top hems.

Finish lower edge with a single or double hem in the same manner as for unlined drapery, first basting hem allowance in place. Slip-stitch hem permanently only after drapery has hung for several days and any necessary adjustments have been made. The hem of lining hangs free, overlapping top of drapery hem by about 2″, but is held loosely in place with a French tack every 12″ to 14″. To make French tack, fasten thread in fabric and take a stitch in lining, holding the two apart about 1″. Take several stitches between the two fabrics, still holding them apart; then work over the threads with a blanket stitch to keep them even and close together.

## PLEATING THE TOP EDGE

The top width of the drapery panel must be pleated to fit the length of the rod. The method of spacing and making the pleats is the same for both lined and unlined draperies and curtains. To determine the size and placement of pleats, subtract the finished width of the drapery from the total width. The difference is the amount to be taken up evenly in pleats. There should be an uneven number of pleats in each panel.

Experiment by pleating a piece of fabric to see how deep the pleats should be to have the effect you want. (The weight of the fabric makes a difference.) For example, if there are 40 inches to be taken up in pleats, and you think each pleat should be about 5″ deep, divide the 40″ by 5″. The result would be 8 pleats. But since an uneven number of pleats is preferable from a design standpoint, you might try dividing the 40″ by 7. This would make the pleats about 5¾″ deep, which might be a little bulky. You would then try dividing the 40″ by 9. This would give you pleats a little less than 4½″ deep. Make a

4½″ pleat in your fabric. If it looks better than the 5¾″ pleat, you would decide to have nine pleats, each 4½″ deep.

To determine where pleats should be placed, first measure the return on the rod. The first pleat should start at this distance from the outside edge of the panel. Make the second pleat 3″ from inside edge of the panel to allow for the standard overlap (which should not be pleated).

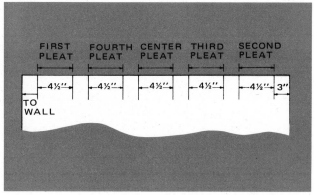

Space the remaining pleats evenly between these two. If making three, five, nine, or seventeen pleats, place third pleat exactly at the center point between the first and second pleats. Place fourth and fifth pleats by bringing center pleat together with each outside pleat. Mark position and width of each pleat with pins or chalk pencil, and space remaining pleats between already-marked pleats in the same manner. Form pleats by bringing each pair of markings together. Pin and stitch along marking from top edge to ¾″ below heading. Be sure to backstitch at each end to fasten thread securely. Now decide which type of pleat to use.

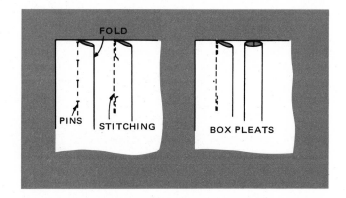

Box pleats are made by spreading the large folds an even distance on both sides of the stitching line and pressing them flat. Stitch across the pleats at the bottom of the vertical stitching to hold the pleats in place.

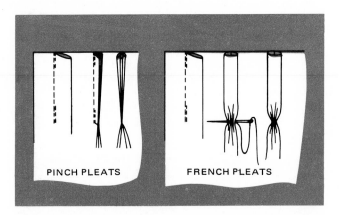

**PINCH PLEATS**     **FRENCH PLEATS**

Pinch pleats divide the fullness of each pleat into three smaller, equal folds. Press firmly in place and stitch across the three folds at the lower edge of the heading. Press pleats above the stitching.

French pleats are similar to pinch pleats, but pleats are not pressed above stitching. Divide the large pleat into three smaller ones and stitch in place by hand by drawing needle and thread through folds several times, pulling thread tight. Fasten thread securely underneath.

If pleater tape was used, the placement of the pleats is determined by the woven pockets in the tape. Simply insert the special pronged hooks in the pockets of the tape and the pleats are made automatically.

There is an easy-to-copy technique for hanging draperies which will give them a professionally-made look. After the draperies are hung on the rod, finger-press each pleat from top to bottom by running your fingers down the edge, forming a fold but not a sharp crease. Place pins about 12" apart down the full length of the pleat. Allow the drapery to hang for a day or two with pins in place. Then remove the pins and the drapery will hang in soft, evenly-spaced folds.

### EASY-TO-MAKE HEADINGS FOR CURTAINS

A plain casing with heading is probably the easiest way to give sheer curtains a decorative finish and is suitable for any informal treatment. Make a deep finished top hem, either single or double, and divide it horizontally with a row of stitching to form both heading and casing. When the rod is inserted in the casing and the fullness of the curtain shirred on the rod, the hem will form a narrow ruffled heading. If a plain casing without heading is desired, as on French doors or within wooden frames, the rod is inserted in a simple hem.

Using ready-made shirring tape is another easy way to make a decorative heading on sheer curtains. It comes in two- and four-cord widths which give the heading a smocked effect. Turn down a ¾" fold at top of curtain and stitch tape to the wrong side of the fabric. Stitch across tape above the top cord and below the bottom cord; if using four-cord width, stitch across one side of each cord between. Stitch tape down one side edge to secure cords; then draw cords from opposite edge so curtain is desired width and stitch. The same effect can be achieved with-

out tape by making a finished top hem and making several rows of stitching through it to form casings. Insert cord through each casing and secure down one side of curtain; pull cords from other side as described above.

### CAFE CURTAINS MADE SEVERAL WAYS

Cafe curtains can be used many ways—and made in several variations. They can be made with pleated or scalloped headings, or with a combination of the two. The method of measuring pleats, and the types of pleats that can be used, are the same as described previously for any draperies or curtains. And the ready-made pleater tapes mentioned earlier can also be used to make cafes. There is also a special pleater tape for making scalloped pinch pleats which is very handy for making cafes. To use this, place scalloped edge of tape along top edge of curtain, right sides together, and stitch along scalloped edge. Trim fabric to match scallops and turn tape to wrong side. Stitch lower edge to fabric and insert pleater pins in pockets to make pleats automatically. Always follow stitching lines on tape to prevent stitching over pockets.

To make scallop-topped cafe curtains without pleater tape, turn 4½" along top edge of panel to right side, then turn 1½" of that 4½" back up (before making

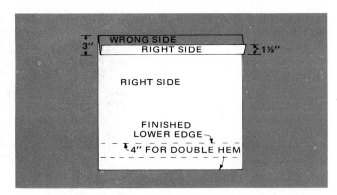

side hems). Cut a 4"-diameter circle from cardboard and draw a line across its center. Allowing 4" for each scallop and ¾" spaces between them, determine how many full scallops will fit across width and plan to center them accordingly, with straight spaces or partial scallops of equal

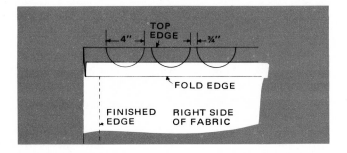

width at each side. Place line on cardboard pattern along top folded edge and trace scallops. Stitch around edges of scallops and trim excess fabric to ¼" from stitching; clip into ¼″ allowances. Stitch a 1½″ seam down each side from top edge to bottom of facing. Trim seams ¼″ beyond stitching and cut away excess above 4½″ fold. Turn scallops right side out and press. Make finished side hems below facing.

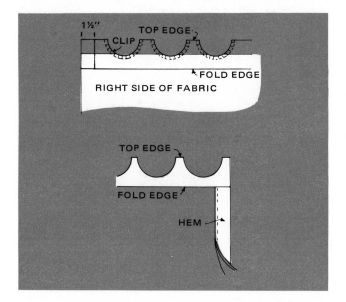

## HOW TO MAKE TIEBACKS

Hold the panels back with a tape measure to determine how long the tiebacks should be. Cut a strip of fabric 1″ longer than desired length and 8″ wide. Cut a 3½″-wide piece of stiffening to finished length. Place stiffening on wrong side of fabric with one edge along center of strip, and ends of stiffening ½″ in from ends of fabric. Stitch along both edges of stiffening.

Fold strip in half lengthwise, right sides together, with fold along one edge of stiffening. Stitch along length, ½″ from raw edges. Turn right side out and press with seam along one edge. Turn ½″ of fabric to inside at each end and slip-stitch closed. Attach a ring to center of each end. Hold tieback in place and attach a cup hook to window frame in desired position; slip rings over hook.

# THE WIDE WORLD OF WINDOW HARDWARE

Leafing through a catalog of window hardware and accessories put out by one of the major manufacturers is an illuminating experience. The variety of rings and rods, clips and hooks, brackets and holdbacks, supports and pulleys, sockets and extenders, track parts and traverse cords, pleater tapes and slides (to mention a few of the products available) is nothing less than mind-boggling. Every conceivable kind of aid you've ever heard of for making and installing curtains and draperies is included—plus lots, we'll wager, you never even dreamed of. We show here only a smattering of the most basic types of hardware and accessories that will help you complete your window treatments. But if *any* problem arises which one of these few examples won't solve, simply see your hardware dealer or dash to the nearest store with a window-accessory department. And in the meantime, here are a few notes which may help you make a selection.

*Adjustable curtain rods* come in sizes from 18″ to 120″ wide—and if 120″ isn't wide enough, extension sections can be added. What's more, they're available in two different styles to take care of curtains of varied weights.

*Standard traverse rods* are made for windows up to 25 feet wide, with projections from 1½″ for sheer curtains up to 5½″ (with extension plates) for draperies over casement curtains or window shades. And *cut-to-measure rods* can be made for windows of any width or shape, however unusual.

*Curtain rod support* should be placed at center of overall width if only one is required. For long rods, an extra support should be placed at or near each corner to provide support for the extra weight when draperies are stacked.

*Rounded pin hooks* fit over a curtain rod. Pin hooks with pointed tops are made to fit snugly on a traverse rod glide.

*Four-pronged pleater hooks* slide into the uniformly-spaced pockets of 4″ pleater tape to make pinch-pleated headings automatically. There are smaller hooks for 3″ cafe tape. *Single-prong hooks* hold drapery ends in place. place.

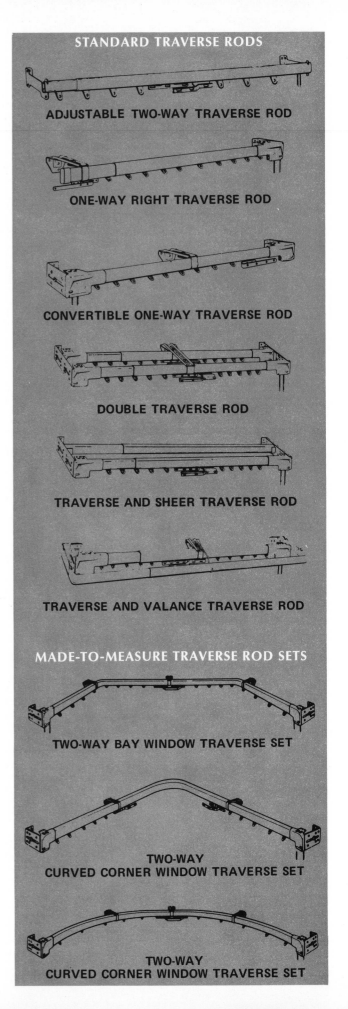

**STANDARD TRAVERSE RODS**

ADJUSTABLE TWO-WAY TRAVERSE ROD

ONE-WAY RIGHT TRAVERSE ROD

CONVERTIBLE ONE-WAY TRAVERSE ROD

DOUBLE TRAVERSE ROD

TRAVERSE AND SHEER TRAVERSE ROD

TRAVERSE AND VALANCE TRAVERSE ROD

**MADE-TO-MEASURE TRAVERSE ROD SETS**

TWO-WAY BAY WINDOW TRAVERSE SET

TWO-WAY CURVED CORNER WINDOW TRAVERSE SET

TWO-WAY CURVED CORNER WINDOW TRAVERSE SET

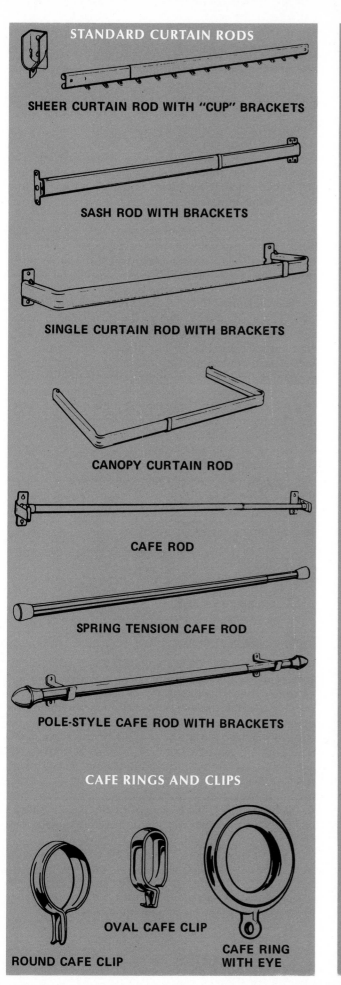

## STANDARD CURTAIN RODS

SHEER CURTAIN ROD WITH "CUP" BRACKETS

SASH ROD WITH BRACKETS

SINGLE CURTAIN ROD WITH BRACKETS

CANOPY CURTAIN ROD

CAFE ROD

SPRING TENSION CAFE ROD

POLE-STYLE CAFE ROD WITH BRACKETS

## CAFE RINGS AND CLIPS

ROUND CAFE CLIP

OVAL CAFE CLIP

CAFE RING WITH EYE

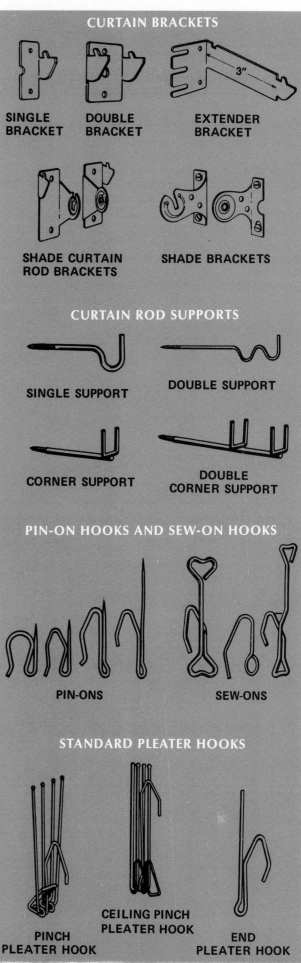

## CURTAIN BRACKETS

SINGLE BRACKET

DOUBLE BRACKET

EXTENDER BRACKET

3"

SHADE CURTAIN ROD BRACKETS

SHADE BRACKETS

## CURTAIN ROD SUPPORTS

SINGLE SUPPORT

DOUBLE SUPPORT

CORNER SUPPORT

DOUBLE CORNER SUPPORT

## PIN-ON HOOKS AND SEW-ON HOOKS

PIN-ONS

SEW-ONS

## STANDARD PLEATER HOOKS

PINCH PLEATER HOOK

CEILING PINCH PLEATER HOOK

END PLEATER HOOK

# HOW TO MAKE
## DECORATIVE VALANCES
## AND CORNICES

Attractive valances and cornices are easier to create than a do-it-yourself decorator might suppose. The two terms are often used interchangeably to refer to any decorative treatment across the top of a window which gives a finished look to curtains or draperies and conceals curtain rods and other fixtures. Such a treatment made primarily of fabric is more properly called a valance (although it may be mounted on a shelf-like board as well as hung on a curtain rod), while a similar treatment based on a box-like foundation of wood or other solid material is a cornice. Either can be used to unify two or more windows, conceal awkward window dimensions, or camouflage structural defects. And either may be simple or elaborate in design, but should harmonize with the style of the room.

There is no hard-and-fast rule regarding the depth of a valance or cornice. It should be determined by the height of the room and the length of the draperies. Approximately one-eighth the total height of the window treatment is usually a good proportion. There are many different types of valances and cornices, and the design possibilities are almost unlimited. But it's always a good

idea to test the design and dimensions by tracing the desired shape onto wrapping paper and cutting out a facsimile which can be placed in the proposed position. You can then judge the proportions and the general effect from a distance. Whatever its style, a valance or cornice should always return to the wall at either end, covering the edges of the drapery and the window molding. The inner dimension should be about four inches wider than the window frame to allow ample clearance for the draperies on both sides.

Both valances and cornices can be made in a simple, tailored style like a rectangular box, or with a shaped lower edge cut in a decorative design and accented with ribbon, braid or other trimming. Valances can be softly swagged or crisply pleated. The box-pleated valance below left is one of a pair made of a flower-striped fabric that coordinates with the all-over floral used for the draperies. The pleats were folded so the stripes match where the pleats meet each other. (See directions on page 139.) Box pleats (or any pleats) should be spaced so that one ends at each front corner.

Shaping the lower edge of a valance to emphasize the design of the fabric it's covered in (if it's covered in a print), or to repeat the silhouette of a distinctive piece of furniture in the room will give your window treatment a "custom-made" look. This type of valance is made on a foundation of firm interfacing or buckram and lightly padded with cotton flannel. After cutting a paper pattern and "trying it on" your window to check its size and shape, cut the outer fabric and the padding one inch larger than the pattern on all sides. Cut the interfacing or buckram the same size as the pattern, and cut the lining

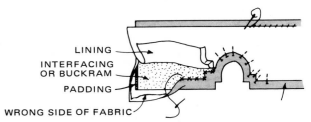

LINING
INTERFACING OR BUCKRAM
PADDING
WRONG SIDE OF FABRIC

fabric ¼" larger than the pattern. Place the padding on the wrong side of the outer fabric and stitch together along all edges. Center the interfacing or buckram on top of the padding and fold the edges of the outer fabric and padding around it. Using heavy-duty thread, catch-stitch the edges of the fabric to the back of the interfacing or buckram, clipping into the one-inch margins at corners and curves to keep fabric and padding flat and smooth. Turn edges of the lining fabric under ½" and slip-stitch to the back of the valance, ¼" from the edges. Sew 2"-wide tape to the back of the valance across the top edge to make a channel for the curtain rod. Place the rod as close as possible to the draperies and hang the valance on it.

If the valance is to be mounted on a board instead of hung on a curtain rod, omit the back channel and stitch the top edge of one-inch twill tape to the back of the valance across the top edge by hand and tack the tape to the top surface of the board with upholsterer's tacks.

# A SIMPLE BOX CORNICE
# IS A CINCH TO MAKE

A simple box cornice is as versatile as it is easy to make, and can be used with striking effect in either a contemporary setting or a traditional one. The fabric that covers it and makes matching draperies defines the mood. Here, a colorful crewel pattern that recalls the prized embroideries imported by the Colonies via sailing ships gives authentic flavor to a living room done in 18th-Century style. The fabric used for the cornice and upholstery was outline-quilted for a luxurious look. (Quilted and unquilted match-mates can often be found; if the fabric you like doesn't come both ways, you could conceivably quilt some yourself.) In this case, the cornice was outlined with contrasting cording for a custom touch. The easy directions are given here.

For each box cornice you'll need:

Two "1 x 6" x 12" for A
One "1 x 6", required width less 1½" for B
¼" plywood, 12" x required width for C
Outer fabric and lining fabric
Covered ¾" cording
Four ½" flat head wood screws
1" wire brads
Tacks or staples
Wood glue

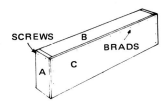

Glue and screw A to each end of B; glue and nail C to A and B as shown. Cut one piece of fabric 14" x width of C plus 4" and two pieces 9" x 14" so pattern will match when 14" edges are joined. On right side of fabric, stitch cording down each side of front piece so it will be along front corner. Stitch 9" x 14" end pieces to front piece, following stitching line of cording. Stitch cording along entire lower edge on right side of fabric.

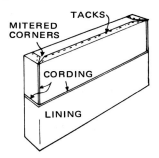

Cut lining fabric 14" x same length as outer fabric. With right sides together, stitch lining to outer fabric along stitching line of cording at lower edge only.

With lining hanging below cornice, place outer fabric on cornice with cording along corners and lower edge. Tack or staple outer fabric to top of cornice and along back edges, mitering corners. Pull lining to inside of cornice and staple or tack to sides along front corners, pleating in any extra fullness. Turn raw edges under and tack along top and back edges.

Tack cording around top of cornice along front and side edges. Cover top of cornice with lining fabric, turning raw edges under and tacking so it covers seam allowances of cording.

# A SCALLOPED CORNICE
# SUITS A TRADITIONAL MOOD

While a box cornice can be either contemporary or traditional, a scalloped one like this is most in keeping with a formal period room. Especially if the fabric is in a richly hued Oriental pattern lavished with gilt fringe. Here, the glowing lacquer red and gold light up the dark wood paneling and traditional furniture, making the window an effective focal point. The cornice is made in much the same manner as the square-cut box cornice on page 133; the only basic difference is that the lower edge is cut in a graceful scalloped design that resembles a softly draped swag. A graph pattern for this particular design is given here, but you could easily substitute any design you prefer—perhaps one that follows the pattern design of your fabric.

For each scalloped cornice you'll need:

   ¾" plywood, 14" x finished length
   "1 x 6" pine, finished length plus 30"
   1½" finishing nails
   Two 3" angle irons and screws
   Tacks or staples
   Outer fabric and lining fabric
   1" thick padding
   Covered cording, twill tape

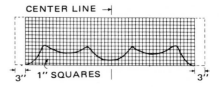

Cut length of plywood 4" wider than window frame. Mark 1" squares on plywood and draw scalloped edge of cornice by enlarging squares in diagram. Pattern is for cornice 48" long but can be adapted to longer length by adding up to 3" on each end or by widening scallops.

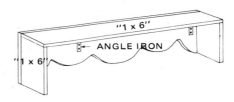

Cut top and two sides from "1 x 6" and assemble cornice, using 1½" nails. Screw angle irons to underside of top along back edge, about 8" in from each end.

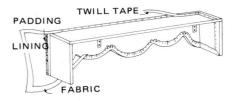

Place padding on front and trim to shape. Cover with lining and outer fabric, centering pattern of outer fabric. Tack or staple fabric to top, then to inside surface of front, starting at widest point and easing fabric around curved scallops and clipping at inside curves. Then pull fabric around ends and tack or staple to inside surfaces. Tack or staple twill tape over raw edge of fabric on top.

Tack or staple cording around bottom edge, then cover raw edges of fabric on inside surfaces with twill tape. Apply fringe to front of cornice, if desired, by blind-stitching it in place. Screw angle irons to window frame in desired position.

A cornice can do more than merely dress up a window. It can continue across a whole wall or even two to promote the illusion (with the aid of draperies) that one or both walls are made entirely of glass. Only the sliding doors and one narrow window in this "sunroom" are actually see-through, but the wrap-around cornice and draperies give the impression they're covering wall-wide expanses of window. Except for the length of the lumber involved, this two-wall cornice is as easy to construct as a simple box cornice. Specific directions on page 133.

A more traditional window treatment shows how effective a shaped cornice can be. Contrasting braid and tasseled fringe emphasize its scallopy curves, giving it a Chinoiserie look that's perfect with Chinese Chippendale furniture. (Notice that the tiebacks are tasseled, too.) Since this window is only 43″ wide, ⅜″ plywood was used for the front panel. And because the panel extends beyond the returns, all three were covered with fabric before the front panel was nailed in place. A pattern is included with the directions on page 140.

# directions for projects

## CORNER CORNICE
### ON PAGE 112

MATERIALS NEEDED:
- "1 x 6" clear pine: one to dimension "X" for A, one to dimension "Y" for D, one 20" for B and E
- "1 x 10" clear pine: one 4" less than A for C, one 4" less than D for F
- 2½" angle irons as required by wall studs plus one (see Diagram 1), with ¾" and 1¾" flat-head wood screws as required
- One 4" mending plate with ¾" screws
- 1¾" finishing nails
- Upholsterers' tacks or staple gun and staples
- Fabric

Remove molding at ceiling where cornice will be placed. Locate wall studs along each wall. Using 1¾" screws, attach an angle iron at each stud location, ¾" down from ceiling (Diagram 1).

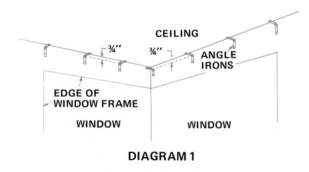

**DIAGRAM 1**

Cut a 45° angle at one end of A and D. Cut C to reach from inside of angle cut on A to ¾" beyond other end of A. Cut F to same length as inside edge of D. Cut B and E to same depth as width of C and F (Diagram 2 shows how

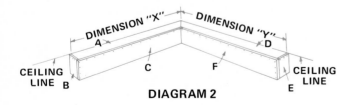

**DIAGRAM 2**

parts fit together when assembled). Nail C to A with right end of C meeting inside of angle cut on A and top edges flush; then nail B to A and C to B. Nail F to D with left end of F ¾" from inside of angle cut on D and right end of F extending ¾" beyond D. Nail E to D and F to E in same manner as before.

Cut 14" strips from full width of fabric and seam together, matching pattern, until long enough to cover B and C plus 6". Place fabric on B and C with fabric design in desired position. Staple to inside faces of B and C at each end. Pull onto top of A, mitering corners, and staple in place (Diagram 3).

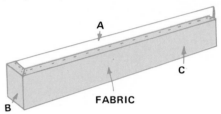

**DIAGRAM 3**

Pull fabric around lower edges of B and C and staple to inside faces, mitering corner and clipping where necessary to keep bottom edge smooth.

Cover faces of E and F in same manner. Place D in position at window with D between top of angle irons and ceiling. Screw through angle irons into D (Diagram 4).

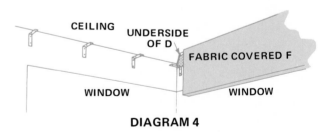

**DIAGRAM 4**

Place A in position and attach in same manner so edge of C goes past end of F. Attach a mending plate across joining of A and D and attach an angle iron around back corner, 2" up from lower edge, attaching it to C and F.

To make draperies, follow directions for lined draperies starting on page 126.

# RUFFLED TIEBACK CURTAINS
## ON PAGES 120–21 (Color Photo)

MATERIALS NEEDED:
  Lightweight decorative fabric such as chintz,
    polished cotton or gingham
  Stiffening for tiebacks
  ⅜" brass rings
  Cup hooks

To determine length of curtains, measure from top of rod to 8" from floor. To determine width of each panel, multiply width of window by one and one-half. Cut lengths of fabric and join together with ½" seams until panel is required width. Press seams open.

**To make right panel of curtain:** With wrong side of fabric toward you, make a finished 1½" hem down left side. Make a double ¼" hem down right side and across bottom (Diagram 1).

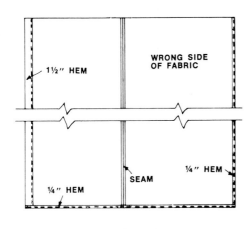

### DIAGRAM 1

Cut 8" wide strips on the lengthwise grain of fabric. Join strips together with tiny French seams until strip is three times the length down one side and across bottom. Make double ⅛" hems along each side of strip and across one end. Gather strip, ½" from top edge—using the ruffler attachment on your sewing machine, if desired—until ruffle equals length plus width of panel (Diagram 2).

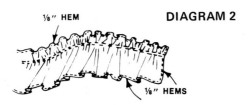

### DIAGRAM 2

Place ruffle along bottom edge of curtain with end hem of ruffle at outside edge of curtain and the gathering line of ruffle along stitching line of curtain hem. Continue po-sitioning ruffle across bottom edge and up center edge, allowing extra fullness at corner to ease ruffle around corner. Stitch together along gathering line. Turn panel ½" to wrong side along entire top edge, including ruffle, then turn 2½" to wrong side and stitch to form bottom of rod casing. Stitch across panel 1" from top edge to form heading and top of casing (Diagram 3).

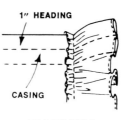

### DIAGRAM 3

Make an 8"-wide valance ruffle three times the width of the window in the same manner as other ruffles, hemming both sides and ends. Gather and attach across top of curtain, placing gathering stitching along stitching at top of casing (Diagram 4).

### DIAGRAM 4

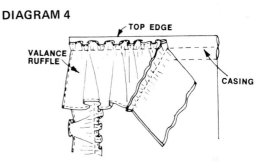

**Ruffled tiebacks:** Hold curtains back with a tape measure to determine length of tiebacks. Cut a strip of fabric 1" longer than finished length and 4" wide. Cut stiffening to finished length by 1½" wide. Place stiffening on wrong side of fabric with one edge along center of fabric and ½" from each end. Stitch stiffening to fabric along both edges.

Fold strip in half lengthwise, right sides together, with fold along one edge of stiffening. Seam along length, ½" from raw edges. Turn right side out and press with seam along one edge. Turn ½" to inside at each end and slip-stitch closed. Make a 4½"-wide ruffle as before, three times the length of tieback; gather and stitch to tieback, placing gathering stitching of ruffle ½" from seamed edge.

Attach a ring to center of each end. Hold tieback in place and attach a cup hook at each side of window frame in desired position.

NOTE: For sill-length ruffled curtains shown on page 121, cut strips for ruffles 4" wide; cut strips for ruffles on tiebacks 3" wide. Ruffles can be any width desired, but should be in proportion to overall size of curtains.

# COVERED BLINDS
## ON PAGE 123

MATERIALS NEEDED:
- Wallpaper
- Rubber base glue
- Wooden venetian blinds
- Single edge razor blades

Lower blind to full length and turn slats into closed position. Remove cord from blind. The design lines of the paper on blinds should line up with the design lines of paper on the walls and on the cornice.

If blinds have a glossy finish, sand lightly before applying paper to insure proper adherence.

Select one of the dominant design lines on the wall and choose the slat of blind which is in line with it.

Measure the circumference of the slat and cut a strip of paper to this measurement plus 1" across full width of paper, making sure design line is in center of strip. Remove slat and apply glue to front only; then stick paper to it in proper position. Fold paper around slat and replace slat in blind to check design line; adjust if necessary. Apply glue to back of slat and stick paper in place, overlapping edges. With razor blade, cut along center of back of slat and remove excess from top edge (Diagram 1).

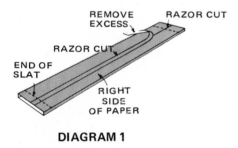

**DIAGRAM 1**

Lift up overlapped edge of paper and pull away excess along edge of paper underneath (Diagram 2).

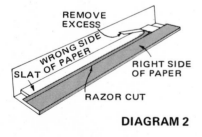

**DIAGRAM 2**

Smooth lifted edge back in place so edges butt tightly. Cut away excess paper at each end, flush with edge of slat (ends are not covered). Cut around holes for cord.

Cover the other slats in same manner. After all are covered, replace cord in blind.

# MINI-AWNINGS
## ON PAGE 123

MATERIALS NEEDED
(for each 24" x 28" awning for 2'-wide window opening:
- 1 yard 44"-wide printed corduroy or other fabric
- 1 yard lining fabric
- 1 yard fusible webbing
- 1 yard ½"-wide guimpe braid
- Fluted dowels, 1⅜" diameter, 15" long, with wooden sockets
- Finials
- 1½" common nails
- 1" finishing nails
- ½" x 1⅜" lath stripping
- White spray paint
- Drapery rod and brackets

NOTE: Any crisp, lightweight, washable fabric in coordinating color is suitable for lining. For best results, preshrink both fabrics, as shrinkage rates may differ. Fusible webbing is packaged in ¾" strips which can be cut in half; it also comes in other widths and by the yard, and is easily cut to desired size. In this project, fusible webbing is used as an easy method of applying braid, which can also be applied by machine or hand stitching.

Cut one 25" x 32½" piece of printed corduroy. (If making two or more awnings, be careful to match pattern. Fabric can be cut evenly by first pulling a crosswise thread or ripping fabric on the cross grain and then following a rib, if using corduroy, to cut fabric lengthwise.) Cut one piece of lining fabric, same size as outer fabric.

As a guide for tracing outline of scallops, draw a 6¼"-diameter circle on cardboard and cut out. From any point on circle, measure in 2" and draw straight line across circle. (This line should measure 6".)

On wrong side of fabric, draw a line across width of fabric, 2¼" from lower edge. Matching line on cardboard guide and line on fabric, mark scallops by tracing around guide four times, starting and stopping ½" from each side edge of fabric (Diagram 1).

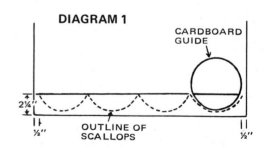

With right sides together, stitch lining to corduroy, ½" from each side edge and along outline of scallops, beginning and ending 2½" from top edge. Trim and notch curves; clip into fabric between scallops (Diagram 2).

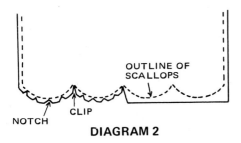

**DIAGRAM 2**

Turn fabric and lining right side out and press so that seams are exactly along edges. Fold ½" along top edges of both fabrics to inside and press, then press ½" to inside along unseamed side edges. Stitch fabrics together close to folded top edges only, through all layers of fabric.

Stitch across width of fabric 1⅞" below line of stitching at top to form top casing. Mark two lines across width of lining, one 6½" from bottom of scallops and one 10½" from bottom of scallops. Bring double thickness of lining and corduroy together along these lines and stitch to form casing for lath strip.

Using fusible webbing, attach strip of guimpe braid along scalloped edge on right side of awning, following manufacturer's directions which accompany fusible webbing.

Make as many awnings as needed in same manner.

Measurements given are for awnings to fit 2'-wide window openings; the number of fluted dowels and wooden sockets required, and the length of lath stripping and drapery rod depend on the number of awnings to be hung (one dowel between every two awnings and one at each end of treatment). Spray-paint fluted dowels, sockets and lath stripping white.

Screw brackets for drapery rod to top of window frame at each side of total window opening at desired height. Insert drapery rod through top casings and place in brackets. Cut lath strip to length of drapery rod; insert in bottom casings. Insert one dowel in one socket and hold against window frame at one side of window. Hold lath strip and awnings out from wall; move socket and dowel on window frame until inside face of lath strip rests against end of dowel and awnings extend from wall without sagging. Mark position of sockets on window frame; nail sockets to frame with 1½" nails. Insert dowels in sockets and nail through lath strip into ends of dowels with finishing nails. Screw finials through lath strip into ends of dowels.

## PLEATED VALANCE
### ON PAGE 132

The box-pleated valance shown on page 132 was mounted on a shelf-like valance board; or it could be made with a channel across the back for a curtain rod, also described on page 132.

Using full width of fabric, cut strips 15" deep so pattern will match when strips are stitched together across 15" ends. Join strips with ½" seams until piece is three times the length of valance board or rod, including returns. Press seams open. Turn ½" to wrong side along lower edge, then turn up 2½" for hem and blind-stitch in place. Divide length of valance board or rod (without returns) into equal parts to determine width of pleats. Pleats in photographed valance are 6½" wide. For this particular floral-striped fabric, with wide and narrow stripes, box pleats were made by folding fabric at centers of the narrow stripes so they match where the pleats meet each other at the center of every other wide stripe. The same effect could be achieved with narrower stripes. However, when planning size of pleats, make sure that one ends at each front corner of the valance. After pleating fabric, cut away any excess at each end and hem so folded edge of hem will be at back edge of cornice board or rod when pleat is at front corner (Diagram 1).

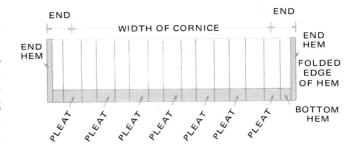

**DIAGRAM 1**

Stay-stitch across top, 1" from edge. Place pleated valance around valance board, with stay-stitching along top edge of board; staple through fabric into top of board (Diagram 2).

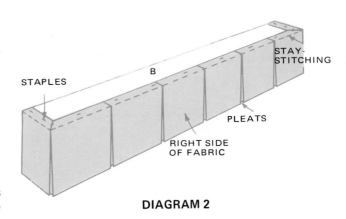

**DIAGRAM 2**

## CHINOISERIE CORNICE
### ON PAGE 135

MATERIALS NEEDED:
(for 43″ window)
  One piece of plywood, ⅜″ x 14″ x 54″, for A
  "1 x 4" pine:
    Two 10″ for B
    One 49½″ for C
  Two 2½″ angle irons with two ⅝″ screws and
    four 1¾″ flat-head wood screws
  1¾ yards of solid-color fabric
  2¾ yards of tasseled trimming
  4½ yards of ¾″-wide flat gold braid
  Four yards of ½″-wide flat gold braid
  1½″ common nails
  Household cement
  Staple gun and staples
  Tissue paper
  Dressmaker's tracing paper
  Tracing wheel

Mark 1″ squares on A. Using Diagram 1 as a guide, enlarge outline of A and pattern for placement of interior braid. Trace both onto tissue paper and set aside. Cut A along outside outline.

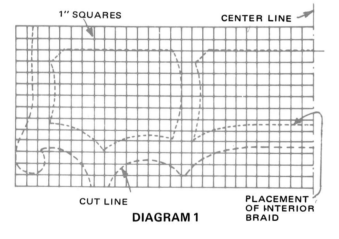

**DIAGRAM 1**

1″ SQUARES    CENTER LINE

CUT LINE    PLACEMENT OF INTERIOR BRAID

Cut fabric to 18″ x 63″ and place A in center of wrong side of fabric. Wrap fabric over top edge and staple to back of A. Pull fabric around side and lower edges, clipping and easing where necessary to go around curves. Staple to back of A so fabric is smooth on front (Diagram 2).

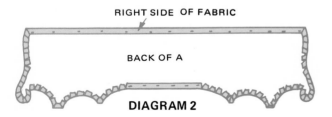

RIGHT SIDE OF FABRIC

BACK OF A

**DIAGRAM 2**

Using two nails at each end, attach one B to each end of C (Diagram 3).

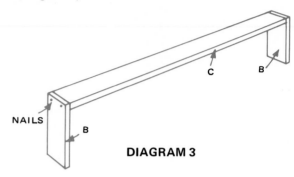

NAILS    C    B    B

**DIAGRAM 3**

Cover outside face and bottom edge of each B with fabric, mitering corners smoothly and stapling to inside face of B and top of C (Diagram 4).

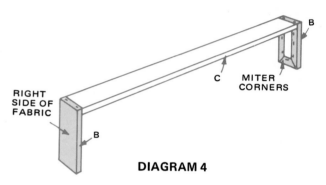

B    C    MITER CORNERS

RIGHT SIDE OF FABRIC    B

**DIAGRAM 4**

Center A on B and C with top edge of A flush with top face of C; nail through A into C, spacing nails about 9″ apart. Nail through A into B with 3 nails on each side. When nailing A to B and C, make sure nail heads are no more than ¾″ in from edge of A so they will be covered by braid (Diagram 5).

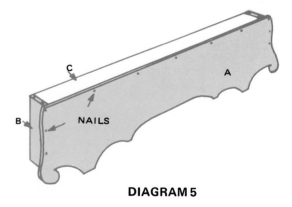

C    A    B    NAILS

**DIAGRAM 5**

Glue tasseled trimming down each side and along lower edge so tassels hang free, holding trimming in place with pins or thumb tacks until glue has dried. Glue ¾″ braid over tape of tasseled trimming and continue along top edge. Using the tissue paper pattern, dress-

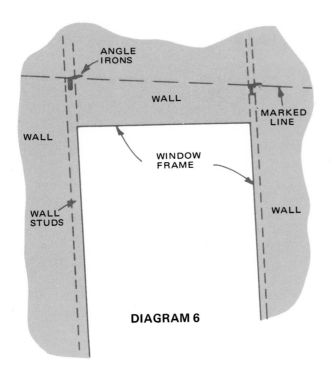

**DIAGRAM 6**

maker's tracing paper and a tracing wheel, transfer pattern for the placement of interior braid to fabric covering front of A. Glue ½″ braid to front of A, following this pattern.

Hold cornice in desired position over window and mark underside of C on wall. Attach one angle iron at each side of window so top of angle is on marked line, screwing into wall studs with two 1¾″ screws for each angle iron (Diagram 6). If cornice is to be hung flush against ceiling, place tops of angle irons ¾″ down from ceiling and remove molding at ceiling line.

Place cornice on angle irons and hold in place with a ⅝″ screw through each angle iron into underside of C.

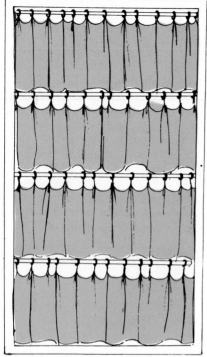

# More Ways with Cafes

One attractive cafe curtain deserves another . . . and another and another. In fact, four short tiers are a decorative way to dress up a tall, slender window. To make them even more so, make deep, scalloped headings and skip the usual overlap; have each tier barely meet the rod below it. This lets in a little light between tiers and lends an airy, lighthearted look. Use spring tension rods and you can remove or rearrange the tiers at will.

A scaled-down cafe curtain used over sheer glass curtains makes a very small window more important without cutting off much light. If the walls are a pale tint, make the glass curtains to match, with a plain casement hem, and attach the rod inside the window frame. Make the border-like cafe curtain in a deeper tone of the same color (or a coordinated print), using scalloped pleater tape, and hang it on a brass rod with decorative finials.

A miniature awning topping a cafe curtain makes a child's room as gay as a circus. Use a single extension rod at the top and an extension canopy rod halfway down the window. For length of awning, measure from top rod to outer edge of the canopy rod and allow for casement hems top and bottom. Baste hems and "try it on" to make sure it's taut before stitching. Add bouncy ball fringe to both awning and scalloped cafe curtain below it.

A cafe curtain and tall tie-back curtains make a fashionable combination for a picture window. Use large brass rods and rings for both sets of curtains. (The scalloped cafe can be a single window-wide

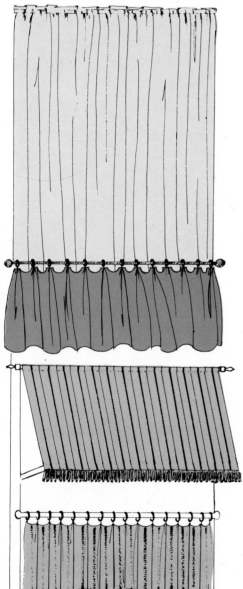

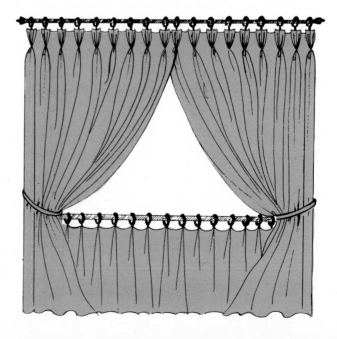

curtain or a pair that parts company at the center for maximum control of light and air.) Make the taller curtains with pleater tape and hook pleater pins into the brass rings. Then tie them back just above the cafe rod, making sure brackets are hidden.

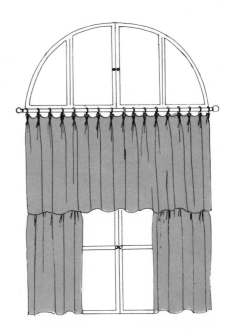

An arched window seems like a decorating problem at first sight, but the problem can be solved by covering it only partially with cafe curtains. The arch itself is probably architecturally attractive as well as high up, so why try to curtain that portion of the window? Instead, make two tiers of sheer cafes, placing the rods at horizontal pane divisions. You could use draperies in the same manner, but cafes offer more flexible control.

A cafe plus a ruffly valance can give a kitchen window a gay provincial look if they're made in traditional tablecloth checks. (Of course, if there's a table, cover it to match.) Making extra-deep headings on both curtain and valance automatically give them a ruffled look when shirred on rods. Use spring tension rods (placed within the window frame) so curtain and valance can be taken down, washed and put up again in double-quick time.

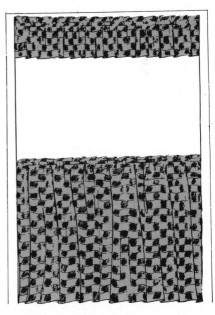

Three frothy tiers of sheer cafe curtains (instead of the usual two) are triply attractive for a little girl's room. Paint wooden poles, finials and brackets a bright color and make the tiers short enough so there's no overlap—then trim each tier with a row of ball fringe to match the fixtures. The colorful poles will show through the sheer fabric. Even more effective: make scallop-topped tiers and hang on wooden rings painted to match the poles.

Cafe curtains can look quite formal when combined with full-length ones at a picture window. Make both sets in three panels—the center cafe twice as wide as the end ones, the full-length versions all the same width. Center one of the full-length panels and tie all three back half-way between the sill and the floor. Use brass rods, with decorative finials on the upper one; the long curtains will hide the brackets for the lower rod.

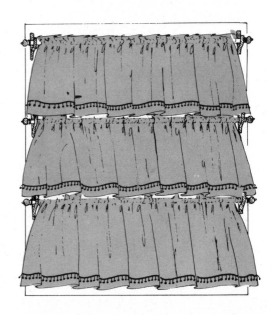

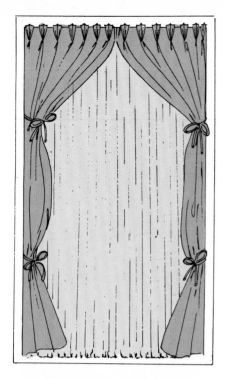

# Curtains Can Dress Up More Than Windows

Camouflage the lack of scenery if a window has no view. Use both sash curtains and tie-backs, but make the sash curtains in an opaque fabric instead of a see-through sheer and install on spring tension rods inside the window frame. Make pinch-pleated tie-back curtains in contrasting fabric and tie back *twice* at equal intervals.

French windows or doors that open into the room need curtains that won't interfere with their function. A sheer fabric gathered on rods, top and bottom, works best. Restrict width of each panel to twice width of glass; if the panels are narrow and the fabric sheer, you can gather it in the middle with a ribbon or bow for a decorative effect.

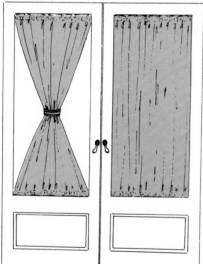

Panelettes are a pretty change from the more-usual shutters—and are almost as flexible when it comes to light control. These small wooden frames are available in a wide range of sizes to fit most windows. In a bedroom, for instance, stretch fabric to match the wallpaper or bedcover on spring rods within each separate frame. Make top and bottom casement hems without headings. You'll have, in effect, a miniature sash curtain within each panel.

Tie-back sash curtains frame a window behind a vanity table in decorative fashion. Use matching fabric and trimming for curtain

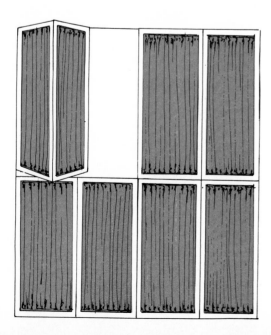

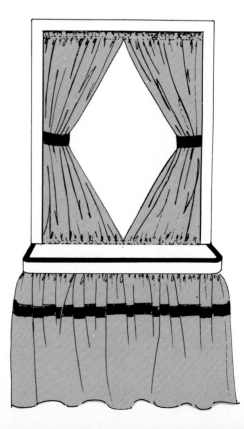

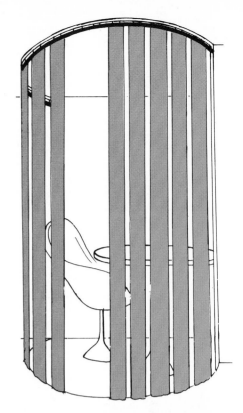

and skirt. Make top and bottom casings with headings on the curtains and gather on spring tension rods placed within the window frame. Fasten the curtains where they meet at center top and bottom so they'll form an interesting diamond-shaped "frame" when held back half-way down with contrasting braid, ribbon or fabric.

Create a dining area by curtaining a corner or an alcove with a semi-circle of ribbons. Install a custom-shaped, ceiling-mounted traverse rod; join floor-length strips at top by stitching between two pieces of tape, leaving 1″ spaces between them. Encase chain weights in narrow hems to keep ribbons taut. Attach tape to rod with small pin hooks.

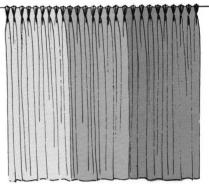

Use dramatic "stripes" of color to camouflage an unattractive wall—with or without windows. Use varying shades of any solid-color fabric—light to dark, dark to light or pale to bright. Allow triple fullness to emphasize the contrast and use convenient pleater tape to make the headings. Install the "curtains" on a ceiling-mounted rod.

Frame rustic doorways in a ski or hunting lodge with tie-back curtains made from colorful fringed blankets. For each pair of curtains, split a blanket so fringe falls along top and bottom edges. Fold top edge down and adjust depth of foldover to make curtains desired length. Make casement hems to encase a wooden cafe rod and use matching cord for tie-backs. Curtains can be quickly released to close off the doorway if the place is drafty.

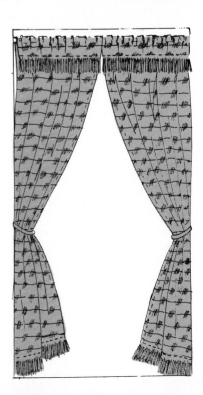

Curtain off a private sunning area on a terrace or in a garden—perfect for private dining, too. Build a simple frame of stock lumber and attach wooden brackets and removable cafe rods along inside top of each side. Make four pairs of full-length cafe curtains in a washable fabric and tie back low at each corner. The same decorative idea could be used for a bed-alcove in a big one-room studio apartment.

# Window Shades

# The Decorator Touch: Window Shades You Can Make

Yes, you can make them. Plain tailored shades in any fabric you please and even decorative Roman shades that look as though they were custom-designed to your order. Surprisingly (considering how spectacular they can look), they're not terribly difficult to turn out. Several helpful products designed specifically for the purpose now make it a cinch to custom-make your own!

Below, two versions of the Roman shade—one boldly splashed with a large-scale Paisley pattern, one whimsically printed with miniature pussycats. The point made here: When you make your own, you can complement the mood of any room as well as carry out any color scheme.

When are window shades more than a means of controlling light? When they're made (by you) to be the focal point of a room. The laminated shades (opposite) are part of a dramatic window treatment that also makes a unified background for the wrap-around seating area. Directions for the fabric-covered cornices and columns start on page 219. Complete directions for making both Roman and laminated shades begin on page 150.

A single flower-sprayed pattern used lavishly *all over* a room can be completely enchanting, as this garden-like living room proves. Very special small touches, such as the extra-deep headings that create valance-like ruffles on the high-tied draperies and matching shades, make a big difference to the look.

# Decorative Window Shades Complete the Pretty Picture

Here, two perfect examples of how much coordinated window shades can add to a room. No other treatment would be quite as effective in this flower-covered living room or the colorful young bedroom. These two rooms also illustrate how charming either a single pattern or a play of pattern-on-pattern can be. Take your pick. Then, by all means, complete the pretty picture with coordinated shades.

What could be more captivating than the cheerful mixture of patterns and melange of colors in this bedroom? The exuberantly patterned wallpaper picks up the pink and green of the precisely checked fabric used to border the draperies and make the scalloped shades, while splashes of bright yellow in furniture and accessories play back the accent color in the wallpaper. Directions for making laminated shades start on page 150.

# basic how-tos

## SEVEN WAYS TO MAKE WINDOW SHADES

Color-coordinated window shades are so attractive, and such a feasible way to tie a decorating plan together, many products have been developed which make it easy for the do-it-yourself home decorator to add this "custom-made" touch to any room. There are heat-sensitized backings you can iron onto the fabric of your choice, pressure-sensitized backings you simply smooth on with the palms of your hands. There are gossamer, web-like materials which will fuse your fabric and backing together when pressed between them (and disappear in the process), and opaque materials with a fusing adhesive on one side which *become* the backing when pressed onto fabric. There are even spray-on adhesives which come in cans and will bond two fabrics together for the desired degree of stiffness. There are also chemical fabric stiffeners you can paint or spray directly on a fabric to make it stiff enough so that no backing is necessary, and others you dip a fabric *into* to obtain the same result. Finally, there are vinyl and vinyl-coated shade cloths which need no backing, and a wide variety of vinyl wallcoverings which may or may not require a backing.

Which of these wonder-workers to choose—and how to proceed after you've purchased the product? Read on; here are general and specific guidelines which should make creating your own window shades as easy as ABC.

## CHOOSING THE FABRIC

If you plan to make window shades to match something else in the room, be sure to choose a fabric that's suitable for the shades as well as for the draperies, upholstery, tablecloth or whatever you plan to coordinate. A medium-weight, closely-woven fabric is the best choice for shades. Very heavy fabrics will not roll up properly; very sheer fabrics don't have enough body to hang well, and may allow adhesive to show through. If using iron-on, self-adhesive or fused-on backing, fabrics such as muslin, chintz, lightweight denim and sailcloth are ideal. In addition to very sheer fabrics, avoid triacetates and light-weight silks, especially for fusing. If you wish to make vinyl or vinyl-coated shades, select the material in a decorator shade department or wallcovering store; vinyls found in dress-fabric departments are usually not suitable for shades.

Before selecting a fabric, consider how much light it will let in, and whether you want room-darkening or light-penetrating shades. Although the type of backing used is the most decisive factor in the transparency or opacity of a window shade, the weave and thickness of the fabric (not necessarily the color) are also important.

Color *does* make a difference in a fabric's insulating property. White and light-colored shades have a reflective quality that helps keep out heat in warm weather, helps keep it in during cold.

## 1. HOW TO USE IRON-ON BACKINGS

Heat-sensitized shade cloths (or backings) are designed for the iron-on method of making window shades. They come in translucent and opaque versions for use with fabrics; some are specially made for use with paper or vinyl wallcoverings. They usually come with the manufacturer's instructions for using the particular product, but here are general directions for both iron-on and self-adhesive backings in case specific directions are not available.

Make sure grain of fabric is straight or can be straightened by pulling diagonally. (Don't purchase a printed fabric which is off-grain and cannot be straightened.) Cut panel 6" longer than window opening and 1" wider than finished shade. Press to remove wrinkles and folds; remove ravelings and lint from both sides. Mark center of top and bottom. Cut backing 18" longer than window and 2" wider than shade. Cut off a 2" strip and an 8" strip (see Diagram 1) and mark center of top and bottom edges on remaining piece. If it is necessary to piece backing, butt edges tightly and hold in place temporarily with masking tape. Remove liner paper from backing (save for pressing) and mark line 2" down from top (Diagram 1).

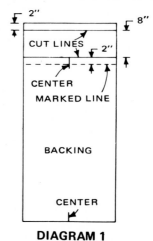

**DIAGRAM 1**

Center fabric on backing, right side up, with top edge along this line, matching center marks, and tape in place (Diagram 2). With iron at correct setting for fabric, press with slow, short strokes from center out to edges. If necessary, use liner paper as a press cloth to prevent glazing, and always use it along edges to prevent iron from touching adhesive backing. If bonding is not perfect, turn

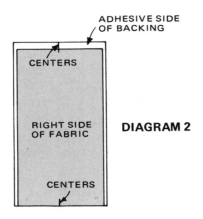

ADHESIVE SIDE
OF BACKING

CENTERS

RIGHT SIDE
OF FABRIC **DIAGRAM 2**

CENTERS

shade over and press backing side, using the paper liner. (The best bond is achieved after shade cools to room temperature.)

Checking measurements carefully, trim side edges so shade is correct width—½" less than roller measures inside metal rings if using bodied fabric, ¼" less if using lightweight fabric. Square off top and bottom edges if necessary.

To make bottom casing for 1¼" slat, fold 1½" to backing side and tape in place temporarily. Using liner paper, press folded edge of fabric only. Remove liner and tape and place 2" strip of backing along folded bottom edge; ½" should extend above casing. Using liner paper, press strip of backing lightly. Insert wood slat in casing, tight against folded edge. Replacing liner paper, press firmly along upper edge of slat. Trim excess backing from side edges (Diagram 3).

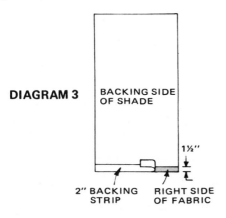

**DIAGRAM 3**

BACKING SIDE
OF SHADE

1½"

2" BACKING
STRIP

RIGHT SIDE
OF FABRIC

If shade is to have scalloped lower edge instead of a straight one, cut a 4" strip instead of a 2" strip from backing for the ironed-on bottom casing. Draw a line across shade 2" from bottom edge on backing side. Cut a circle from cardboard to use as a pattern for scallops. Dimension of circle should depend upon the width of the shade; a 7½" circle is a good dimension for a 48"-wide shade. From any point on circle, measure in 2" and draw a straight line across circle; this line should measure 6¾". Scallops can meet or be separated by straight spaces. (See Diagram 1 on page 138 for tracing a scalloped edge where

scallops meet.) If using a 7½" circle and separated scallops are desired, allow 6¾" for each scallop and 2¼" between them to determine how many full scallops will fit across width; plan to center them accordingly, with partial end scallops of equal size filling any remaining width. Matching line on cardboard guide and line on backing, outline scallops by tracing around cardboard, leaving 2¼" between scallops. Cut around scallops. On 4" strip of backing previously cut from main backing, score and pull 1" of liner paper from each long edge of backing, leaving 2" at center. Place strip on backing side of shade, with bottom edge of strip ½" above top of scallops and remaining liner paper inside; press strip in place. Allow shade to cool and trim ends. Glue trimming along scalloped edge if desired and insert slat in casing formed by liner-covered section of 4" strip.

Remove liner from 8" backing strip and place lower edge along top edge of fabric, adhesive side down, overlapping 2" of backing (Diagram 4). Tape corners and cover with liner paper; press 2" strip where backing meets backing, holding upper edge of strip away from table as you press.

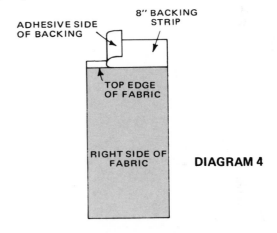

ADHESIVE SIDE
OF BACKING

8" BACKING
STRIP

TOP EDGE
OF FABRIC

RIGHT SIDE OF
FABRIC **DIAGRAM 4**

Make sure upper edge of backing strip is straight and parallel with upper edge of fabric. Place upper edge of strip along black line of roller (making sure it is straight), cover and press lightly, just enough to anchor edge of backing to roller (Diagram 5). Wind backing around roller

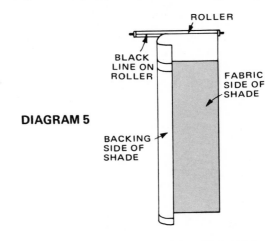

ROLLER

BLACK
LINE ON
ROLLER

FABRIC
SIDE OF
SHADE

**DIAGRAM 5**

BACKING
SIDE OF
SHADE

very evenly, pressing to bond it to roller. Continue rolling until you reach end of adhesive. Attach shade pull to lower edge of shade with screw eye; hang shade on brackets.

This method of attaching the shade to the roller, known as the "reverse roll," is preferred by professional decorators because it hides the roller, which the conventional method, or "regular roll," does not. For reverse roll, the spring end (the flat tip) of the roller must be mounted on the right in order for the shade to roll; a reverse bracket is required for this installation. For regular roll, the spring end must be mounted on the left. If you prefer the regular roll, reverse the 8″ backing strip at the top of the shade and attach it to the backing side rather than the fabric side.

Follow the same procedure when using iron-on backings with wallcoverings as with fabric, being sure to test the temperature of the iron on scraps of the covering first.

## 2. SELF-ADHESIVES ARE SIMILAR TO IRON-ONS

The basic difference between iron-on and self-adhesive backings is that iron-ons are *heat*-sensitive, self-adhesives are pressure-sensitive. Most self-adhesive backings can be laminated to fabric by pressing the fabric onto the backing and smoothing from the center outward with the palms of one's hands. Except for pressing with an iron, the directions given above for measuring, cutting, laminating and rolling can be followed with these products. Some are recommended for use only with fabrics; others can be used with fabrics or wallcoverings.

## 3. TWO WAYS TO FUSE FABRIC AND BACKING

Two types of fusible materials originally designed as dressmaking aids can be used to fuse fabric to a backing to make a window shade. The newer of the two is a gauze-like material which literally melts when it is placed between two fabrics and heat is applied. It comes in narrow widths and is sold in fabric and sewing-notion departments. Because this web-like material "disappears" when fused, it can be overlapped slightly if it must be pieced without adding extra bulk to the shade. However, the fusing process itself adds a certain amount of stiffness, so a lightweight fabric such as muslin should be used for the backing. If the outer fabric is lightweight and smoothly woven, it can also be used for the backing.

To make a shade with this type of fusible material, cut it, the outer fabric and backing all 12″ longer and 1″ wider than the window opening. Place fusible material between fabric and backing and cover fabric with a wet press cloth. Using steam setting on iron, press by applying firm pressure for ten seconds at a time, or until press cloth is dry. Do not glide iron back and forth. Working from the center outward toward edges, overlap each pressed area slightly until the entire shade has been covered. Allow fabric to cool, then check the bond and repeat pressing if necessary.

Checking measurements carefully and using a yard-stick to mark straight lines, trim width to ¼″ less than roller width if using lightweight fabrics, ½″ less if using heavier fabrics. Square off top and bottom edges if necessary. Side edges can be kept from fraying by painting a ⅛″ strip of clear nail polish or white glue down each side. Make hem by turning ½″ to backing side, turning up another 1½″ and topstitching. Attach top of shade to roller with masking tape, a staple gun and staples, or by applying strong, all-purpose adhesive to both surfaces, making sure that the shade is absolutely straight along roller.

If outer fabric is quite lightweight (no heavier than muslin), side edges can be given a more finished appearance by wrapping outer fabric around them. Cut fusible material and backing ¼″ *less* than the width of the roller and outer fabric 2″ *wider* than the roller. Cut two 1″-wide strips of fusible material the length of the shade. After shade has been fused and before making hem, place strips on backing along side edges; wrap fabric around edges and overlap strips. Fuse outer fabric to backing by pressing as before.

The second type of fusible material which can be used to make window shades is actually an iron-on interfacing used in dressmaking. One side is coated with a fusing adhesive; the other side remains intact and becomes the backing when fabric is fused to the coated side. If it must be pieced, edges must butt together closely; overlapping would create a bulky ridge down the shade. Cut this material and the outer fabric both 12″ longer and 1″ wider than the window opening. Place fabric right side up on adhesive side of backing and use a *dry* press cloth and hot, *dry* iron. A stiffer shade will result than when using the separate, "disappearing" type of fusible material described above. For this reason, side edges should be left plain; wrapping with fabric would probably create too much bulk.

## 4. SPRAY-ON ADHESIVES CAN ALSO BE USED

Several spray-on adhesives designed for craftwork or for bonding carpet and floor tiles (as well as cork, cardboard and fabric) can also be used to make window shades. Using this method, shade can be made with either plain or wrapped side edges; cut fabric and backing as described above. Place backing on newspapers, shake spray can well and spray the backing lightly and evenly (too heavy an application could cause discoloration of the backing). Place fabric over sprayed surface, wait a few minutes until adhesive is "tacky," and press by smoothing outward from the center with the palms of your hands. After bond is complete and fabrics are dry, shade can be sprayed with a fabric protector to make it soil-resistant and cleanable by sponging. Complete shade as described above. One note of caution: Be sure to use these (and any other) spray-on products in a well-ventilated room.

## 5. VINYL WINDOW SHADES ARE EASY TO MAKE

A wide variety of vinyl and vinyl-coated fabrics and wall coverings which are suitable for window shades can be found in decorator shade departments and wallcovering stores and departments. Happily, most require no backing; if you choose a very lightweight vinyl-coated wallpaper, use a self-adhesive backing. Shade cloths in this category include vinyl-coated cottons, fiberglass and all-vinyl versions in a wide variety of textures, all of which are washable. These are sold in window shade departments and stores, which will usually cut them to your order. Both shade cloths and wall coverings are available in translucent and opaque types. As with other materials, lightweight vinyls should be cut ¼″ less than the width of the roller; heavier ones should be ½″ less. Make a 1½″ finished hem as before and use a staple gun and staples to attach shade to roller. Insert a 1¼″ slat in the bottom hem.

### 6. SOME ADHESIVES REQUIRE NO BACKING

There are also chemical adhesives that impart sufficient body to fabrics so that no backing is necessary. Most are of the spray-on variety, but one is a chemical dipping solution. It can be applied by dipping the fabric into it, by painting it on both sides of the fabric with a roller, or by using a spray-topped bottle to spray it on both sides of the fabric. At least two others are aerosol sprays which can also be sprayed directly on both sides of the fabric. Be sure to press the fabric first and hang in such a position that it can be sprayed from both sides and allowed to dry before proceeding. Press again if necessary, and cut and finish as when making vinyl shades. Again, always be sure to use any aerosol sprays in a well-ventilated room.

### 7. ROMAN SHADES ARE DOUBLY DECORATIVE

The cords which raise a Roman shade do so by creating decorative folds that add an interesting dimension. Any firmly-woven fabric can be used. You'll need a "1 x 2" board as wide as the window opening, a ⅜″ brass rod the width of the shade, Roman shade tape and traverse cord, two angle irons with screws, ½″ screw eyes and a small awning cleat.

Cut fabric 2″ wider than finished width of shade and 3″ longer than window opening. To make bottom hem, turn ½″ to wrong side of fabric, then turn up another 1″ and stitch. Turn 1″ to wrong side along each side edge and press. Cut strips of Roman shade tape 1½″ longer than hemmed shade; sew to wrong side of fabric along side edges, covering raw edges of fabric, and then at equal intervals of 10″ to 14″ across back of shade, making sure rings on all tapes are in straight lines across shade. Stop stitching just above bottom hem, leaving bottom ends of

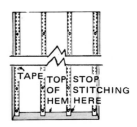
**DIAGRAM 1**

tape unattached. Turn up ends of tape to form loops; stitch in place so lower edges of loops are just above bottom hem (Diagram 1). Stitching will not be noticeable on a patterned shade if thread is carefully matched to background color. If using solid-color fabric, conceal stitching with strips of decorative braid sewn to front of shade and turned under at hem. Cover brass rod with a fabric casing and insert through loops of tape on back of shade; tack tapes to covering with a few hand-stitches. Attach a "1 x 2" board flat against inside top of window recess with a 1½″ angle iron at each end. Turn top edge of shade to wrong side and tack or staple to top edge of board so shade hangs straight and to proper length. Attach screw eyes to underside of board, 1″ in from front edge, spaced to match centers of rings on each strip of tape (Diagram 2). Cut one length of cord for each row of rings on back of

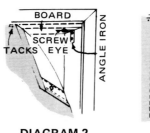
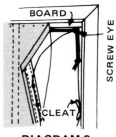
**DIAGRAM 2**  **DIAGRAM 3**

shade, making it long enough to go up shade and through screw eye, across board to the right, and down right side. (Each cord will be a different length.) Tie one cord to each ring of bottom row; thread it up through each ring of tape and through all screw eyes across top to right side of board. With shade in lowered position, knot all cords together under last screw eye on right, and cut off remainder of all cords *except one*. Install the awning cleat to hold cord at a convenient height on window frame (Diagram 3).

# Solutions for Problem Windows

Almost every homemaker considers her particular windows a decorating problem, and she may be right. Practically any window is a problem (or at least a challenge) because the way it's treated is so important to the plan of the room. Here, some solutions for difficult and not-so-difficult problems.

Even the home of your dreams may have problem windows. For instance, if you've found the perfect apartment with a marvelous terrace off the living room, you've probably also found that it has triple-width windows and a narrow door placed so close together they create a definite problem. But this can easily be solved by treating the two as a single unit. Just use floor-length draperies on two rods—one the width of the door, the other as wide as the windows—attached so closely under the cornice that there seems to be no separation at all when both draperies are drawn. Either the window or door draperies can be opened independently, or both can be opened for maximum light and view.

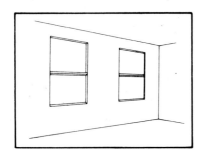

A pair of windows broken up by a narrow space poses a problem. Treating the windows separately would emphasize the broken-up look of the wall, so treat all three areas as a single unit by outlining them with a single framework. Paint the sides to match the wall and cover the front with the dominant stripe of a wallpaper-printed fabric. Then hang two-tier cafe curtains on the lower two-thirds of each side—covering the bottom half of each window with a light-admitting sheer and hiding the wall below with a tier of the floral-striped fabric.

Would you believe these are the same two windows? In a more formal room, cover the awkward space between them with a mirror that adds new dimension and reflects everything in sight. The windows on either side are treated equally to charming Toile de Jouy under-draperies and sweeping over-draperies in a coordinated solid color, with an over-all valance to match. The draperies can be closed to cover the mirror, opened halfway as shown here, or opened all the way to put both mirror and windows (and the scenery beyond them) on view. Double traverse rods make the treatment completely flexible—and give you a choice of decorative options at a moment's notice.

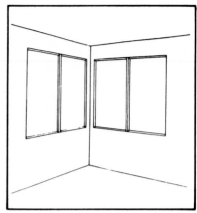

Corner casements can hardly be called a problem—the only problem is which of many attractive ways to treat them! Here, they inspired a compact conversation grouping—a great space-saving idea for small rooms. Note that the sectional couches and long fabric loops used in lieu of drapery-rings pick up the print's dominant color and toss pillows in varied shapes repeat the pattern to tie it all together.

And here, we circled the square to convert the same casement corner into a colorful dining area. It's the imaginative use of fabric that completely changes the look. A great sweep of pinch-pleated, floor-length draperies is hung on a curved ceiling track to make a charming backdrop for important luncheons or dinners à deux. And the choice of fabric is virtually unlimited. You could use a sheer dress fabric or a luxurious cut velvet; the mood could be pleasantly casual or decidedly formal. To make the whole setting a delightful unit, circle the hem of a harmonizing solid-color tablecloth with a wide band of the print used for the drapery.

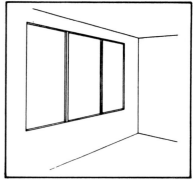

Chances are, you're faced with a wide window (triple-sashed to boot) somewhere in your house or apartment. If it's centered on a narrow wall with useless space on either side, try extending both cornice and draperies to the wall's full width—suddenly the whole room will look much wider! The draperies and matching shades are in the same fabric, trimmed with contrasting braid.

If, on the other hand, you want to *detract* from the look of width, try this contrasting treatment. It's based on a wooden valance board (with gracefully draped swag and short cascades) that extends only far enough beyond the windows to allow the draperies to cover the frame. This and the laminated window shades are in solid color to contrast—but also harmonize—with the striped draperies. (A coordinated pattern could also be used.) The swag, cascades and draperies are all edged with two-tone fringe to complete the well-coordinated look. Directions for making both lined and unlined draperies begin on page 124.

# 4
# CHILDREN'S ROOMS

# Storybook Rooms

# Raggedy Ann and Andy Live Here

Tall tales of wonder and fantasy spell enchantment for small children, and spark the kind of imagination that later turns into creativity. You can spur that process by providing a colorful environment with a touch of built-in fantasy, where both a child and his imagination can grow. Where to look for inspiration? To the classics, of course, and the beloved storybook characters that never grow old.

Raggedy Ann and Andy live happily (by day, at least) in the bright-eyed room at the right. The clean, poster-y look, strong primary colors and simple furniture make an ideal setting for Raggedy Ann's (and her young owner's) adventurous escapades. The free-form plaid "wallpaper" was rolled on with a roller and the scrubbable, self-adhesive carpet tiles can be replaced in case of serious mishap. The straight curtains and scalloped cafes at the window make a versatile combination for controlling light (as well as discouraging Raggedy Ann's usual method of egress on nocturnal adventures). Directions for making the scalloped cafe curtains and the cornice are on page 168.

To paint a plaid wall, use white or pale background color, medium second color and dark third color. Paint wall with two coats of background color. Mark center of wall at ceiling line. Measure 4½" to the left of this point and drop a plumb line to floor. Measure down plumb line to 9" from ceiling and draw a horizontal line across wall, using a level for accuracy. Measure 9" to right of plumb line and draw a second vertical line to outline center colored stripe. Measure 9" down from level line and draw a second horizontal line across wall to outline top colored stripe. (Starting stripes at center and at ceiling will make any unevenness in plaid due to uneven wall measurements fall at corners and at floor where they will be least noticeable.) Continue marking vertical lines every 9" across width and horizontal lines every 9" to floor. Starting with center vertical stripe, paint every other one second color; starting with second horizontal stripe, paint every other horizontal stripe to match. Roll paint on in an almost free-hand manner so stripes cover marked lines and have slightly uneven edges. Apply only one coat; don't go over any stripes to make edges straighter. Using third color, paint squares where vertical and horizontal stripes overlap.

# Winnie-the-Pooh Eats Here

It's a good place to eat honey, because it's right next to Christopher Robin's tree house.

Christopher's tree house (in the Hundred Acre Wood, of course) is a double-decker bunk bed, so Pooh and all his friends—even gloomy old Eeyore—can stay overnight in case it rains. The trunk part of the tree was cut out of plywood, and the "grain" drawn on free-hand with a paint brush. The inside walls were sheathed in rough casing lumber and painted dark green so anyone sleeping inside the tree will feel nice and cozy. The scallopy little table with its tree-trunk base was also made of plywood, and is surprisingly easy to put together. You'll find directions for making it and the tree-house bunk beds starting on page 170.

# The Easter Bunny Sleeps Here

Feminine bunnies prefer flowers to cabbages—so naturally, any lady bunny would love having a room like this one for tea parties with friends as well as for sleeping.

You can create an equally magical world of imaginative flowers for your own favorite bunny (perhaps with a little help from the bunny's father). Start with a ruffly bedspread in a flower-sprayed print—you'll find dozens to choose from in any fabric department. Make a super-size flower cut from layers of fiber board painted to complement the printed bedspread and attach it to the wall for an enchanting headboard. The table that looks like another big flower has the same ingenious base as the one in Pooh Bear's habitat on page 163, here turned ups-a-daisy.

Even the whimsical little chairs, which are a cinch to construct, have flowers for backs. (You don't have to be an artist to give them happy-flower faces!) You'll find complete directions and diagrams for making the flower headboard, the flower table and the flower-face chairs starting on page 173. Basically, all you need for the furniture and headboard are fiber board, plywood and paint. Assuming you already own a mattress and boxspring, these simple materials plus fabric for the bedspread could be the extent of your purchases for this storybook room. And we guarantee that young bunny will be delighted!

# Make an Imaginative Menagerie to Brighten a Young Bedroom

*Pamela Octopus*

*Myrtle Turtle*     *No-Animal Animal*     *Goggle-Eyed Spider*

*Fanny Elephant*     *Loopy the Lion*     *Gertie Giraffe*

A menagerie, says Webster, is a "collection of wild or foreign animals . . . especially one kept for exhibition." Well, these whimsical creatures aren't wild, but they're definitely denizens of other worlds—and will be proudly kept on exhibition in the private domain of any young collector lucky enough to be their keeper. They're easy to make from any colorful scraps of fabric you have on hand—the more unlikely the merrier.

Use decorative fabrics or dress fabrics, preferably with soil-resistant finish. Make at least one member of the menagerie to match curtains or draperies or something else in the room, and stuff them all with polyester fiberfill for bouncy firmness. (In spite of their amusing personalities, they're really comfortable lounging pillows.) Easy-to-follow directions and diagrams for making all seven charmers start on page 176.

Notice, too, the other bright ideas exhibited by this preteen room. A wealth of stowaway space is provided by the wall-long expanse of unfinished chests painted white. The handy desk is simply a piece of ¾″ plywood attached to the wall and one chest, and edged with a 2″ lath strip for a substantial look. The bookcase is made of "1 x 8" clear pine, each shelf painted a different color borrowed from the bright print curtains.

# directions for projects

## SCALLOPED CORNICE
## FOR RECESSED WINDOW
### ON PAGE 161

MATERIALS NEEDED:
(for each cornice)

    One piece of plywood, ¼" x 7¼" x width
        of window, for A
    "1 x 4" pine x width of window plus 14½",
        for B and C
    Compass
    Padding
    Two 2½" angle irons with four ¾" and four 1¾" flat-
        head wood screws
    Jigsaw or sabre saw
    Staple gun and ¼" staples
    1" common nails
    1½" finishing nails

Using a compass, mark scalloped outline as shown in Diagram 1 on plywood for A. (Diagram 1 is for a 36"-wide window.) Mark center arc first and continue scallops to each end of plywood, elongating last scallop on either end so ends are full depth of scallops.

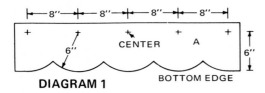

**DIAGRAM 1**

For wider windows where centers of last scallops will be 4" or more from ends, have two arcs meet at center point as shown in Diagram 2.

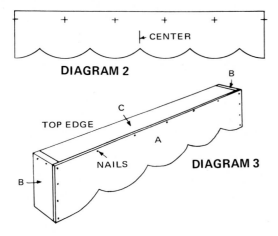

**DIAGRAM 2**

**DIAGRAM 3**

Cut along scalloped edge with jigsaw or sabre saw.

Cut two 7¼" lengths of "1 x 4" for B. Using 1" nails, nail through each end of A into B with outside edges flush. Measure across top between B; cut C to this length and nail C flush with top of A in same manner. Using 1½" nails, nail through B into C at each end (Diagram 3).

Cut padding to fit front surface of cornice only; staple in place. Cut a 10"-wide strip of fabric 2" longer than cornice. Place top edge of fabric 1" over top edge of cornice and wrap 1" of fabric around each end; staple in place. Pull fabric around lower edge of cornice, clipping and easing as necessary so fabric fits smoothly around scallops. Staple in place on inside of A (Diagram 4).

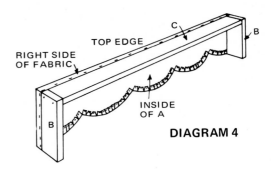

**DIAGRAM 4**

Using 1¾" screws, attach angle irons to each side of window frame, 2" in from side edges and with tops of angle irons ¾" below top of recess.

Place cornice on angle irons so C fits between angle irons and top of recess. Screw through angle irons into C with 1" screws.

## SCALLOPED CAFE CURTAINS
### ON PAGE 161

MATERIALS NEEDED:
    36"-wide fabric
    Scalloped pleater tape
    Pleater hooks and two end hooks
    Cafe rod and rings

Cutting across width, cut pieces of fabric 5" longer than finished length of cafe curtains. Cut enough pieces to equal 2½ times window width plus 12" after pieces are seamed together. Allow for matching fabric at seams.

Stitch pieces together to form one curtain, taking ½" seams and matching fabric design. Press seams open. Allowing at least 3½" of fabric uncovered at each side, cen-

168 • CHILDREN'S ROOMS

ter tape on fabric, right sides together, and cut it so you have ¾″ of tape and a single pocket beyond the last scallop at each end. Trim fabric so it extends 3½″ beyond tape at each end (Diagram 1).

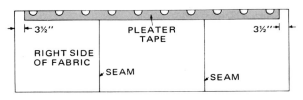

**DIAGRAM 1**

Stitch up one end of tape (so pocket on end is left open for end pin). Following marking on tape, stitch across top edge, around scallops and down other end of tape, leaving pocket open for end pin as before (Diagram 2). Cut away top corners of fabric on a diagonal line and cut out centers of scallops. Clip around scallops, through pleater tape and fabric, from outer edge to stitching, being careful not to clip stitching (Diagram 3).

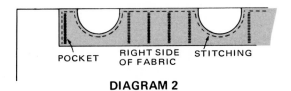

**DIAGRAM 2**

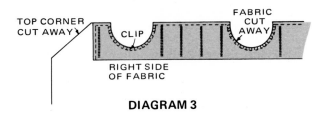

**DIAGRAM 3**

Turn right side out. (Diagonally-cut corners allow 3½″ side allowances to turn in under pleater tape.) Press to form smooth scallops. Make a 2″ hem down each side edge and stitch in place. Stitch across bottom edge of tape (Diagram 4).

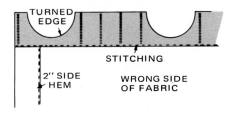

**DIAGRAM 4**

Turn ½″ to wrong side across lower edge of curtain; then turn up a 4″ hem. Attach brackets for rod to window frame at required height. Insert pleater pins in pockets of tape. Place rings on rod; insert hooks of pins in rings and hang curtains on rod.

# RUFFLED PILLOW COVERS
## ON PAGES 161, 162, 184, 190

MATERIALS NEEDED:
    Fabric
    Buttonhole twist

Cut fabric for front of pillowcase 1″ longer and 1″ wider than pillow. Cut two pieces for back of pillowcase, each 1″ longer than pillow and 4¼″ wider than half of pillow width. Decide how wide ruffle around edge of pillow is to be; cut a strip of fabric (or piece together a strip) twice this width plus 1″ and 2½ times as long as the circumference of the pillow.

Fold strip for ruffle in half, right sides facing, and stitch short ends together to form complete circle; press seam allowances open. Fold fabric in half lengthwise, wrong sides together and raw edges even; press folded edge. Using buttonhole twist in bobbin, run a row of machine gathering around ruffle, ½″ from raw edges. Place ruffle around front of pillowcase with raw edges of ruffle and front section even and pull up bobbin thread, gathering fullness evenly around all sides. Baste ruffle to front section ½″ from edges, allowing extra fullness at corners to fall to inside (see Diagram).

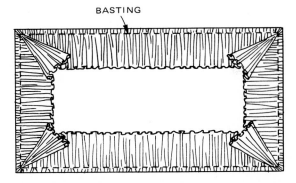

On one long side of each back section, turn ¼″ to wrong side, and then another ½″; stitch hems. Place one back section partially over the other so hemmed edges overlap by 3″ and total width is the same as front section. Baste together ½″ from side edges. Place back section over front section, right sides together, with ruffle between them and all edges flush. Stitch together ½″ from edges. Turn pillowcase right side out and insert pillow.

Either ready-made eyelet ruffling or straight eyelet edging can be used for the ruffle around the pillow cover; if using straight eyelet edging, gather one edge as described above and stitch to front section in same manner as fabric. If using eyelet ruffling, no additional gathering is necessary.

## TREE TRUNK TABLE
### ON PAGE 163

MATERIALS NEEDED:
>    One piece of plywood, ¾″ x 30″ x 30″,
>        for top
>    One piece of plywood, ¾″ x 24″ x 48″,
>        for base
>    Four small hooks and screw eyes
>    Plywood basecoat and paint

**Top:** Draw 1″ squares on 30″ plywood square and enlarge pattern from Diagram 1. Cut along marked line.

Apply basecoat and paint according to manufacturer's directions.

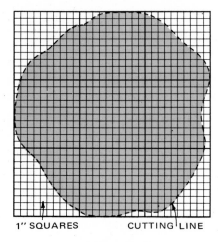

DIAGRAM 1

**Base:** Cut two 21″ x 24″ pieces from 48″ plywood. On one piece, draw 1″ squares and enlarge pattern from Diagram 2. Cut along marked line.

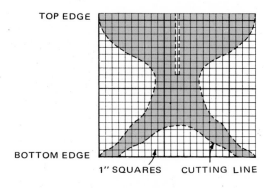

DIAGRAM 2

Cut a 9″ x ¾″ center notch by boring a ¾″ hole 9″ from top edge; saw from *top* edge into this hole. Square inside corners with a file (Diagram 3).

Place this section of base on other 21″ x 24″ piece and trace outline, including notch. On second section, cut

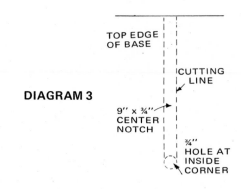

DIAGRAM 3

notch from *bottom* edge to center in following manner; lengthen lines of first notch until they reach bottom edge; bore hole where notches meet and cut as before (Diagram 4). Base will be assembled in "egg crate" fashion with the pieces at right angles to each other; length of notches may have to be adjusted so unit will stand firmly. For tree trunk table, rest flat end of base on floor (see photo).

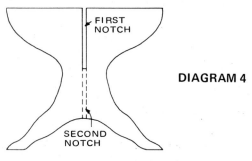

DIAGRAM 4

Apply basecoat and paint according to manufacturer's directions. Attach a screw eye to base at each side of center notch; attach hooks to top to hold top firmly in place on base.

## TREE-HOUSE BUNK BEDS
### ON PAGE 162

MATERIALS NEEDED:
>    Four pieces of plywood, each ½″ x 48″ x 96″ for
>        F, H, J, K
>    Clear pine:
>        Two "1 x 6" x 96″ for C
>        Four "1 x 6" x 80″ for E
>        Two "1 x 3" x 96″ for B
>        Four "1 x 3" x 75″ for D
>        One "1 x 3" x 75″ for G
>        Four "2 x 3" x 96″ for A
>    No. 8 flat-head wood screws: 1″, 1¼″, and 1¾″
>        sizes
>    ⅛″ drill bit (for boring pilot holes)
>    Backsaw
>    Chisel
>    Try square

Jigsaw or sabre saw
1½" finishing nails
Plywood basecoat and paint
Wood filler and wood glue
Two 5" x 39" x 75" mattresses
Purchased ladder
Two screw eyes with ⅝" shank and two cup hooks.

NOTE: Bed is designed for room with 96" ceiling; adjustments in lengths of A, H, J and K must be made for other ceiling heights.

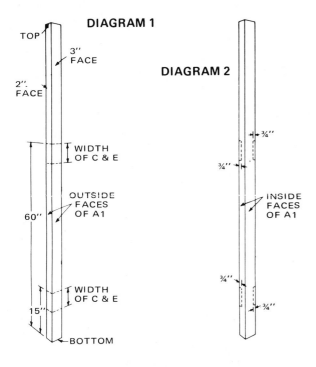

**DIAGRAM 1**

**DIAGRAM 2**

Cut four "2 x 3" to ½" less than ceiling height for A. On one A, mark outline of notches on two adjoining sides (for A1), making each notch same height as width of C and E; place top of lower notch 15" from bottom, and place top of upper notch 60" from bottom (Diagram 1). Continue markings around corners onto inside faces; mark lines on inside faces ¾" from outside corners to indicate depth each notch is to be cut (Diagram 2). Mark a second A1 in same manner.

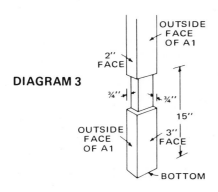

**DIAGRAM 3**

Cut notches in following manner. Using a backsaw, cut along marked lines on outside faces to a depth of ¾"; using a chisel, cut out notches as shown in Diagram 3. Be sure that C and E fit snugly into notches so outside faces of C and E are flush with outside faces of A.

Make two uprights A2 by placing notches at same heights from bottom as on A1, but on the two adjoining sides shown in Diagram 4.

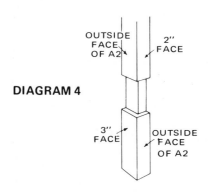

**DIAGRAM 4**

Cut four B, each 44½" long. Cut four C, each 48" long. Bore seven pilot holes for 1¼" screws in each B in positions shown in Diagram 5.

**DIAGRAM 5**

Bore four pilot holes for 1¾" screws in each end of both C in positions shown in Diagram 6.

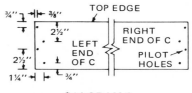

**DIAGRAM 6**

Apply glue to B. Place B on C so top edge of B is ½" down from top edge of C and C extends 1¾" past each end of B. Screw B to C with 1¼" screws (Diagram 7). Assemble other B and C in same manner.

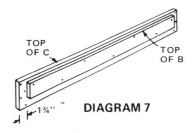

**DIAGRAM 7**

Apply glue to each end of C; with A1 at right end and A2 at left end, place C in notches on 2″ faces of A1 and A2 so ends of C are flush with outside corners of each A. Use a try square to be sure all four inside angles are 90°; screw C to A1 and A2 with 1¾″ screws through pilot holes 1¼″ from each end (Diagram 8). Assemble other A and C in same manner.

Apply glue to each end of E; place E in notches on 3″ faces of A1 and A2 so ends of E are against C and outside faces of E are flush with outside faces of A and with ends of C. Check inside angles as before, then screw through C into end of E with 1¾″ screws and through E into A with 1¼″ screws (Diagram 10).

Measure length from inside of C at head to inside of C at foot; measure width between inside of E at each side. Cut two F to these dimensions. Cut a notch at each corner to go around each A. Apply glue to top edge of each B and D; place F on B and D so top of F is flush with top of C and E; nail through F into B and D with 1½″ nails, 1″ from each A and about 10″ apart (Diagram 11).

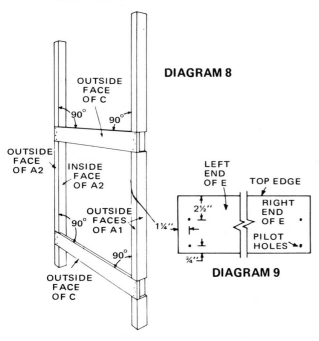

**DIAGRAM 8**

**DIAGRAM 9**

Cut four D, each 74½″ long, and cut four E, each 78½″ long. Drill nine pilot holes for 1¼″ screws in each D in same manner as for B, placing them 1¼″ from each end and 9″ apart. Drill two pilot holes for 1¼″ screws in each end of both E, as shown in Diagram 9.

Glue and screw D to E in same manner as for B and C, using 1¼″ screws and having ends of E extend 2″ past each end of D.

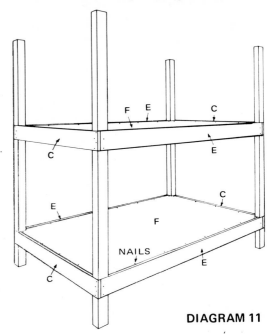

**DIAGRAM 11**

To make rail G for upper bunk (see photograph), cut G ¼″ shorter than length of bed from inside of A1 at head to inside of A2 at foot. Attach a cup hook to A1 and to A2, 1″ from outside face and 7½″ up from top of E. Attach screw eyes to inside face of G so they will fit over cup hooks to hold G in place.

Fill nail holes and cracks; sand all surfaces smooth. Apply basecoat and paint according to manufacturer's directions.

Draw 2″ squares on the 48″ x 96″ panel of plywood for H and mark outline of tree trunk from Diagram 12. Using a jigsaw or sabre saw, cut along marked lines and across top so H is ¼″ less than ceiling height. Drill eighteen pilot holes for 1″ screws ¾″ in from edges and one in center in positions shown in Diagram 12.

Following Diagram 13, mark and cut J in same manner; drill twelve pilot holes in positions indicated.

Following Diagram 14, mark and cut K in same manner; drill ten pilot holes in positions indicated.

Fill edges of plywood; apply basecoat and paint to inside faces and all edges of H, J and K. Using 1″ screws, attach H to A and C at foot end of bed so edges of H are flush with outside faces of A; attach J to side at foot end

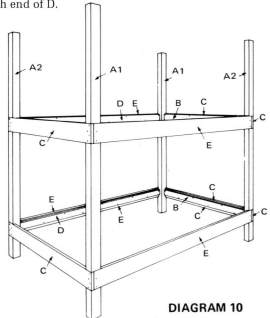

**DIAGRAM 10**

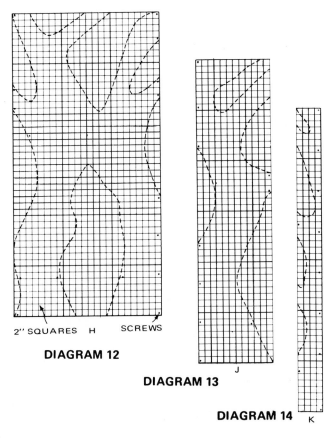

**2" SQUARES**  H  **SCREWS**

**DIAGRAM 12**

**DIAGRAM 13**

**DIAGRAM 14**  K

so left edge of J is flush with outside face of H; attach K to head end so right edge of K is flush with outside face of A (see photo).

Turn screws until heads are slightly below surface; fill and sand. Apply basecoat and paint; with fine artist's paint brush, draw wood grain in darker shade of green on outside surfaces of "trunk" (see photo).

# FLOWER HEADBOARD
## ON PAGE 164

MATERIALS NEEDED:
    One piece of fiber board, ½" x 48" x 96"
    Basecoat and paint
    Two screw eyes with ⅞" threaded shanks
    Picture wire and hook
    1" and 1½" wire brads
    Compass, cardboard strips
    Jigsaw or sabre saw

Make a "compass" from 1"-wide strips of cardboard joined firmly together end to end (with staples or tape) to a length of 26". Mark cardboard in center of width at the following points: Make first mark X ½" from left end; starting at X each time, measure 5½" for A; 6" for B; 6⅜" for C; 8½" for D; 11¾" for E; 12⅞" for F; 15³⁄₁₆" for G; 18"

for H; 19¹⁄₁₆" for J; 24" for K. Using a nail, make a small hole in cardboard just large enough to hold pencil point firmly at each mark from A to K (Diagram 1).

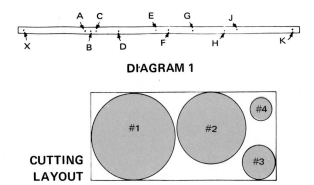

**DIAGRAM 1**

**CUTTING LAYOUT**

Draw four circles on fiber board in positions shown in Cutting Layout, using X mark on "compass" as center point for each one. Place thumb tack or small nail through X and put pencil point through hole K for circle #1; through hole H for circle #2; through hole D for circle #3 and through hole B for circle #4. Cut out all circles with jigsaw or sabre saw.

Draw petaled edge on circle #1 in following manner: Place X at center of circle as before and draw an inner circle with pencil at J. Place X on inner circle (this will be point #1) and pencil at E; swing compass to mark point #2 on inner circle; place X on point #2 and swing compass to mark point #3; place X on point #3 and swing compass to mark point #4; continue around inner circle until it is divided into ten equal parts (Diagram 2).

Draw a straight line from point #1 to point #2; from #2 to #3; from #3 to #4; continue around circle, connecting all adjacent points. Measure each straight line to determine exact center of each one (Diagram 3).

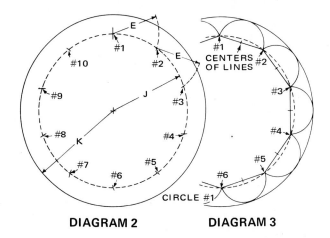

**DIAGRAM 2**  **DIAGRAM 3**

Place the point of a regular compass on center mark of first straight line and set compass so pencil reaches point #1; swing pencil arc connecting points #1 and #2; repeat on each straight line to form ten semi-circular petals as shown in Diagram 3. Cut along scalloped edge.

Draw petaled edge on circle #2 in same manner; Place X at center of circle as before and draw an inner circle with pencil at F. Place X on inner circle (this will be point #1) and pencil at G; swing pencil to mark point #2 on circle; continue to mark off five equal spaces (Diagram 4).

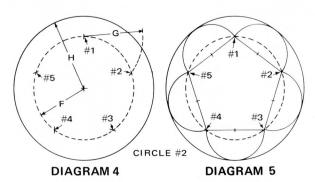

**DIAGRAM 4**       **DIAGRAM 5**

Connect points #1 and #2 with a straight line as before and mark center of line; repeat in other four spaces. Set compass from center of first line to point #1 and swing arc to #2; continue around for other four petals (Diagram 5). Cut along scalloped edge.

Draw petaled edge on circle #3 in same manner: Place X at center of circle and mark an inner circle with pencil at C; divide circle into seven equal parts with pencil at A (Diagram 6). Connect adjacent points with straight lines; determine center of each line, and draw petals as before (Diagram 7). Cut along scalloped edge.

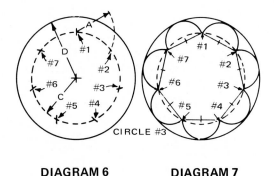

**DIAGRAM 6**       **DIAGRAM 7**

Apply basecoat to both faces and all edges of each circle to prevent warping. Paint both faces and all edges of each circle in desired color.

Center circle #2 on #1 and nail together, placing 1″ brads so heads will be covered by #3 and driving brads at an angle. Center circle #3 on #2 and nail together with 1½″ brads in same manner. Center circle #4 on #3 and attach with 1″ brads toenailed through edges of #4 into #3; touch up with paint, if necessary.

Attach two screw eyes to back of circle #1, positioned so their shanks will go into circle #2 also. Attach picture wire and hang in position on wall.

# FLOWER TABLE
## ON PAGE 164

**MATERIALS NEEDED:**
    One piece of plywood, ½″ x 36″ x 36″, for top
    One piece of plywood, ¾″ x 24″ x 48″, for base
    Four small hooks and screw eyes
    Jigsaw or sabre saw
    Plywood basecoat and paint
    Compass

**Top:** On the 36″ plywood square, draw diagonals from opposite corners to locate center. Using cardboard compass described in directions for making flower headboard, page 173, place X at center and pencil at H; draw circle (Diagram 1). Cut out with jigsaw or sabre saw.

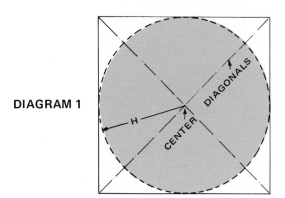

**DIAGRAM 1**

Make the following new marks on cardboard compass, measuring from X for each one: 7¹¹⁄₁₆″ for P; 14¾″ for Q; 16⅜″ for R; 7½″ for S.

Draw petaled edge in same manner as for headboard: Place X at center of circle, and draw an inner circle with pencil at Q; place X on inner circle (this will be point #1) and pencil at P; swing compass to mark point #2 on inner circle. Continue around to divide circle into twelve equal parts (Diagram 2).

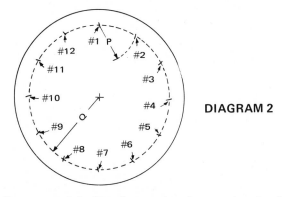

**DIAGRAM 2**

Draw a straight line from point #1 to point #2, from #2 to #3, etc., until all adjacent marks are connected by straight lines. Mark center of each line. Place point of regular compass on center mark of straight line and set compass so pencil reaches point #1; swing arc to #2; continue marking arcs based on each straight line to form twelve petals (Diagram 3).

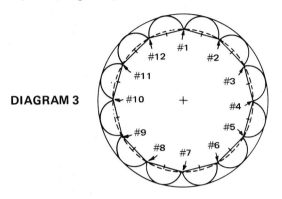

**DIAGRAM 3**

Place X of compass on center and draw a third circle with pencil at R (Diagram 4).

Cut around each petal to circle R, along circle R and then around next petal. Apply basecoat and paint according to manufacturer's directions. Place X of compass at center and pencil at S; draw circle and paint for flower center (Diagram 5).

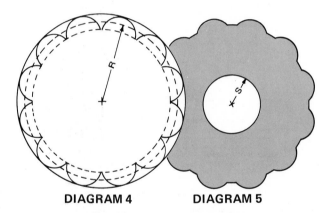

**DIAGRAM 4**     **DIAGRAM 5**

**Base:** Cut and finish base from 48″ piece of plywood in same manner as base of tree trunk table on page 170. Rest branched end of base on floor for flower table (see photo on page 164.)

# FLOWER-FACE CHAIRS
## ON PAGE 164

MATERIALS NEEDED:
(for four chairs)
 One piece of plywood, ¾″ x 48″ x 60″
 2″ finishing nails
 Wood glue
 Wood filler
 Plywood basecoat

Enamel paint in desired colors
Small artist's brush (for faces)
Compass

Using Cutting Layout, cut following pieces from plywood; four A, 10¼″ x 14″; four B, 10¼″ x 10¼″; four C, 14″ x 27¼″.

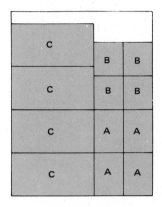

**CUTTING LAYOUT**

On one A, mark center line and two rounded corners as shown in Diagram 1. Cut corners on marked lines. Using this one as a pattern, draw curved corners on other three A and cut.

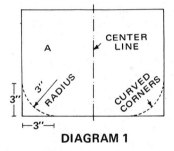

**DIAGRAM 1**

Drive three nails in A along center line, placing them 1″ from front and back edges and one at center. Tips of nails should just protrude from other side of A. Apply glue to one edge of B. Place A on B so nails in A are at center of thickness of B and front and back edges of A and B are flush. Drive nails so heads go below surface of A (Diagram 2).

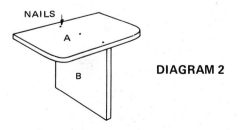

**DIAGRAM 2**

Mark one 14″ x 27¼″ piece for C as follows: Draw a line across piece at point 11″ from bottom edge, then draw a second line ¾″ down from first one. Draw two lines down center of lower section, 6⅝″ from each side edge. Draw center line X through exact center of upper section and mark a point 7″ from top edge for center of circle. Set compass at 5″ and draw circle (Diagram 3).

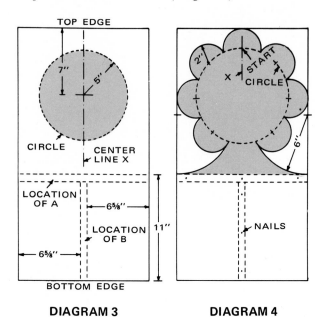

**DIAGRAM 3**          **DIAGRAM 4**

Set compass at 2″ and place point on intersection of line X and top of circle. Draw an arc from circle on one side of X to circle on other side. Continue around circumference of circle so arcs meet at circle. Set compass at 6″; place point on side edge 6″ above first marked line and swing arc from side edge up to scallop where scallop meets circle; repeat on other side. Cut out along scalloped and curved edges, then use this C as a pattern for other three C. Drive three nails into center of horizontal, ¾″-wide "stripe," placing one at center and one 1″ from each end. (These nails will be driven into A.) Drive three nails along center of vertical ¾″-wide "stripe," placing one 1″ from bottom edge and others 4″ apart. (These nails will be driven into B.) Tips of all nails should just protrude from other side of C (Diagram 4).

Apply glue along back (straight) edge of A and along back edge of B. Place C against B and A with bottom and side edges even. Drive nails into A and B so heads are countersunk as before. (See photo of assembled chair, page 164.)

Fill all cracks and edges of plywood with wood filler. Sand smooth, then apply plywood basecoat according to manufacturer's directions. Paint desired colors.

Draw a circle for face with compass set at 4¾″. Paint circle off-white, then draw in features with artist's brush, using photograph as a guide. For flower chairs without faces, simply paint the center circle a different color and omit features.

Assemble other three chairs in same manner.

# STUFFED OCTOPUS
## ON PAGE 167

**MATERIALS NEEDED:**
  ¼ yard fabric
  4½ yards large ball fringe; 1 yard each of 3 colors;
    1½ yards of fourth color
  Iron-on tape for eyes and mouth, black and white
  Polyester fiberfill for stuffing
  Four yards florists' wire (optional)

Enlarge graphs in Diagram 1 to make patterns or cut one 6″ x 17″ rectangle and two 6″-diameter circles directly from fabric. Using Diagram 2 as a pattern, cut two small black circles and two larger white circles of iron-on tape for eyes, and one heart-shaped piece of black iron-on tape for mouth.

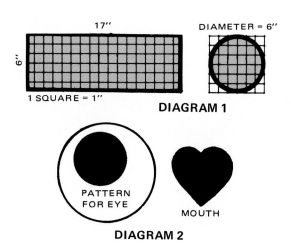

**DIAGRAM 1**

**DIAGRAM 2**

Place black circles on white circles for eyes; iron eyes and mouth onto rectangle of fabric in positions indicated in Diagram 3.

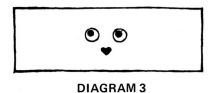

**DIAGRAM 3**

Fold rectangle in half, right sides facing, and pin ends together ½″ from edges (Diagram 4). With right sides together and edges flush, baste one circle to top edge of main section and one circle to bottom edge (Diagram 5). Stitch together with ½″ seams; clip seam allowances around both circles. Remove pins from pinned side seam and turn right side out. Stuff through opening and slip-stitch opening closed.

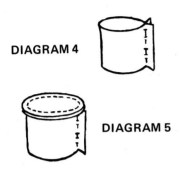

**DIAGRAM 4**

**DIAGRAM 5**

Mark eight positions for placement of "tentacles," spacing them evenly around bottom circle (about 2″ apart). Cut eight 18″-long strips of ball fringe, two of each color, and sew in place by hand, alternating colors. Sew remaining ball fringe around top edge of octopus, turning ends under at back edge. If desired, stitch a length of wire to underside of each tentacle for extra stiffness.

## STUFFED TURTLE
### ON PAGE 167

MATERIALS NEEDED:
⅝ yard printed fabric
½ yard solid-color fabric
Iron-on tape for eyes, black and white
Scrap of red felt for tongue
1½ yards moss fringe
Polyester fiberfill for stuffing

Enlarge graphs in Diagram 1 to make paper pattern for each section. Adding ½″ for seam allowance around each section, cut two main sections from printed fabric; cut one upper and one lower head section, eight foot sections and two tail sections from solid-color fabric. On wrong side of lower head section, mark dots as indicated on diagram; bring two rows of dots together to form tuck on inside and stitch. Cut two black ovals and two white ovals from iron-on tape for eyes, in sizes shown in Diagram 2. Place black ovals on white ovals and iron onto upper head section in positions shown in Diagram 1. Cut one tongue section from red felt in size shown in Diagram 3; pin in place on right side of upper head section so that straight end of tongue is flush with raw edge of fabric and curved end of tongue points inward.

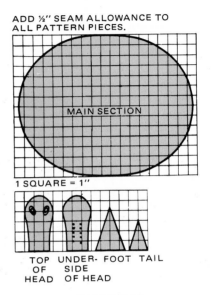

ADD ½″ SEAM ALLOWANCE TO ALL PATTERN PIECES.

MAIN SECTION

1 SQUARE = 1″

TOP OF HEAD    UNDER-SIDE OF HEAD    FOOT    TAIL

**DIAGRAM 1**

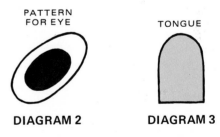

PATTERN FOR EYE

TONGUE

**DIAGRAM 2**    **DIAGRAM 3**

With right sides facing, pin upper head section to lower head section; pin two tail sections together; pin each of four pairs of foot sections together. Stitch, leaving bottom edges open, and turn right sides out. Stuff head, tail and foot sections, filling to ¾″ from ends; baste ends together. Pin stuffed head, tail and feet to right side of one main section in positions shown in sketch, with all raw edges flush and head, tail and feet pointing to inside. Pin main sections together, right sides facing; stitch together ½″ from edges, leaving opening between feet on one side of turtle. Clip curves, turn right side out and stuff. Turn raw edges to inside and slip-stitch closed.

Slip-stitch moss fringe to top of turtle ½″ above seam-line, overcasting ends where they meet at back edge.

## STUFFED NO-ANIMAL ANIMAL
### ON PAGE 167

MATERIALS NEEDED:
> ½ yard fabric
> Two large tassels
> Iron-on tape for eyes, black and white
> ½ yard giant rickrack for mouth
> Polyester fiberfill for stuffing

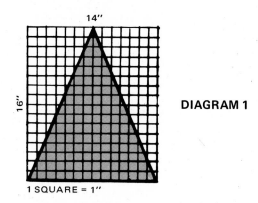

**DIAGRAM 1**

14″

16″

1 SQUARE = 1″

Enlarge graph in Diagram 1 and cut two triangles of fabric, each 16″ high and 14″ wide at base. Using Diagram 2 as pattern, cut two black circles and two white ovals of iron-on tape for eyes. Place circles on ovals and iron onto one triangle of fabric, placing them 4″ from apex and ½″ apart.

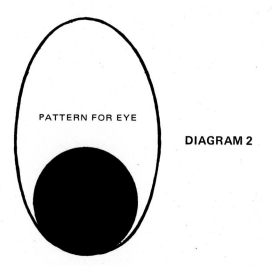

PATTERN FOR EYE

**DIAGRAM 2**

Place triangles together, right sides facing; stitch together ½″ from edges, leaving 4″ along bottom edges open. Turn fabric right side out and stuff triangle through opening. Slip-stitch opening closed.

Press 10″-long piece of rickrack into curved shape with warm iron. Turn ends under and pin "mouth" in place; slip-stitch to fabric. Sew two tassels to top point of triangle.

## STUFFED SPIDER
### ON PAGE 167

MATERIALS NEEDED:
> ½ yard fabric
> One yard black carpet fringe
> Iron-on tape for eyes, black and white
> Polyester fiberfill for stuffing

**DIAGRAM 1**

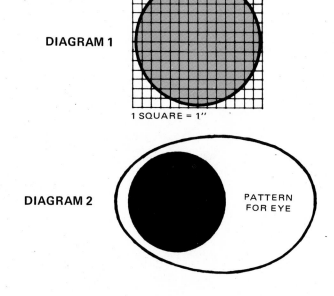

1 SQUARE = 1″

**DIAGRAM 2**

PATTERN FOR EYE

Enlarge graph in Diagram 1 or draw 14″-diameter circle on paper for pattern. Cut two circles from fabric. Using Diagram 2 as pattern, cut two black circles and two white ovals of iron-on tape for eyes. Place black circles on white ovals and iron onto one fabric circle, placing them 1″ from edge and ½″ apart.

Place fabric circles together, right sides facing; pin and

stitch together ½″ from edge, leaving 4″ opening opposite eyes. Clip into seam allowance at 2″ intervals around entire circle. Turn right side out and stuff through opening; slip-stitch opening closed.

Pin fringe in place along seam line, with ends meeting at center back. Slip-stitch fringe in place, joining ends by overcasting.

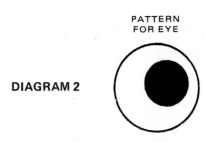

**PATTERN
FOR EYE**

**DIAGRAM 2**

## STUFFED ELEPHANT
### ON PAGE 167

MATERIALS NEEDED:
 One yard fabric, 36″ wide or wider
 ⅛ yard interfacing for ears
 Iron-on tape for eyes, black and white
 ½ yard ball fringe for collar
 Yarn for tail
 Polyester fiberfill for stuffing

Enlarge graph in Diagram 1 to make paper pattern for each section. Adding ½″ for seam allowance around each section, cut two main sections, four ear sections and one head section from fabric, with arrows on cross grain if fabric is striped. Cut two black circles and two white circles of iron-on tape for eyes, in sizes shown in Diagram 2. Place black circles on white circles and iron one white

circle onto each main section in position shown in Diagram 1.

Place two main sections together, right sides facing, and pin and stitch one side of head section to each piece, starting just above eyes. Pin and stitch remainder of two main sections together, clipping seam allowances around curves and leaving 6″ between small circles on diagram open. Turn right side out and stuff trunk, head and body through opening; slip-stitch opening closed.

Cut two pieces of interfacing from pattern for ears. Place two ear sections together, right sides facing; place matching piece of interfacing on one wrong side; stitch together, leaving lower edges with pleat markings open. Clip curves and turn ears right side out. Make pleats as marked and turn raw edges to inside. Slip-stitch ears to main sections.

Sew ball fringe around elephant's neck for collar. Grouping several strands of yarn for each of three sections, make a braided tail about 6″ long. Tie a knot in tail 1″ from one end and trim ends of yarn evenly. Sew other end of tail in place along seamline.

## STUFFED LION
### ON PAGE 167

MATERIALS NEEDED:
 ½ yard fabric, 36″ wide or wider
 Scraps of contrasting fabric for eyes, mouth
 Scraps of interfacing for ears
 Black iron-on tape for nose, pupils of eyes
 Black yarn, one small skein
 One yard tassel fringe
 Polyester fiberfill for stuffing

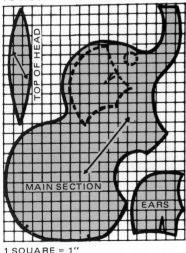

ADD ½″ SEAM ALLOWANCE
TO ALL PATTERN PIECES.

TOP OF HEAD

MAIN SECTION

EARS

1 SQUARE = 1″

**DIAGRAM 1**

Enlarge graph in Diagram 1 to make paper patterns for all sections. Adding ½″ for seam allowance or ¼″ for applique allowance around each section, cut two main sections and four ear sections from fabric, two eyes and mouth from contrasting fabric, nose and pupils of eyes from black iron-on tape. Diagram 2 is actual-size pattern for eyes.

ADD ½″ SEAM ALLOWANCE
TO ALL PATTERN PIECES.

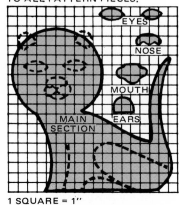

1 SQUARE = 1″

**DIAGRAM 1**

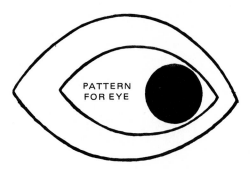

PATTERN
FOR EYE

**DIAGRAM 2**

Applique eyes and mouth to front main section by hand or machine. Iron black nose in place above mouth; iron pupils onto eyes. Using black yarn, embroider whiskers, markings on mouth and outline of legs with basic outline stitch.

Place two main sections together, right sides facing; stitch together ½″ from edges, leaving 8″ along bottom open. Clip curves and turn right side out. Stuff head, body and tail through opening; slip-stitch opening closed. Sew fringe around face by hand.

Cut two pieces of interfacing from pattern for ears. Place two ear sections together, right sides facing; place matching piece of interfacing on one wrong side and stitch together, leaving bottom edges open. Clip curves and turn right side out. Turn raw edges to inside and slip-stitch to front main section in positions indicated in Diagram 1. Sew piece of tassel fringe around end of tail.

# STUFFED GIRAFFE
## ON PAGE 167

MATERIALS NEEDED:
    One yard fabric
    Iron-on tape for eyes, black and white
    ¾ yard moss fringe
    Three colored pipe cleaners for top of head
    Polyester fiberfill for stuffing
    One yard florists' wire for tail and back

Enlarge graph in Diagram 1 to make paper pattern for each section. Adding ½″ seam allowance around each section, cut two main sections, one bottom section, one face section, one tail section and four ear sections. Using Diagram 2 as a pattern, cut two pieces of white iron-on tape and two pieces of black iron-on tape for eyes. Place black pieces on white pieces and iron onto face section,

ADD ½″ SEAM ALLOWANCE
TO ALL PATTERN PIECES

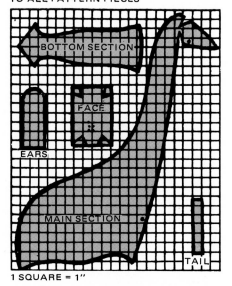

1 SQUARE = 1″

**DIAGRAM 1**

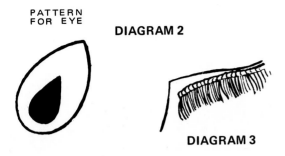

PATTERN
FOR EYE

**DIAGRAM 2**

**DIAGRAM 3**

fringe in seam at tip of ear and leaving straight edges open. Clip curves and turn right side out. Fold each ear so it fits notch at top of head. Pin ear in notch and stitch notch together from wrong side. (Diagram 4).

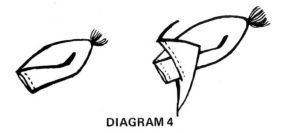

**DIAGRAM 4**

in positions shown on sketch. Stitch edges of lower notch in head of each main section together from wrong side.

Cut an 18″-long piece of moss fringe. Pin woven edge of fringe to right side of one main section along giraffe's back ⅜″ from raw edge, with fringe pointing inward (Diagram 3). Fold tail section in half lengthwise with right sides facing, and stitch ½″ from edge along one end and length. Turn right side out. Pin tail to one main section in position shown in sketch. With right sides facing, join two main sections from top of head to tail, stitching ½″ from edge and making sure woven edge of fringe is caught in seam. Cut a length of wire long enough to reach from top of head to tail and continue inside tail. Sew by hand along inside of seam line and insert in tail. Stitch tail in place on seam line.

Place two ear sections together, right sides facing, and stitch together ½″ from edge, catching small piece of

With right sides facing, pin and stitch bottom section to bottom edges of two main sections, ½″ from edges.

On face section, bring dots together to form tuck on inside and stitch. Stitch four darts at edges of face section to shape face. Pin face section to main sections, right sides facing, and stitch. Stitch remaining seams, except between dots on front seam. Clip curves and turn right side out.

Stuff through neck opening, stuffing head, main section and neck. Turn raw edges to inside and slip-stitch opening closed. Bend pipe cleaners and sew in place at top of head. Sew a small piece of fringe around end of tail.

# Room to Grow

# Plan Ahead to Give a Small Boy's Room a Big Future

The room above is a tiny 9′ x 10′ in size, but it was planned with big expectations. Right now it's a nursery for a very small boy, but it won't be long before he and it grow up. The first thing the expectant parents did was strip away a double closet to make room for the built-in crib, which was constructed to fit the 56″-wide opening. Purchased, ready-to-paint storage units make a base for the crib, so very little building was involved. The walls of the former closet form three sides of the crib, and bumper guards are hung in decorative fashion from lath strips attached to the walls. (The loops are equipped with snap fasteners, so the bumpers can be removed in a snap.) The mattress is a standard-size crib mattress; directions for covering it and for making the bumper guards *and* the mammoth stuffed mouse start on page 192.

No, it didn't grow in size—at left you see a little more of it, but it's still the same room. However, its scope and use *have* expanded, because it's now the domain of an active nine-year-old (a Little Leaguer, naturally) who reads, does homework, plays and sleeps within its limited environs. The niche that was originally a double closet now houses bookshelves, a headboard-night table and the head of a single bed, with room left over for open storage bins to hold sports equipment. The shelf below the window that was originally used as a changing table now serves as a desk, with the storage units from below the crib now taking the place of drawers.

A plaid corduroy bedspread and window shade give the lively red, white and blue color scheme a decidedly masculine flavor. A director's chair is covered in the same fabric. The bedspread is a simple throw with a band of contrasting fabric added around the bottom. Directions for making basic bedspreads start on page 45. Directions for laminating a window shade to match are on page 150. Directions for director's chair are on page 56.

# A Room-Full of Checks for a Feminine Young Charmer

There's no mistaking to whom this bedroom belongs! It was obviously designed to delight a very young lady who loves ruffles and frills—and she'll dream happily in it long after her present pets have gone to animal heaven. The high-key color scheme of hot pink and white will still please her feminine psyche, and the gingham-checked bedcover and curtains will come up crisp and sassy after many a sudsing. The bedcover is the simplest of throws (see page 45), and it camouflages the fact that the studio-couch bed includes a second, pull-out bed for an overnight guest. The pretty canopy effect is achieved by simply adding an extra pair of tied-back curtains, complete with ruffles, above the bed. The curtains are straight, hemmed panels of fabric with valance ruffles attached before being gathered on a single long rod. Everything is easy to make—there's certainly no intricate sewing involved. The room's charm lies in its fresh and totally feminine ambiance. See page 124 for basic curtain directions, page 169 for ruffled pillow covers, and page 132 for valances.

# A Bed-Full of Flowers for a Feminine Young Lady

She may become a leader of the feminist movement in a decade or two, but right now she's definitely a Miss, not a Ms., with a predilection for pretty, feminine things. She likes ruffles and flowers and fresh, clean colors—and she'd *love* to sleep in a ruffly canopy bed because it would make her feel like the Princess in her favorite fairy tale. Happily, you don't have to buy a fancy (and expensive) tester bed to make her dream come true. You can construct the open-topped canopy frame from stock lumber, and make all the frilly trappings on your sewing machine. The frame fits around a 30″ x 75″ mattress and boxspring so it won't seem overpowering in a small girl's small room, but you can easily adjust the measurements to suit a wider bed, if that's what you plan to use.

Incidentally, this lightly scaled canopy bed with its partially enclosed feeling would be a fine transition between a crib and a full-size bed. If you choose a multi-color flower print on a snowy white background, you can paint the "posters" and top molding any color that appears in the print as a starting-point for your color scheme, perhaps painting the walls a pale tint of the same color and adding contrasting accents also taken from the print. Directions for making the canopy frame, the bed drapery and the quilt that doubles as a bedspread start on page 194. Notice that no head pillow is used (it's better for children to sleep without one), so the quilt is cut to fit flat, with a few toss pillows added for lounging.

# Bunk Beds Make Sharing More Fun

To many boys and girls, sleeping in a bunk bed means pure bliss—and more than compensates for sharing a room. Fortunately so, since bunk beds may be the only solution when a very small room must be divided by two.

These contemporary bunk beds and the companion twin-desk unit are easy to build with ¾″ plywood and stock lumber. Uprights are held in place with spring-action "metal sleeves," also available at lumber yards. Stationary ladder is part of the clean-lined design. (For very young occupants, add horizontal railing to top bunk.) Directions begin on page 195.

# Fill Her
# Teen Years
# with Bouquets

Choose a wallcovering that comes with matching fabric (or vice versa) and convert a teen-age bedroom into a garden of flowers. Many delightful floral patterns are coordinated in this manner; you can usually buy both wallcovering and fabric where the wallpaper is sold. Covering both walls and windows with the same pretty pattern makes a small room look larger because it unifies the background, and makes what otherwise might be architectural eyesores (such as the slanting walls opposite) practically unnoticeable. Contrasting all the colorful pattern in this flower-bower is a spectacular scalloped coverlet that's easy to make. Directions for it begin on page 196, and directions for making the gathered dust ruffle appear on page 53.

# directions for projects

## STUFFED TOY MOUSE
### ON PAGE 183

MATERIALS NEEDED:
- ⅞ yard 44"-wide printed fabric
- ¼ yard 44"-wide blue fabric
- Scrap of white fabric
- ½ yard black felt
- Three pounds shredded polyester foam

Enlarge graph and draw parts of mouse, adding ½" seam allowance all around each part. Trace each part except ears on printed fabric, tracing two side sections for head and three side sections for body; cut out. Trace four ear sections on black felt and cut out (two are needed for each ear). From black felt, cut 1¼" x 15½" strip for whiskers; slash 6" into each end three times, making four equal whiskers on each side; taper end of each whisker by trimming to a point.

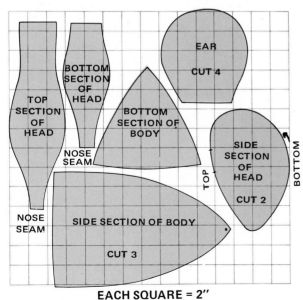

**EACH SQUARE = 2"**

From blue fabric, cut one 7"-diameter circle for the nose and four 2½"-diameter circles, two for each eye. From white fabric, cut two 1"-diameter circles for pupils of eyes, cutting a small pie-shaped piece from each, as shown in photograph on page 183.

With right sides of fabric together, stitch three triangular body sections together so they form a pyramid, carefully matching the three points at the top. Stitch the bottom section of body to the side sections, leaving a 7" opening along one side for stuffing. Turn covering for body to right side and stuff with shredded foam; turn seam allowances of opening inside and slip-stitch opening closed.

With right sides of fabric together, stitch narrow ends of the top and bottom head sections together. The nose will be attached along this seam later. Beginning at the nose, stitch the bottom section of head to bottom edges of the two side sections of head, stopping ⅜" before reaching wide end of bottom section. Starting at the nose seam, stitch top section of head to top edges of the two side sections of head, stopping stitching at edge of bottom section. Turn covering for head to right side. Stuff head with shredded foam, turn under raw edge of bottom section and slip-stitch opening closed.

Using double thread, run a line of small gathering stitches around nose section, ¼" from edge. Draw up thread until opening is approximately 2" wide; fill nose with shredded foam, pull gathering thread tight and knot securely. Sew nose in place along seam at front of head where top and bottom sections of head are joined.

With right sides together, stitch two small blue circles together to make each eye, leaving a small opening for turning to right side. Turn right side out, press, and slip-stitch opening closed. Attach white pupils with fusible webbing or white glue. Glue eyes in place on head or stitch on by hand. Stitch two black ear sections together to make each ear, leaving straight edges open. Turn to right side, press, and slip-stitch opening closed. Stitch one ear to each side of head with small running stitches. Attach whiskers under nose. Stitch head to body with small slip stitches.

## MATTRESS COVER FOR CRIB
### ON PAGE 183

MATERIALS NEEDED:
(for standard 27" x 52" x 4" thick mattress)
- 3½ yards 44"-wide corduroy or other fabric
- 9¼ yards cording, to be covered
- 24"-long zipper

From fabric, cut two 28" x 53" pieces to cover top and bottom of mattress; two 5" x 53" pieces, one 5" x 28" piece and two 3" x 28" pieces for boxing strips; and eight 2" strips x full width of fabric to cover cording. (Two 3"-wide pieces will be used for side on which zipper is inserted.) Cut all pieces, except 2"-wide strips, with long edges parallel to selvages.

Following manufacturer's directions, center and apply zipper to 28"-long edges of two 3"-wide pieces.

Cut cording into two equal lengths. Seam 2"-wide strips of fabric together into two equal lengths and cover cording. (Fold strip in half lengthwise, right sides together; place cording inside, along fold. Stitch as close to cording as possible, using cording foot if available.) Trim seam allowances of cording to ½".

Place top fabric section on mattress, right side up; place covered cording around top section with stitching line of cording along edge of mattress and seam allowances of cording flush with raw edge of fabric, clipping into seam allowances at corners. Trim cording to fit, allowing 1" for overlap. Pull out one end of cording from its cover and cut off ½"; turn raw edge of covering to inside. Stitch cording in place, following stitching line of cording. Where ends of cording meet, slip raw end of casing inside turned-in end and slip-stitch closed.

With right sides together and raw edges even, pin one 5" x 53" boxing strip along each side of top section; pin one 5" x 28" boxing strip along one end and 28" boxing strip with zipper at other end. Holding ends of boxing strips together at each corner, mark placement of each seam so boxing fits smoothly along cording. Stitch seams at corners.

With right sides together and raw edges flush, stitch boxing to top section; open zipper and stitch boxing to bottom section in same manner. Press seams open. Turn cover to right side and insert mattress.

## BUMPER GUARDS FOR CRIB
### ON PAGE 183

MATERIALS NEEDED:
(for three bumpers, two 15" x 29" x 2" thick, one 15" x 52" x 2" thick)

    Five yards 44"-wide corduroy or other fabric
    17½ yards cording
    Four 24"-long zippers
    Nineteen two-part snap fasteners, ½" diameter
    Two pieces, 15" x 29" x 2"-thick firm polyure-
        thane foam padding
    One piece, 15" x 52" x 2"-thick firm polyure-
        thane foam padding

Following Cutting Layout for fabric, cut four 16" x 30" sections and two 16" x 53" sections to cover fronts and backs of three bumpers; six 3" x 16", two 3" x 30", one 3" x 53", four 2" x 30" and two 2" x 53" strips for boxing; one 4" x 77" and two 4" x 66" strips for loops; fifteen 2"-wide strips x full width of fabric to cover cording. Cut all pieces, except 2"-wide strips for covering cording, with long edges parallel to selvages.

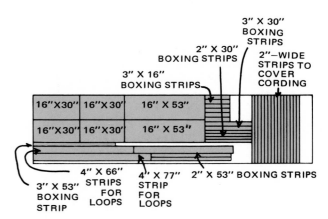

**CUTTING LAYOUT FOR FABRIC**

Join 2"-wide strips and cover 17½ yards of cording (see directions for mattress cover for crib, at left). Stitch cording around the three front sections and the three back sections for bumper covers in the same manner as for mattress cover.

Cut 4"-wide strips for loops into nineteen 11"-long sections. Fold each 11"-long strip in half lengthwise with right sides together; stitch long edges together ½" from raw edges. Turn each strip to right side. (If desired, stitch 18"-long piece of cording or string to one end of strip before stitching long edges together; stitch with cording or string inside strip and projecting from other end to facilitate turning strip to right side after stitching by pulling cording or string through.) Press each strip so seam is flat along one edge. Finish one end of each strip by folding raw edge in ⅜"; stitch across end close to fold. Following manufacturer's directions, attach top half of snap fastener ½" from each finished end and bottom half of fastener 1" from each unfinished end.

To attach nine strips for loops to back section of long bumper, place them over cording with snap fasteners on top, and with raw edges of loops, cording and back section flush. Space loops 4¼" from each end and 3¾" apart. Stitch unfinished end of each loop to back section along stitching line of cording. In same manner, stitch five strips to back section of each end bumper, spacing them 3¾" from each end and 3½" apart.

Following manufacturer's directions, center and apply one 24" zipper to long edges of two 2" x 30" boxing strips. With right sides together and taking ½" seams, stitch two 3" x 16" boxing strips and two 3" x 30" boxing strips together, alternating shorter and longer strips, to form complete ring. Stitch boxing strip to one 16" x 30" front section, with seams at corners. Open zipper. Stitch boxing strip to 16" x 30" back section with loops, with seams at corners and zipper portion of boxing strip at opposite side from loops. In same manner, complete cover for other end bumper of the same size.

Following manufacturer's directions, center and apply two 24" zippers to long edges of two 2" x 53" boxing strips, with zipper pulls meeting at center of length. With right sides together and taking ½" seams, stitch two 3" x 16" boxing strips and two 3" x 53" boxing strips together, alternating shorter and longer strips, to form complete ring. Stitch boxing strip to 16" x 53" front section with seams at corners. Open zipper. Stitch boxing strip to 16" x 53" back section with loops, with seams at corners and zipper portion of boxing strip at opposite side from loops; insert foam padding.

## QUILTED SPREAD
### ON PAGE 187

MATERIALS NEEDED:
(for 30" x 75" mattress)
     5½ yards 45"-wide fabric
     5½ yards 45"-wide lining fabric
     Polyester batting
     Buttonhole twist

From outer fabric, cut one 31" x 117" center section and two 21½" x 76" side sections. Cut lining and batting to same dimensions for each section, piecing batting if necessary by butting lengths together and catch-stitching in a few places. Place batting between outer fabric and lining, right sides outside, and baste together along center of length and width and around all edges of each section.

On each section, fold one end diagonally so the crosswise edge is flush with one lengthwise edge, right sides of outer fabric together. Mark diagonal line along fold on lining fabric to establish true diagonal for quilting lines. Draw parallel lines 7" from first line in one direction; fold other end on same side in same manner and mark diagonal lines in opposite direction. Using buttonhole twist, machine-stitch through all thicknesses along lines in one direction; stitch along lines in opposite direction.

With right sides together, center and pin one side section to each long edge of center section. Stitch together with ½" seams, starting and ending stitching ½" from ends of side sections and backstitching at both ends. (The resulting cross-like shape permits side and end drops to fall over side and end rails of frame while fitting around posts.)

Overcast all raw edges by hand or machine. If top of mattress is 21" from floor, turn ½" to wrong side along overcast edges and stitch hem. If mattress is lower, center spread on bed and mark hem ½" from floor; turn and stitch hem.

## CANOPY FRAME AND
## RUFFLED BED CURTAINS
### ON PAGE 187

MATERIALS NEEDED:
(to fit around 30" x 75" bed)
     "3 x 3" pine:
          Four 80" for A and B
          Two 32" for C
          Two 77" for D

     2" crown molding:
          Two pieces 39" long
          Two pieces 84" long
     "1 x 6" pine:
          Two 37" for end rails
          Two 83½" for side rails
     32" length of ¾" dowel
     Twelve flat-head wood screws
     Eight 4" round-head bolts with nuts and washers
     1¾" finishing nails
     Wood glue
(for four pairs of 78"-long curtains and valance)
     27¾ yards of 45"-wide fabric
     Eight adjustable 12"–20" sash curtain rods
     Tacks

**Canopy Frame:** NOTE: Be sure to purchase "3 x 3"'s (actually 2½" x 2½") which are finished on all four sides (S4S) and be sure they are straight and true. Allow them to dry at room temperature for at least two weeks before starting construction.

Make a template to fit end of "3 x 3" and mark a ¾" circle in *exact* center (Diagram 1).

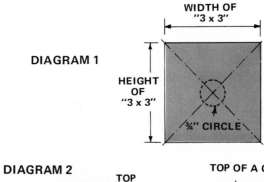

DIAGRAM 1

WIDTH OF "3 x 3"

HEIGHT OF "3 x 3"

¾" CIRCLE

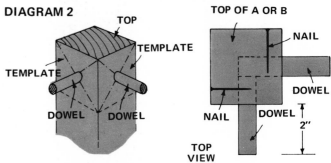

DIAGRAM 2

TOP

TEMPLATE

TEMPLATE

DOWEL   DOWEL

TOP OF A OR B

NAIL

DOWEL

NAIL   DOWEL

2"

TOP VIEW

Place template on one face of A, flush with top, and mark center of ¾" hole. Bore a ¾" hole 2" deep in position marked. Repeat on one *adjoining face* of A. Bore two holes in same manner at top of each B. Cut eight 4" lengths of dowel. Apply glue and insert a dowel into each hole in A and B, pushing the first dowel in the full 2", and the second dowel up against the first one. Trim dowels so all project 2" from faces of A and B. Bore pilot holes into two remaining faces of each A and B for finishing nails, placing them 1" in from side edges so nails will go through dowels; drive nails in place (Diagram 2).

Using template, mark center of ¾" hole on both *ends* of each C and D. Bore ¾" holes 2" deep in positions marked.

On each C and D, bore two pilot holes for finishing nails 1″ in from each end, placing both on the same face (Diagram 3).

**DIAGRAM 3**

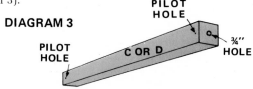

PILOT HOLE

PILOT HOLE

C OR D

¾″ HOLE

Place one C between two A and check to be sure top edges line up when dowels go into ends of C. Apply glue and place hole in one end of C over dowel on left A and push in place. Apply glue to dowel on right A and place in position with dowel of A going into hole in C. Nail through pilot holes in C so nails go through dowels.

Place second C between two B and check to make sure top edges are even when dowels go into ends of C. Glue and nail second C and two B together in same manner as for first C and A.

Place one D between each A and B, checking to make sure top edges are even, and assemble in same manner as before to complete basic frame (Diagram 4).

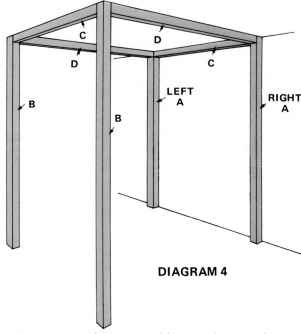

C

D

D

C

LEFT A

B

B

RIGHT A

**DIAGRAM 4**

Miter pieces of crown molding to fit around top of frame; nail to frame ¾″ above lower edge.

Measure up 5″ from bottom of each A and B and draw line across both outside faces of each to mark placement of side and end rails. Place one 37″-long end rail against one end of frame with bottom of rail along marked lines on A and ends of rail flush with outside faces of A; screw through rail into A. Screw second end rail to B in same manner.

Place one 83½″ side rail against one side of frame with bottom of rail along marked lines on A and B and ends of rail flush with outside faces of end rails; bolt to A and B. Bolt second side rail to other side of frame in same manner.

Countersink all nailheads. Fill all holes and crevices with wood filler. Sand all surfaces and edges with medium, then fine sandpaper. Apply basecoat and paint, following manufacturer's directions.

**Ruffled Bed Curtains:** Cut eight panels of fabric for curtains, each 76″ long x full width of fabric. Cut eight 5″-wide strips for attached ruffles, each 280″ long. Cut six additional 5″-wide strips for valance ruffle, each 108″ long. Cut four 3″-wide strips for ties, each 40″ long.

Trim or clip selvages on curtain panels to prevent puckering. Make side hems by turning ¼″ to wrong side and then an additional ½″; stitch. Make top casings by turning under ¼″ and then 1″; stitch. Make bottom hems in same manner as for side hems.

Make double ⅛″ hems on all sides of 280″-long strips for attached ruffles. Gather length of each ruffle to fit evenly around one long edge and short bottom edge of each curtain (see photo). Stitch to right side of curtain ½″ from side and bottom edges, reversing ruffled sides to form four pairs. Insert sash rods in casings of two pairs of curtains for sides of bed; extend rods to 20″ length and attach to top of frame as close as possible to lower edge, starting 2″ in from each corner. Insert remaining rods in remaining curtains; adjust rods to 16″-length and attach to ends of frame in same manner.

Fold each tie section in half lengthwise, with right sides together; stitch ¼″ seams along edges, leaving about 4½″ open in center. Refold so seam is centered on back of tie; press seam open; stitch across ends. Turn right side out and slip-stitch opening closed. Tie in place.

With right sides facing and taking ½″ seams, join edges of six strips for valance ruffle to form complete ring. Make ⅛″ double hems along both raw edges. Gather length along one edge, fitting ruffle evenly around top of frame. Tack in place around frame and over curtains.

## BUNK BEDS
### ON PAGE 188

MATERIALS NEEDED:
(for 30″ x 75″ mattresses)
    Clear pine:
        Six "2 x 3" x ceiling height, for uprights
        Four "1 x 3" x 77″, for sides of beds
        Four "1 x 3" x 32″, for ends of beds
        Four "1 x 3" x 19½″, for ladder treads
        Four "1 x 2" x 18″, for ladder braces
    Two 32″ x 77″ panels of ¾″ plywood for bases
    Nine 36″ lengths of ⅞″ dowel
    Six "Timber Toppers" (metal sleeves) No. 50
    Finishing nails
    Wood glue
    Orange and purple semi-gloss enamel
    Two 30″ x 75″ mattresses

NOTE: Purchase clear pine stock lumber which is finished on all four sides (S4S) and be sure all pieces are straight and true. Allow them to dry at room temperature for two weeks before starting construction. If using other than 30″ x 75″ mattresses, adjust measurements of lumber accordingly. "Timber Toppers" are metal sleeves with springs which hold uprights securely in place at floor and ceiling.

Measure the distance from floor to ceiling where each individual upright will be placed, as floor-to-ceiling measurements at different points may vary. Cut each upright to floor-to-ceiling measurement minus 3½″. Before assembling unit, sand all parts and paint uprights, dowels, ladder treads, braces and metal sleeves orange; paint bases and side and end pieces purple. Apply two coats to all parts, allowing first coat to dry thoroughly before applying second.

Glue and nail the "1 x 3" side and end pieces to the plywood bases, making butt joints with the 32″ lengths between ends of 77″ lengths and all bottom edges flush. Drill 1″ holes centered on the flat sides of uprights as follows: Drill four holes in two uprights, 15″, 40″, 52″ and 85″ from floor end (left-hand pair of uprights in photo). Drill three holes in two uprights, 15″, 40″ and 52″ from floor end (right-hand pair in photo). Drill two holes in two uprights, 15″ and 52″ from floor end (center pair in photo).

Drill three holes along center of each 77″-long side piece, placing holes 4″, 25″ and 72″ from end where ladder will be placed. See photograph for placement of dowels through uprights and side pieces.

To construct ladder, glue and nail the four "1 x 2" braces between center front upright (with two holes) and right front upright (with three holes), placing them 10″ from floor and 10″ apart. Cut ¾″ x ¾″ grooves in uprights directly above each brace on each side; fit the 1″ x 3″ treads into the grooves, gluing and nailing them in place with back edges of treads and uprights flush.

Countersink all nails; fill all holes and crevices with wood filler and touch up with paint. Place metal sleeves on uprights and assemble unit.

## SHELF UNIT
### ON PAGE 189

MATERIALS NEEDED:
    Six "2 x 3"s, each ceiling height for uprights
    ¾″ plywood:
        Two 8″ x 77″ for upper shelves
        One 19″ x 77″ for lower shelf
    "1 x 2" for shelf edging:
        Six 78½″ lengths
        Four 8″ lengths
        Four 8¾″ lengths
    "1 x 2", 75″ long, for brace for bottom shelf
    Six "Timber Toppers" (metal sleeves; see Bunk
        Beds) No. 50

NOTE: Purchase clear pine stock lumber which is finished on all four sides (S4S) and be sure all pieces are straight and true. Allow them to dry at room temperature for two weeks before starting construction. Bunk Beds

(above) and Shelf Unit were designed so that ¾″ plywood for both units could be cut from two 4′ x 8′ sheets.

Nail "1 x 2" edging around 8″-wide shelves, making butt joints with 8″ lengths between ends of 78½″ lengths and all top edges flush. (Outside measurements of shelves with "1 x 2" edging added will be 9½″ x 78½″.)

Cut opening and two grooves in 19″-wide bottom shelf to accommodate "2 x 3" uprights as follows, remembering that actual measurements of a so-called "2 x 3" are approximately 1½″ x 2½″ (be sure to take precise measurements of lumber being used): Cut 1½″ x 2½″ opening through center of shelf, with long edge of opening parallel to long edge of shelf, and back edge of opening 8¾″ from back edge of shelf. To do this, mark 1½″ x 2½″ rectangle in correct position and drill hole in center of rectangle, then insert narrow saw blade and cut out rectangle. Cut 1½″ x 2½″ groove in each end of shelf, with back edges of grooves 8¾″ from back edge of shelf and grooves aligned with center opening. Nail two 78½″ lengths of "1 x 2" edging and four 8¾″ lengths in place around shelf with all top edges flush. Nail 75″ length of "1 x 2" to underside of shelf just behind grooves.

Drill two 1″ holes through each upright, centering them on 2½″ sides and placing them 46″ and 67″ from floor ends. Drill corresponding holes for dowels through "1 x 2" edging around 8″ shelves, drilling three holes in center of width on each long side, one in exact center of length and one 1¼″ from each end.

Sand all parts smooth; paint uprights and dowels orange and shelves purple, applying two coats and allowing first coat to dry thoroughly before applying second.

Before placing uprights in vertical position, nail three uprights to back of bottom shelf, one flush with each end and one in exact center, with top of shelf (which serves as desk) 29″ from floor ends. Insert remaining uprights through opening and in grooves of lower shelf; nail through brace below shelf into uprights. Place metal sleeves on ends of uprights. Insert dowels through holes in uprights and corresponding holes in 8″ shelves to hold shelves in place.

Countersink all nail heads; fill holes and crevices with wood filler and touch up with paint.

## SCALLOPED COVERLET
### ON PAGE 190

MATERIALS NEEDED:
(for 36″- to 39″-wide bed)
    Five yards 54″-wide white fabric
    5¼ yards 54″-wide green fabric

    Polyester batting
    Green yarn
    Tapestry needle

From white fabric, cut two panels 50″ wide x 90″ long. From green fabric, cut two panels 54″ wide x 94″ long. From batting, cut one panel 54″ wide x 94″ long. Make sure all panels are true rectangles and corners are square.

To make scallop pattern for white panels, draw a 10″-diameter circle on paper; divide in half and cut out semicircle. Using semicircle as pattern, trace scallops around all four edges of each white panel, with straight edge of semicircle 5″ in from edge of fabric. Start with complete semicircle in one corner and trace five complete semicircles along each short side and ten complete semicircles along each long side. Semicircles will overlap at each corner, forming three-quarters of a circle (Diagram 1). Cut out around scallops.

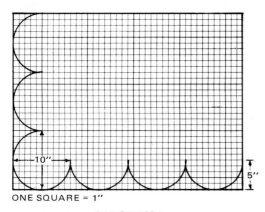

ONE SQUARE = 1″

**DIAGRAM 1**

Place scalloped white panels together, right sides facing and all edges flush. Stitch together ½″ from edges, following outline of scallops; leave opening in center of one short side wide enough to turn panel to right side. Clip seam allowances around curves and into points between scallops. Turn panel to right side and press so stitching is along exact edge of scallops. Turn seam allowances of opening to inside, clipping around curves and into points, and slip-stitch opening closed.

To make scallop pattern for green fabric, draw a 14″-diameter circle on paper; divide in half and cut out semicircle, then draw a straight line 5″ from straight edge. Starting in one corner of one green panel, trace full depth of semicircle at outside edge, but trace only to marked line on other side of pattern. Continue tracing shallow scallops to marked line only, except at corners, overlapping semicircles at each corner (Diagram 2). As before, there will be five scallops along each short side and ten

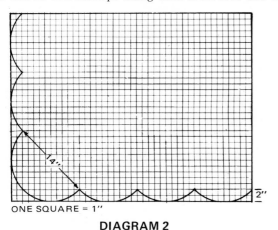

ONE SQUARE = 1″

**DIAGRAM 2**

scallops along each long side. Trace matching scallops on second green panel and cut around scallops.

Center batting on wrong side of one green panel with outside curves of scallops flush with edges of batting. Pin and baste together down center length, across center width and along all edges. Place green panels together, rights sides facing and all scalloped edges flush; pin together. Stitch together ½″ from scalloped edges of green panels, carefully following scalloped outline, and leaving opening in center of one short side wide enough to turn panel to right side. Trim away excess batting as close to stitching as possible and clip seam allowances of green fabric around curves and into points of scallops. Be sure to remove all pins.

Turn to right side and press so stitching is along exact edge of scallops. Turn seam allowances of opening to inside and slip-stitch closed.

Mark placement for tufts on finished white panel in the following manner: Mark five tufts 4½″ in from one short end, placing one in center of each scallop. Tufts in centers of corners will also be 4½″ in from side edges. (See Diagram 3.) Mark four tufts in second row from same end, placing them 5″ in from points of end scallops and on a line with first points of side scallops. Continue marking alternating rows of five tufts and four tufts as indicated by Diagram 3, forming a diamond pattern, with tufts in each row 10″ from each other. Diagram 3 shows slightly more than one-half of panel; fifth row of tufts will be in exact center of complete panel.

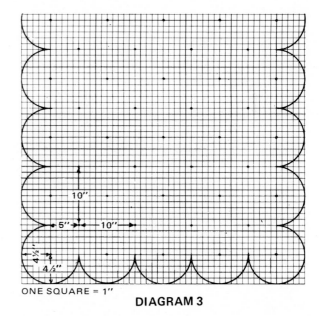

ONE SQUARE = 1″

**DIAGRAM 3**

Center white panel over finished green panel; green panel should extend an even 2″ beyond white panel around all scalloped edges. Baste panels together down center length, across center width, and around all edges. Using three strands of green yarn and tapestry needle, insert needle through both panels at each marking for tufts from right side to wrong side and back up to right side. Tie yarn securely on right side and trim ends 2″ from knots.

# Fun Things to Do with Fabric

A battered storage hassock was transformed into the colorful toy chest opposite when it was covered with a decorative fabric. If fabric is wide enough, wrap front and sides with one piece, allowing enough margin on all sides to turn raw edges under. Use strips of fusible web to fasten the upper raw edge to wrong side of fabric, then glue fabric to hassock with fabric paste, mitering corners to cover top edges. Glue back and bottom raw edges to hassock and cover back with a separate piece of fabric. Pad top with a layer of polyurethane foam and make a fitted cover for top in same manner as for a boxed cushion, allowing extra to cover lower edge and turn edges under. Smooth cover over top and glue to sides and lower edge. Protect fabric-covered surfaces of base with plastic spray or several coats of clear shellac.

Give an unpainted chest a custom look by covering the fronts of the drawers with printed fabric. Remove the knobs and paint them and the chest to complement the print. Cut fabric to cover each drawer front, allowing 3″ above top edge and 2″ overlap along sides and bottom. Center fabric on drawer and glue in place, then cut square of excess fabric away at each corner. Glue overlap to sides and bottom of drawer. Wrap 3″ allowance around top edge of drawer and glue to inside.

Cover easy-to-build cubes with vinyl-coated fabric to make a colorful "table" and "chairs." Twelve-inch cubes can be covered with a 40″ square of fabric. To cover 24″ cube, first size entire cube with sizing glue. Cut two pieces of fabric to cover opposite sides, allowing 2″ at bottom and ½″ extra along remaining edges to go around corners onto adjacent sides and top. Glue to cube. Cut one piece to cover remaining sides and top. Glue to cube, going up one side, across top and down last side. Wrap fabric around lower edges of cube and tack to inside.

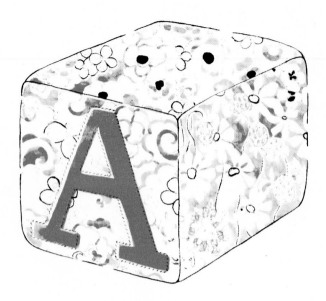

Make a super-size "alphabet block" for decorative seating in a young lady's room. Build a 12″ x 12″ cube of ½″ plywood (or buy an inexpensive plastic one) and pad with 2″-thick fiberfill or foam padding. Stitch together a flower-printed slipcover, seaming all except three lower edges. Applique contrasting letters on two sides, slide cover over cube and slip-stitch closed.

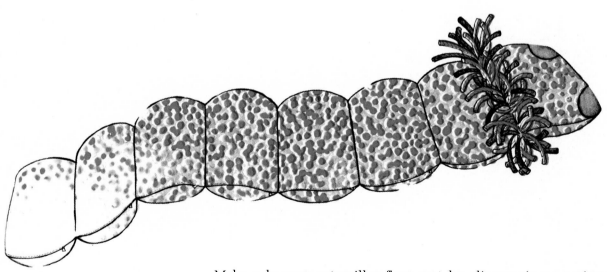

Make a bouncy caterpillar floor mat by slipcovering a series of foam-filled pillows—or the blow-up plastic kind, which are even bouncier. Make separate covers, each with its own zipper, and snap or stitch them together. Applique two big felt eyes on one end, and add a fuzzy collar of fluffy rug yarn.

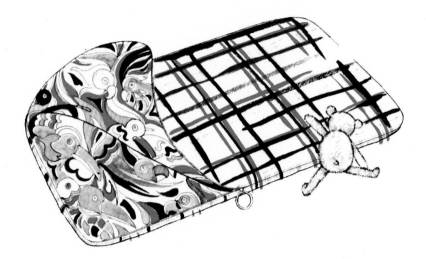

Zip up several lightweight sleeping bags to make those indoor slumber parties less of a scramble. Stitch together two big rectangles of fabric with a layer of fiberfill between them. Fold in half, apply a zipper across the bottom and a long separating zipper along the unfolded side. Unzipped, it will also do very nicely as a cozy coverlet.

# 5
## MORE
## GENERAL
## IDEAS

# Floor-Length Tablecloths Round Out a Decorating Plan

One of the quickest (and easiest) tricks in a professional decorator's book is the coordinated round tablecloth. It can be made of almost any fabric, to match draperies, slipcovers, upholstery or what-have-you, and can be used in any room to tie a color scheme together. What goes on underneath is nobody's business; the "table" may be packing boxes topped with a circle of plywood. Here, a flower-splashed cloth matches a fabric-covered lambrequin to create a colorful dining area in a one-room apartment. Directions for making lambrequin, page 218. Directions for making tablecloths start on page 210.

An easy-to-make round tablecloth can be contemporary or traditional, to complement the mood of any room. Make it in an abstract print to match straight, fabric-covered panels and it's as modern as today. But make it in a blooming print of full-blown cabbage roses to match a curvaceous loveseat and it becomes as Victorian as a bell jar. See directions for round tablecloths on page 210  Directions for making draperies start on page 124.

# Pillows, Cushions and Mattress Covers Can "Make" a Room

The final, perfect touch that adds a fillip of contrast or ties a color scheme together is often a splash of bright pillows or a few trimly covered cushions. Happily, they can be made in a flash—even at the last moment—and at very little expense. A mattress cover (which is basically a grown-up cushion cover) is just as easy to make, and offers even larger possibilities for color coordination.

Crisply-tailored mattress covers and a lineup of cushions both furnish and decorate this twenty-four-hour living room. The mattresses are placed on a U-shaped platform to make a room-size "conversation pit" that turns into comfortable sleeping quarters by night. The pillow covers that carry out the calm and restful color scheme are simply squares of fabric stitched together—corded or not.

Above right, two more ways to dress up a day-or-night bed. For the casual country look so much in favor, cover the bed with a bandanna-print throw and add lots of ruffly pillows—all in the same print, but in four scrambled colors. Make the cover, ruffle and cording different every time. You're the tailored type? Slipcover the bed in stark white sailcloth zapped with stripe-covered cording and add a mass of bright pillows that pick up the colors of the stripes. Directions for making pillows, cushions and mattress covers start on page 220.

Colorful pillows or cushions are often the final, perfect touch that ties a room together—and the touch that gives either one a well-finished look is trim, straight cording. You can buy cording already covered in many colors—sometimes even in colorful stripes. But it's easy to cover your own—to match or contrast any covers you make by following the directions below.

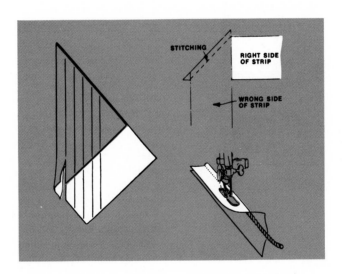

## COVERING AND APPLYING CORDING

Cut 2″-wide strips of fabric on the true bias by folding one straight end of the fabric diagonally so the crosswise edge is flush with one lengthwise edge after selvages have been evenly trimmed. (Always cut off *all* selvages, whatever you're making.) Press the fold lightly and measure from the fold across the doubled fabric, continuing across any remaining single layer. With right sides of the strips facing, seam them together on the lengthwise grain. Keep width of strip even by extending points of strips being joined beyond width by ¼″ and taking ¼″ seams (see Diagram). Press each seam as stitched, then press seam allowances open. One yard of 36″-wide fabric will make approximately 17 yards of seamed-together bias strip; one yard of 44″ fabric will make almost 21 yards. Fold strip in half lengthwise, wrong sides together, and press. Place cord in fold. Using adjustable cording or zipper foot, stitch close to cord without crowding against it. Trim fabric ½″ from stitching for seam allowance.

With ½″ seam allowances of fabric and cording even, stitch cording to right side of fabric piece, following stitching line of cording. Place corresponding fabric piece over cording, right sides of fabric together and all seam allowances even, and stitch between cording and previous row of stitching, crowding cording foot against the cord.

To join cording, cut covered cord ½″ longer than required. Pull one end of cord out from covering and cut off ½″. Turn ¼″ of covering to inside, concealing raw edge. Starting with this end, apply cording as described above. Where ends of cording meet at starting place, slip second end into turned-in edge of covering and continue stitching.

# basic how-tos

## HOW TO MAKE FLOOR-LENGTH ROUND AND OVAL TABLECLOTHS

The Yardage Chart which follows tells you at a glance how much fabric you need, depending upon the size of the table and the width of the fabric you plan to use. It also tells you how many lengths to cut and how long to cut them. All specifications are for tables 29" high, and all yardage requirements are for solid-color fabrics or all-over patterns which don't have to be matched. (The large flower print on page 204 had to be carefully matched at the seams, so extra fabric was required.) In all sizes given, the hemmed edge of the cloth will be ½" from the floor. If it is not necessary for the cloth to be full length, one of smaller diameter than that indicated for the size of the table can be used.

**Cutting:** Cut the number of lengths required according to the chart, with each length the number of inches indicated. When two or four lengths are required, cut *one* width of fabric lengthwise into two half-widths.

**Seaming:** It is not desirable to have a seam running across the center of a cloth (and therefore the table); to avoid this, seam lengths together in the following manner: *Two lengths:* Seam one-half-width to each side of a full width. Seams will fall near edge of table or in the skirt. *Three lengths:* Seam the three full widths together evenly. *Four lengths:* Seam three full widths together, then seam one half-width to each side of the three joined widths.

When stitching seams, place right sides of fabric widths together, with selvages even. Stitch ½" from edge unless deeper seams are necessary (when color or pattern of fabric does not reach to selvages). Press allowances open.

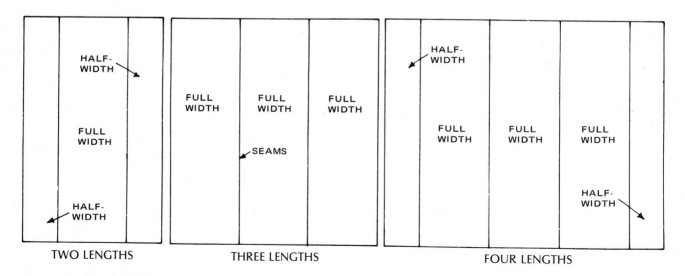

# YARDAGE CHART FOR ROUND AND OVAL TABLECLOTHS

| CLOTH | SIZE OF TABLE | SIZE OF CLOTH BEFORE HEMMING | YARDS REQUIRED | | | | NUMBER OF LENGTHS REQUIRED | | | | NUMBER OF INCHES EACH LENGTH SHOULD BE CUT |
|---|---|---|---|---|---|---|---|---|---|---|---|
| | | | 36" | 45" | 48" | 54" | 36" | 45" | 48" | 54" | |
| A | 30" diameter round | 89" diameter | 7½ | 5 | 5 | 5 | 3 | 2 | 2 | 2 | 90" |
| B | 36" diameter round | 95" diameter | 8 | 8 | 5½ | 5½ | 3 | 3 | 2 | 2 | 96" |
| C | 48" diameter round | 107" diameter | 9 | 9 | 9 | 6 | 3 | 3 | 3 | 2 | 108" |
| D | 54" diameter round | 113" diameter | 9½ | 9½ | 9½ | 9½ | 3 | 3 | 3 | 3 | 114" |
| E | 60" diameter round | 119" diameter | 13¼ | 10 | 10 | 10 | 4 | 3 | 3 | 3 | 120" |
| F | 42" x 54" oval | 101" x 113" | 9½ | 9½ | 9½ | 6½ | 3 | 3 | 3 | 2 | 114" |
| G | 48" x 72" oval | 107" x 131" | 11 | 11 | 11 | 7½ | 3 | 3 | 3 | 2 | 132" |

## MARKING AND HEMMING ROUND CLOTHS

**With Satin-Stitched or Decorative Edging:** If you wish to finish cloth with satin-stitched or other decorative edging instead of a hem, fold fabric in half as shown, matching seams and raw edges, and pin the two layers together. Mark center of width along the folded edge. To make string compass for marking half-circle, tie a knot at one end of string and place it on center mark; stretch string taut and tie a second knot to indicate cut line on cloth. For cloths designated "A" through "E" on yardage chart, second knot should be following distance from first knot: A, 43½"; B, 46½"; C, 52½"; D, 55½"; E, 58½". Working on a flat surface, mark half-circle by moving string and pinning through both layers of fabric along line indicated by second knot. Turn fabric over and mark positions of pins with chalk. Turn over again and remove pins, again marking line with chalk. Satin-stitch along marked line and trim fabric along edge of stitching.

**With one-inch hem:** To make cloth with hemmed edge, fold fabric in half and then in half again, as shown, to form a square four layers thick; pin layers together. Using string compass as described above, mark cutting line by pinning along arc made by second knot. Second knot should be following distance from first knot: For cloth A, 44½"; B, 47½"; C, 53½"; D, 56½"; E, 59½". Cut along marked line through all four layers of fabric and stay-stitch the edge, easing fabric in slightly so there will be less fullness when the hem is turned. Measure one inch from cut edge and turn, pulling up bobbin thread as necessary, and stitch hem.

## MARKING AND HEMMING OVAL CLOTHS

Oval tables vary greatly in shape, so an oval cloth must be cut to fit the particular table. Center seamed fabric on table carefully and hold in place with heavy objects

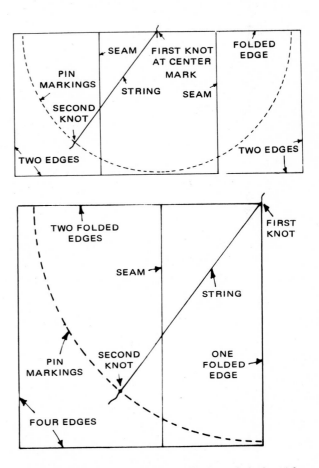

around the edge of the table; mark edge of cloth ½" from floor. Satin-stitch along marked line and trim, or make a one-inch hem in following manner: Stay-stitch one inch beyond marked line, easing fabric in slightly around curves. Cut along stitching, turn hem on marked line and stitch.

# FOUR FOOL-PROOF WAYS TO COVER
## WALLS WITH FABRIC

If you've always thought of fabric-covered walls as a "decorator" kind of thing requiring professional installation, think again. Here are four different ways you can do the job yourself, the method determined only by the area and the kind of fabric you want to use. Any one will camouflage problem walls, disguising bumps and cracks paint cannot conceal. But the big bonus is that very "decorator" look you may have thought unobtainable. By using fabric, you can cover your walls with the perfect pattern and texture. The possibilities for coordination are unlimited.

### FABRIC STAPLED TO FURRING STRIPS

The most usual method of covering walls with fabric is to staple it to furring strips and then conceal the staples with painted lath strips, decorative braid or contrasting beams. Almost any type of fabric can be used, even a loosely-woven one, because adjustments can be made if the fabric should sag. But it's best to choose a moderately-sized, all-over pattern to avoid any matching problems.

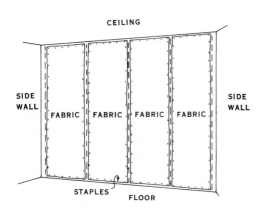

Start by attaching ¼" x 2" lath stripping along ceiling and floor lines. Measure the wall to determine how many fabric widths are required and apply lath strips vertically where the fabric panels will meet, spacing them at equal intervals across the wall and making sure that the last panel is the same width as the first. Try to use a width which will keep door and window openings within a panel or panels. Cut lengths of fabric equal to the height of the wall, plus an extra inch at top and bottom if you plan to use only vertical cover-up strips. Begin by stapling the left side of the first fabric panel to the furring strip in the left-hand corner, stapling it first halfway down the panel to anchor the fabric while working. Bring the fabric across to the second furring strip and staple it in the center also. Working from side to side to keep pattern and grain line straight, staple fabric to both furring strips, up to ceiling line and down to the floor. Turn under one-inch hems at top and bottom, nail to top and bottom furring strips with finishing nails (as few as possible) and work fabric back over each nailhead. If you plan to use decorative stripping along ceiling and floor lines,

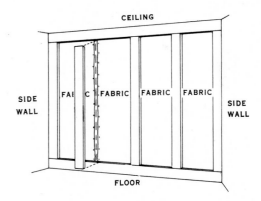

simply trim away excess fabric and staple to furring strips as before. Then go on to the next panel and continue in the same manner across the wall. When all fabric panels have been stapled in place, cover each meeting of the stapled edges with painted or fabric-covered lath strips or other decorative stripping.

A crewel-patterned fabric used for slipcover and drapery also covers one wall, unifying the whole room. Painted "2 x 4"'s that match the other walls conceal the stapled edges of the fabric, suggesting a paneled wall.

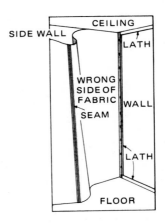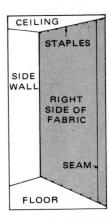

## FABRIC APPLIED IN PRE-SEWN PANELS

The velvet-clad walls above the paneled dado in the living room opposite were covered via the "pre-sewn" technique, in which the fabric is applied in one-wall units. Not the easiest method of covering walls, the elegant result is well worth the extra effort, especially for formal or traditional rooms where a solid-color fabric is used. First, figure out how many fabric widths you need, discounting door and window openings. Make these openings four inches *less* than their actual measurements and allow one-inch seam allowances on both sides of each width. (Seam allowance will be used for blind-tacking along outside edges.) In planning the layout for each wall-size panel, try to place seams at the edges of doors and windows. Measure the height of the wall and add four inches at top and bottom of each fabric length so you can get a good "grip" when pulling the fabric taut. If using solid-color fabric, multiply the total length by the number of widths required. If you have chosen a patterned fabric, you must allow for matching the pattern across all walls. In this case, if the total length includes less than a complete design motif, the remaining depth of the repeat must be added to each length so all lengths can be matched.

After the fabric lengths have been cut, trim off all selvages so the fabric will stretch evenly, and stitch the lengths together to conform to your pre-planned layout. Press all seam allowances flat. Each wall covering will look like a huge sheet with cut-outs for doors and windows.

To prepare the walls for covering, remove all floor and ceiling molding. Frame each wall—ceiling, floor and sides—with ¼" x 2" lath stripping. Two vertical strips will meet at each corner. Frame each door and window opening in the same way. Remove the switch plate and frame the area it occupies with the same ¼" x 2" lath stripping.

Now you're ready to begin the actual application. Take the first pre-sewn wall panel and blind-tack the left side to the lath stripping in the left-hand corner of the wall, working from top to bottom. To do this, turn the right side of the fabric against the adjacent side wall so the wrong side of the fabric faces you. Staple an even 1" margin of the fabric (wrong side out) to the left edge of the lath stripping. Now place upholsterers' tape (or ½"-wide strips of cardboard) over the fabric, fitting it snugly into the corner, and tack it to the lath stripping through the fabric. When the fabric is turned back to the right side, it

will wrap around the cardboard tape, leaving a clean, straight edge tight against the corner.

Fold the fabric to the right side as indicated above, and bring it across the wall to the furring strip in the right-hand corner. Pulling it taut, staple the center of the fabric length to the center of the lath strip. This secures it temporarily so you can make sure the fabric is straight and door and window cut-outs in correct position.

Going back to the corner in which you started, begin stapling the fabric panel to the top and bottom furring strips, working along top and bottom edges alternately as you pull the fabric taut. Measure from seam to seam as you staple to make sure you are pulling evenly and the fabric remains straight. Trim away excess fabric along ceiling and floor.

Continue to the corner and staple the right edge of the fabric panel, not to the opposite lath stripping on the same wall, but to the corner stripping on the adjoining wall, leaving just enough "give" to blind-tack the fabric panel for the adjacent wall in place. Repeat the procedure for the remaining walls. When you come to the right edge of the final panel, fold the raw edge of the fabric around upholsterers' tape (or cardboard strips), pull the fabric taut and straight, and nail it directly to the last furring strip with finishing nails, carefully working the fabric back over each nailhead. If you plan to apply molding along the corners, the last raw edge of fabric can be stapled directly to the furring strip without wrapping it around cardboard. Pull the fabric taut around door and window openings and staple directly to the lath strips that frame them, trimming away excess fabric.

Now for the finishing touches. Conceal staples along floor and ceiling with painted or fabric-covered molding. (If original molding was removed, simply replace it.) Staples around doors and windows can be covered the same way, or with a decorative braid glued over the staples and raw fabric edges. If, in spite of your best efforts, you're not happy with the way the corners of the room look, cover inconspicuous quarter-round molding with fabric and apply.

## FABRIC WRAPPED AROUND FIBERBOARD PANELS

The easiest method of covering walls with fabric is to wrap fiberboard panels with the fabric and then nail the panels to the wall. Because it's also the most expensive method (due to the additional cost of the panels), it's recommended primarily for single walls or limited areas.

First, measure all areas to be covered. Cut fiber-board panels to fit, allowing for the thickness of the first panels to be applied if covering the ceiling or more than one wall. Cut fabric 4″ wider and longer than each panel. Center any pattern on the panel and wrap the 4″ allowance around the top edge, stapling it in the center on back of panel. Repeat at bottom edge and sides. With fabric held in place by one center staple on all four sides, start at center of one side and staple fabric to back of panel for about 6″ on either side of the original staple. Do the same on the opposite side, pulling the fabric taut with equal tension so the pattern and fabric grain remain straight. Continue working in this manner until fabric is stapled along both side edges, then repeat along top and bottom edges. Miter corners as indicated by the diagrams. Nail panels to the wall with finishing nails and carefully work the fabric back over each nailhead. Cut all panels so the pattern matches across the entire wall or area.

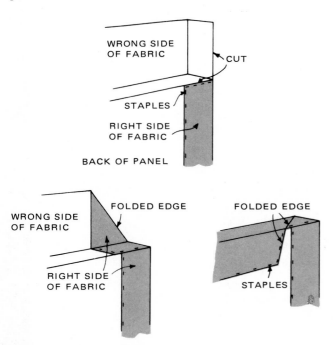

## FABRIC APPLIED LIKE WALLPAPER

Fabric applied like wallpaper is the best method for covering bathroom and other walls that don't readily accept nails or staples. Closely-woven cottons such as chintz or sailcloth are preferable to fabrics made of silk or other fibers. (Silk, for instance, must be backed by paper or adhesive.) Test a sample of the fabric to be sure it's colorfast, won't shrink or be stained by wallpaper paste.

If using plain fabric, estimate the yardage you'll need the same way you would for wallpaper. Measure the number of widths required to cover all walls, allowing an extra ½″ on each panel for overlap. When planning the layout for each wall, try to place the edges of fabric widths at the edges of doors and windows. Multiply the height needed for each panel by the number of widths required. Then subtract the height of windows and doors from this figure.

If you have chosen a patterned fabric, extra yardage must be allowed for matching. Measure the depth of the pattern repeat and determine how many repeats are required for each length of fabric. If the length includes less than a complete design motif, the remaining depth of the pattern repeat must be added to each length to allow for matching. Multiply the total length of the number of fabric widths needed. Remember to allow for ½″ overlap on each width and to deduct the height of doors and windows.

Trim off all selvages and fold the fabric back and forth neatly, accordion-style, for easier handling. Mix wallpaper paste a little thicker than you would for applying wallpaper. Apply paste to the wall, not to the fabric. Start at the ceiling line and unroll the fabric a foot or so at a time, smoothing it and brushing out air bubbles as you work. At the bottom, trim fabric along the baseboard with a razor blade.

Apply the remaining fabric widths, overlapping each one by ½″. (The fabric will tend to contract as paste dries.) Remove any excess paste along the edges with a damp sponge.

To make the library alcove at the left, the ceiling panel was cut first, then the back panels, allowing for the thickness of the ceiling panel. The side panels were cut last, allowing for the thickness of the back panels they butt against. The alcove was planned to partially surround the sofa slipcovered in the same print that covers the panels, creating a warm and inviting spot for reading.

# directions for projects

## LAMBREQUIN
### ON PAGES 111, 204

MATERIALS NEEDED:
(for lambrequin 115″ wide x 96″ high)
> One piece of plywood, ¾″ x 48″ x 96″ for A and B
> "1 x 4" clear pine:
> > one 115″ for C
> > two 95¼″ for D
> Six 2½″ angle irons with twelve ⅝″ screws
> Six hollow-wall fasteners
> Four 1½″ flat head wood screws
> Four 3″ mending plates with ⅝″ screws
> 1½″ finishing nails
> Upholsterers' tacks or staple gun and staples
> 3⅔ yards 44″-wide flannel for padding
> 4¼ yards 45″-wide fabric
> Wood glue

From plywood, cut one 13½″ x 88″ piece for A and two 13½″ x 96″ for B. Using mending plates, attach A and B as shown in Diagram 1, placing plates 2″ from edges of A and checking with a try square to make sure corners are square.

**DIAGRAM 1**

Drill two pilot holes at each end of C, placing them ⅜″ from ends and 1″ from side edges. Glue and screw C to both D with 1½″ screws. Using 1½″ finishing nails, glue and nail A and B to C and D, keeping all outside edges flush (Diagram 1).

Hold lambrequin in place against wall and mark inside edges of C and D on wall. Using hollow-wall fasteners, attach angle irons in positions shown in Diagram 2.

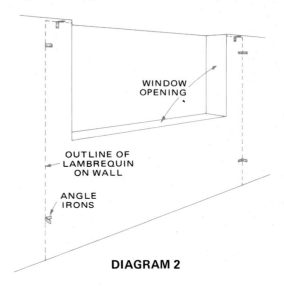

**DIAGRAM 2**

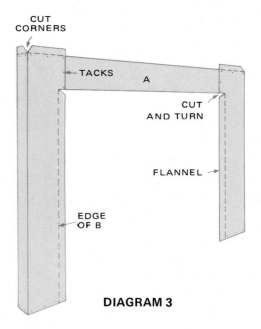

**DIAGRAM 3**

Cut 98″-long piece of flannel in half lengthwise and place on outside faces of B and D as indicated by Diagram 3; staple in place close to top and bottom edges and along back edge of D. Cut diagonally into corners as indicated, and staple to top of C; pull through opening and staple to inside faces of A and B.

Cut two 16"-deep strips of flannel across width of flannel. Cover A as shown in Diagram 4, trimming so that edges butt against flannel covering B. Staple to top of C and inside face of A.

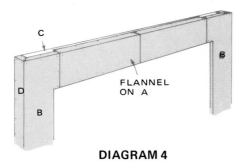

**DIAGRAM 4**

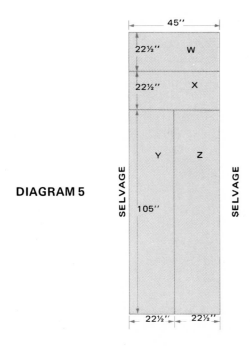

**DIAGRAM 5**

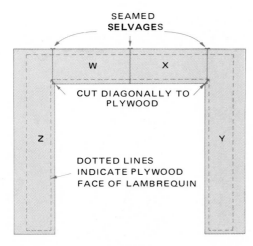

**DIAGRAM 6**

Pattern of fabric on A and B should run in the same direction and be matched where joined by seams. Cut fabric as shown in Diagram 5 and seam together to cover lambrequin as shown in Diagram 6. Clip diagonally from each inside corner of fabric to inside corner of plywood, pull fabric around inside edges of plywood and staple to back. Touch up tiny triangle of plywood left uncovered on inside edge of each corner with paint to match background of fabric.

Pull fabric along each side around outside of D and staple to inside. Clip diagonally at front corners from top of fabric to top edge of A and turn clipped edges under (Diagram 7). Pull fabric extending above sides onto top of C and staple in place; then pull fabric extending above front face of lambrequin onto top and staple in place.

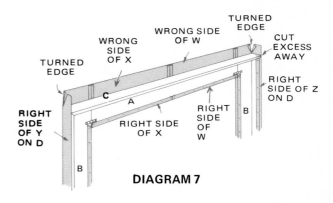

**DIAGRAM 7**

Clip diagonally into bottom corners of fabric, turn clipped edges under and staple to inside faces of B and D in the same manner. Hold lambrequin in place against wall and screw through angle irons into C and D with ⅝" screws.

## CORNICES AND COLUMNS
### ON PAGE 146

MATERIALS NEEDED:
 For each column:
  One "1 x 12", ceiling height, for A
  Two "1 x 4"s, each ceiling height, for B
  One "1 x 4", 24" long, for C
 For each cornice:
  One "1 x 10" of required width, for D
  One "1 x 3" of required width, for E
  Three 2½" angle irons with ¾" and 1¾" flat-head
   wood screws
 Fabric
 2" finishing nails
 Staple gun and staples

Start nails into both long sides of A, ⅜" in from edge and about 12" apart; nail A to two B so edges of A are flush with outside faces of B (Diagram 1). Assemble other columns in same manner.

Cut two C for each column so they will fit snugly between two B at top and bottom of column (Diagram 2).

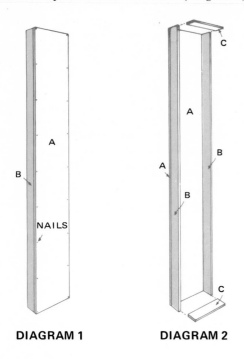

**DIAGRAM 1**          **DIAGRAM 2**

Determine position of each column along wall; nail one C to floor and one C to ceiling at each position. (When attaching C at corner, place end of C ¾″ from side wall so B can be inserted later.) Determine positions of studs; using 1¾″ screws, attach an angle iron to each one across area where cornice will be placed so tops of angle irons are ¾″ below ceiling (Diagram 3).

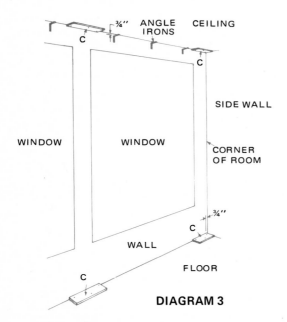

**DIAGRAM 3**

Start nails into one long side of D in same manner as for A and attach D to E as shown in Diagram 4.

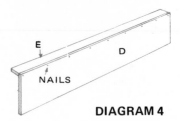

**DIAGRAM 4**

Cut strips of fabric 24″ wide and 2″ longer than A so pattern will be in same position on each column. Wrap fabric around column and staple to inside faces of A and B. Place columns around each C and hold in place with one nail through each B into C at top and bottom; make a tiny slit in fabric at each nail; carefully pull fabric back over nailhead so it will not show. Attach curtain rods and hang casement curtains in place; hang shades. Cut 13″-deep strips of fabric to cover cornice so pattern will match pattern on columns when in place. Staple fabric to top edge of D, wrap fabric around side and bottom edges and staple in place. Place cornice in position on angle irons with E between ceiling and angle irons; using ¾″ screws, screw through angle irons into underside of E to hold cornice in place.

## KNIFE-EDGED SQUARE PILLOWS

MATERIALS NEEDED:
   Fabric
   Zipper, same length as one side of pillow
   Covered cording

Cut fabric for top and bottom sections of cover to size of pillow plus ½″ seam allowance on all four sides. Place cording around right side of top section with all raw edges flush and stitch, clipping seam allowances to go around corners (Diagram 1).

Place zipper, wrong side up, along one edge on wrong side of top section so teeth of zipper are on top of cording and stitching line of zipper is along stitching line of cord-

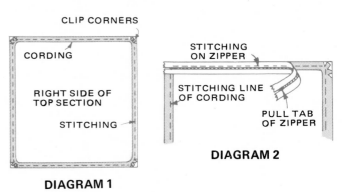

**DIAGRAM 1**          **DIAGRAM 2**

ing (Diagram 2). Stitch in place. Turn zipper over so right side faces up and seam allowances are turned to wrong side of fabric.

Turn under ½″ along one edge of bottom section of cover. Place folded edge over zipper, covering teeth, and stitch bottom section to zipper along stitching line of zipper (Diagram 3). Open zipper and place bottom over top,

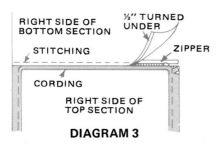

**DIAGRAM 3**

right sides together and all edges even. Stitch around remaining three sides of cover, following stitching line of cording.

NOTE: Covers for knife-edged triangular and rectangular pillows are made in the same manner as cover for square pillow.

## BOXED SQUARE CUSHIONS

MATERIALS NEEDED:
Fabric
Zipper, same length as one side of cushion
Covered cording

Cut fabric for top and bottom sections of cover to size of cushion plus ½″ seam allowance on all four sides. Place cording around right side of top section with all raw edges flush and stitch, clipping seam allowances to go around corners. Apply cording to bottom section in the same manner.

Cut fabric for five boxing strips 1″ longer and 1″ wider than side of pillow. Using two of these strips, insert zipper as follows: Fold ½″ to wrong side along one strip and stitch along one side of zipper; fold 1″ to wrong side along other strip and place over zipper so folded edge covers stitching on first side and stitch along other side of zipper. Cut strip so "X" equals width of other three strips (Diagram 1).

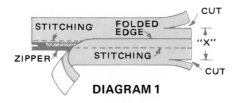

**DIAGRAM 1**

Stitch ends of boxing strips together, right sides facing, with ½″ seams. Place boxing around top section with a

seam at each corner, keeping raw edges flush and clipping at corners as necessary. Stitch boxing to top, following stitching line of cording (Diagram 2).

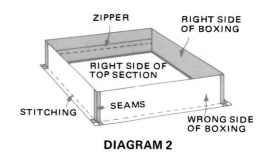

**DIAGRAM 2**

Open zipper and attach boxing strip to bottom section in same manner. Turn right side out.

## BOXED ROUND CUSHIONS

MATERIALS NEEDED:
Cushion form
Fabric
Covered cording (optional)
Zipper

Cut two circles of fabric 1″ wider in diameter than diameter of cushion form. If cushion is to be corded, apply covered cording around top and bottom sections, following directions on page 209.

Boxing is made in two sections, with zipper inserted in one of them. Zipper should be long enough so cover can be put on form and removed quickly and easily. For example: For a 16″-diameter round cushion with 2″-deep boxing, cut one boxing strip 3″ wide x 34″ long; cut second strip 5″ wide x 19″ long. Fold 5″-wide strip in half lengthwise and press; cut on folded line. With right sides of 2½″-wide strips facing, stitch strips together with a 1″ seam. Stitch first 2½″ with regular machine stitch, backstitching to reinforce end of 2½″ seam; continue stitching, using machine basting stitch, for length of zipper (in this case, a 14″-long zipper); stitch remainder of seam with regular machine stitch, reinforcing beginning of regular stitching. Press seam open. Open zipper and place face down with one tape on one seam allowance. Place bottom of zipper at beginning of machine basting, with teeth on seam line. Machine-baste along guideline, stitching through zipper tape and seam allowance only.

Close zipper and turn face up, with seam over zipper teeth. Starting at top, stitch down one side of zipper, across bottom, up other side and across top, stitching close to zipper teeth through zipper tape, seam allowances and strip. Press; remove machine basting.

The two strips (one with zipper inserted) should now be the same width. Place the two strips around boxing of cushion form, with right sides of strips against cushion;

mark seam lines to join them. Remove from cushion form and stitch the two strips together; press seams open (see Diagram).

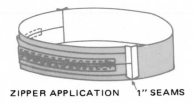

ZIPPER APPLICATION    1″ SEAMS

Open zipper. With right sides together and all seam allowances even, stitch completed boxing strip to top section and then to bottom section of cover. Turn cover to right side and insert cushion form.

# RUFFLED ROUND PILLOWS

MATERIALS NEEDED:
(For each 15″-diameter pillow)
    44″-wide fabric:
        ¾ yard for ruffle
        ½ yard for cover
    1⅓ yards covered cording
    Padding
    One 14″ zipper

From cover fabric, cut one top section A, 16″ x 16″, and two bottom sections B, each 8½″ x 16″. Place two B with right sides together and all edges even; make a ½″ seam along one long side, stitching 1″ with regular machine stitching, 14″ with basting stitches, and the last 1″ with regular stitching. Press seam allowances open. Place B wrong side down over zipper so basting line is centered on zipper; stitch around zipper. Remove basting (Diagram 1).

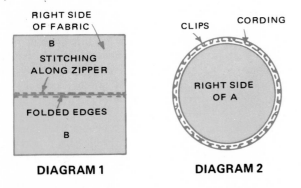

DIAGRAM 1          DIAGRAM 2

Place A and B together, mark a 15″ diameter circle on one, and cut through both at same time. Place covered cording on right side of A so stitching line of cording is ½″ from raw edge of A; clip seam allowance of cording to go around circle (Diagram 2).

Across full width of fabric for ruffle, cut three pieces, each 7″ long. Seam short edges together to make one long

piece, and trim to 110″ length. Seam two remaining 7″ edges together to form a complete circle. Finish ruffle and attach to A in same manner as for ruffled rectangular pillows (see Diagram 4, page 223). Open zipper part way. Place A and B with right sides together and seam allowances even and stitch around circle, following stitching line of cording. Turn cover to right side and stuff with padding.

# RUFFLED RECTANGULAR PILLOWS

MATERIALS NEEDED:
(For each 16″ x 22″ pillow)
    44″-wide fabric:
        1 yard for ruffle
        ¾ yard for cover
    Two yards covered cording
    Stuffing
    One 20″ zipper

From cover fabric, cut one top section A, 19″ x 25″, and two bottom sections B, each 10″ x 25″. Place two B with right sides together and all edges even; make a ½″ seam along one long side, stitching 2½″ with regular machine stitching, 20″ with basting stitches and the last 2½″ with regular stitching. Press seam allowances open. Place B wrong-side down over zipper so basting line is centered on zipper; stitch around zipper. Remove basting (Diagram 1).

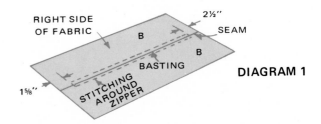

DIAGRAM 1

With right side up, fold fabric at corner so raw edges of two adjoining sides are even. To form corner, measure 1½″ in from point of fabric along raw edges and stitch straight down from there to diagonal line of fold. Repeat at other three corners (Diagram 2).

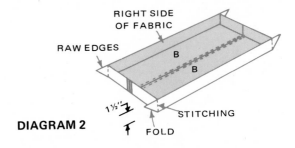

DIAGRAM 2

Place covered cording on right side of B with raw edges even and stitch in place, following stitching line of cording and turning folded corners to ends of cover as shown (Diagram 3).

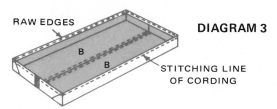

**DIAGRAM 3**

RAW EDGES

B
B

STITCHING LINE OF CORDING

Across full width of fabric for ruffle, cut four pieces, each 7″ long. Seam short edges together to make one long piece 7″ wide. Seam two remaining 7″ edges together to form a complete circle; press seams open. With wrong sides together and raw edges even, fold in half to 3½″ width. Run two rows of gathering stitches ¼″ and ½″ from raw edges. Pull up bobbin threads and pin ruffle around B over cording so all raw edges are even; adjust gathers evenly, allowing extra fullness at corners. Stitch ruffle in place, following stitching line of cording (Diagram 4).

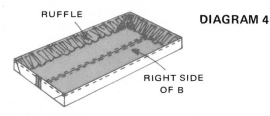

**DIAGRAM 4**

RUFFLE

RIGHT SIDE OF B

Form corners on top section A in same manner as for bottom. Open zipper part way. Place top and bottom with right sides together, raw edges of fabric, cording and ruffle even, and seams at corners meeting; stitch all around, following stitching line of cording. Turn to right side and stuff.

## ROUND BOLSTERS

MATERIALS NEEDED:
Round foam bolster, same width as bed or sofa
Zipper, same length as bolster
Two button molds, to be covered
Cording, to be covered
Nylon thread or buttonhole twist
Fabric

Measure circumference of bolster. Cut fabric 1″ wider than circumference and 1″ longer than bolster. Fold under ½″ of fabric along both long sides; place folded edges along center of zipper and stitch along both sides of zipper.

Cut 2″-wide bias strips of fabric and cover cording (see page 209); trim to ½″ beyond stitching line. Place cording around both ends of fabric, with raw edges of cording and fabric flush. Stitch, following stitching line of cording (Diagram 1).

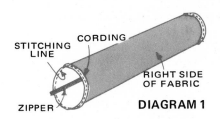

STITCHING LINE
CORDING
RIGHT SIDE OF FABRIC
ZIPPER
**DIAGRAM 1**

Cut two strips for ends to length equal to circumference of bolster plus 1″, and to width equal to one-half of diameter of bolster plus 1″. Fold one strip in half, right sides together, with raw edges of short ends flush. Stitch ½″ from edge (Diagram 2). Repeat for other end strip.

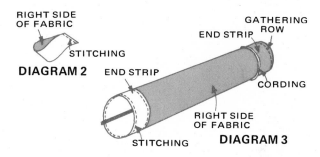

RIGHT SIDE OF FABRIC
STITCHING
**DIAGRAM 2**
END STRIP
GATHERING ROW
END STRIP
CORDING
RIGHT SIDE OF FABRIC
STITCHING
**DIAGRAM 3**

Place one strip around each end of bolster, right sides together and edges flush. Stitch, following stitching line of cording. Turn strips to right side. Using nylon thread or buttonhole twist, run a gathering row of stitching around loose end of each strip, ½″ from edge (Diagram 3). Cover buttons. Pull up gathering row as tightly as possible to form end. Sew button in center of each gathered end.

## SQUARE BOLSTERS

MATERIALS NEEDED:
Fabric
Cording, to be covered
Fastener tape, 2″ shorter than bolster

Cut two squares of fabric the same size as end of bolster, plus ½″ seam allowance on all four sides. Cut bias strips of fabric 2″ wide, seam together and cover cording (see page 209). Trim seam allowances of cording to ½″ beyond stitching line. Place cording around edge of each square, on right side of fabric, with seam allowances of fabric and cording even. Stitch cording in place, following stitching line of cording and clipping seam allowances of cording to go around corners (Diagram 1).

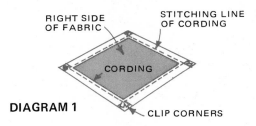

RIGHT SIDE OF FABRIC
STITCHING LINE OF CORDING
CORDING
**DIAGRAM 1**
CLIP CORNERS

Cut fabric 1″ longer than bolster and 1¾″ wider than circumference of bolster. Turn ½″ of fabric to right side along one long edge and center one-half of fastener tape along folded edge; stitch in place, covering raw edge of fabric. Turn ½″ of fabric to wrong side along other long edge and apply other half of fastener tape in same manner, with both strips of tape starting and ending 1″ from ends.

Place fabric around bolster so fastener tape is along center of one side. Make a small clip in seam allowance at each corner. Remove fabric and place one end around each square end piece, with right sides together, seam

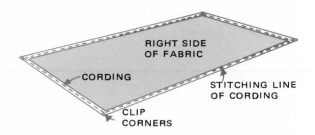

**DIAGRAM 1**

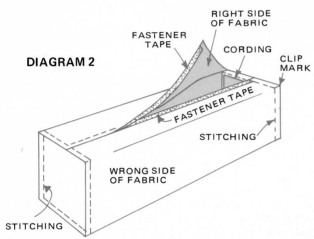

**DIAGRAM 2**

allowances even, and a clip mark at each corner of square. Stitch together, following stitching lines of cording (Diagram 2). Edges of opening, with two halves of fastener tape facing each other, will overlap.

## MATTRESS COVERS

MATERIALS NEEDED:
    Fabric
    Eleven yards of cording, to be covered
    Six yards ½″-wide elastic

Cut 2″-wide bias strips of fabric and cover cording (see page 209); trim fabric ½″ from stitching line. Place fabric for top section of cover on mattress, centering design if fabric is patterned. Mark edge of mattress on all four sides with tailor's chalk. Remove fabric and straighten lines if necessary, measuring to make sure width and length remain constant. Trim fabric ½″ beyond seam lines. Place cording around edge on right side of fabric, with stitching line of cording over seam line of fabric and all seam allowances even; clip seam allowances of cording to go around corners. Stitch together, following stitching line of cording (Diagram 1).

Cut four boxing strips 1″ wider than depth of mattress, cutting two 1″ longer than length of mattress, and two 1″ longer than width of mattress. If fabric is patterned, cut

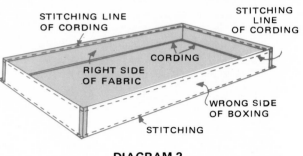

**DIAGRAM 2**

strips so pattern will match after strips are seamed together. Stitch together with ½″ seams and press seam allowances open. Place boxing on top section with a seam at each corner, right sides together and all seam allowances even. Stitch boxing to top, following same stitching line as before. Stitch cording along free edge of boxing, on right side of fabric, in same manner as before (Diagram 2).

Cut four additional strips of fabric for under-mattress section to same sizes as boxing strips and stitch together with ½″ seams. With right sides together, stitch under-mattress section to boxing, matching seams at each corner and with seam allowances even, following stitching line of cording. Make a ¾″ casing along lower edge of under-mattress section, leaving a 1″ space open for inserting elastic. Cut ½″-wide elastic 15″ shorter than distance

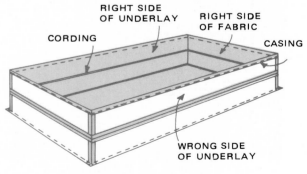

**DIAGRAM 3**

around under-mattress section. Thread elastic through casing, stitch ends of elastic together, and slip-stitch opening closed (Diagram 3). Turn cover to right side and place over mattress like a fitted sheet.